First World War
and Army of Occupation
War Diary
France, Belgium and Germany

41 DIVISION
Headquarters, Branches and Services
Commander Royal Artillery
1 May 1916 - 31 December 1916

WO95/2620/3

The Naval & Military Press Ltd
www.nmarchive.com
Published in association with The National Archives

Published by

The Naval & Military Press Ltd

Unit 10 Ridgewood Industrial Park,

Uckfield, East Sussex,

TN22 5QE England

Tel: +44 (0) 1825 749494

www.naval-military-press.com

www.nmarchive.com

This diary has been reprinted in facsimile from the original. Any imperfections are inevitably reproduced and the quality may fall short of modern type and cartographic standards.

© **Crown Copyright**
Images reproduced by permission of The National Archives, London, England, 2015.

Contents

Document type	Place/Title	Date From	Date To
Heading	WO95/2620 41 Div Commander RA May 16-Dec 16		
Heading	41st Division C.R.A. 1916 May-1916 Dec		
War Diary	Aldershot	01/05/1916	01/05/1916
War Diary	Merris	05/05/1916	26/05/1916
War Diary	Steenwerck	27/05/1916	30/06/1916
Miscellaneous	Report on Bombardment of "Work" U 28 a 4.6. Appendix "A"	08/06/1916	08/06/1916
Miscellaneous	Report on Bombardment of hostile work U.21.b.9.7.-U.22.a.c.9. Appendix" B	11/06/1916	11/06/1916
Miscellaneous	Headquarters, 41st, Division.	01/08/1916	01/08/1916
War Diary	Steenwerck	01/07/1916	31/07/1916
Miscellaneous	Report On Operations Night July 2/3 Appendix. B.		
Miscellaneous	Right Group		
Miscellaneous	Programme Of Shoots Night 2/3rd. July 1916		
Miscellaneous	Programme Of Shoots Night 2/3rd. July		
Miscellaneous	Report on Artillery Operation July 6th. and night July 6th/7th.		
Miscellaneous	Report on Wire Cutting, Saturday July 8th., and Artillery co-operation In raid night July 9th/10th.	10/07/1916	10/07/1916
Miscellaneous	War Diary Appendix D	06/07/1917	06/07/1917
Miscellaneous	Wire Cutting Saturday July 8th		
Miscellaneous	Bombardment Saturday July 8th night July 9/10		
Miscellaneous	War Diary Appendix. E.	11/07/1916	11/07/1916
Miscellaneous		07/07/1916	07/07/1916
Miscellaneous	124th Infantry Brigade. Wirecutting For Enterprise July 10/11		
Miscellaneous	Bombardment		
Miscellaneous	Final Bombardment Night July 10/11		
Miscellaneous	122rd Inf Bde Appendix F.		
Miscellaneous	Bombardment (Casual) Night July 12/13th		
Miscellaneous	Barrage & Bombardment Night July 12/13th		
Miscellaneous	Appendix G Wire Cutting 8 a.m.-12 noon 12-7-17.	12/07/1918	12/07/1918
Miscellaneous	Programme for Night 13 July 1916	13/07/1916	13/07/1916
Miscellaneous	Artillery Support For Aid of 124th Inf. Bde. Night July 13/14th Appendix H		
Miscellaneous	Barrage From O.C' to O.15'		
Miscellaneous	C.R.A. S 510. No. 6	14/07/1916	14/07/1916
Miscellaneous	Minor Enterprise 124th Infantry Brigade Night July 15/16		
Miscellaneous	Report on Operation Of 14.7.16	15/07/1916	15/07/1916
Miscellaneous	C.R.A. S 510. No. 5 Appendix I	14/07/1916	14/07/1916
Miscellaneous	Minor Enterprise 124th Infantry Brigade Night July 15/16.		
Miscellaneous	Artillery Support For Aid of 124th Inf. Bde. Night July 15/16th		
Miscellaneous	Barrage From O.O' to O. 25'		
Miscellaneous	CRA S490 Appendix J	13/07/1916	13/07/1916
Miscellaneous	Town Shoot		
Miscellaneous	Pont Rouge	13/07/1916	13/07/1916
Miscellaneous	Headquarters, 41st. Division Appendix K	27/07/1916	27/07/1916

Miscellaneous	S 583	22/07/1916	22/07/1916
Miscellaneous	Amendment to S 583	24/07/1916	24/07/1916
War Diary	Steenwerck	17/08/1916	23/08/1916
War Diary	Pont Remy	24/08/1916	01/09/1916
War Diary	Argoeuves	02/09/1916	02/09/1916
War Diary	Ribemont	03/09/1916	06/09/1916
War Diary	Bellevue Fm	07/09/1916	18/09/1916
War Diary	Pommiers	19/09/1916	30/09/1916
Miscellaneous	41st Divisional Artillery Operation Order No. 3 Appendix A	01/09/1916	01/09/1916
Miscellaneous	41st. Divisional Artillery Operation Order No.4 Appendix B	02/09/1916	02/09/1916
Miscellaneous	March Table		
Heading	41th Div R.A. H.Q. October. 1916		
War Diary	Pommiers	01/10/1916	31/10/1916
Miscellaneous	File	12/10/1916	12/10/1916
Miscellaneous	41st Divisional Artillery Operation Order No. 20 Appendix A	30/09/1916	30/09/1916
Miscellaneous	A Form. Messages And Signals.	30/09/1916	30/09/1916
Miscellaneous	A Form. Messages And Signals.		
Miscellaneous	41st Divisional Artillery Group Operation Order No. 22 Appendix C	03/10/1916	03/10/1916
Miscellaneous	Amendment to 41st. Divisional Artillery Group Operation Order No. 23 Appendix D		
Miscellaneous	41st Divisional Artillery Group Operation Order No. 23	05/10/1916	05/10/1916
Miscellaneous	41st Divisional Artillery Group Operation Order No. 24. Appendix. E.	10/10/1916	10/10/1916
Operation(al) Order(s)	41st Divisional Artillery Group Operation Order No. 24	10/10/1916	10/10/1916
Miscellaneous	A Form. Messages And Signals.	11/10/1916	11/10/1916
Miscellaneous	12th Signals. C.R.A. Right Group	11/10/1916	11/10/1916
Miscellaneous	Amendments to 41st Divisional Artillery Group Operation Order No. 25. Appendix F	11/10/1916	11/10/1916
Miscellaneous Map	41st Divisional Artillery Group Operation Order No. 25	11/10/1916	11/10/1916
Operation(al) Order(s)	41st Divisional Artillery Group Operation Order No. 26	13/10/1916	13/10/1916
Operation(al) Order(s)	41st Divisional Artillery Group Operation Order No. 27. Appendix. H	14/10/1916	14/10/1916
Operation(al) Order(s)	41st. Divisional Artillery Operation Order No. 28. Appendix I	14/10/1916	14/10/1916
Operation(al) Order(s)	41st Divisional Artillery Group Operation Order No. 29 Appendix J	15/10/1916	15/10/1916
Miscellaneous	41st Divisional Artillery Group Operation Order No. 30. Appendix K	16/10/1916	16/10/1916
Miscellaneous	Amendment to 41st. D.A.G. Order No.31. Appendix L	17/10/1916	17/10/1916
Operation(al) Order(s)	41st Divisional Artillery Group Operation Order No. 31.	17/10/1916	17/10/1916
Miscellaneous Map	Appendix 'A'.		
Operation(al) Order(s)	41st Divisional Artillery Group Operation Order No. 34.	22/10/1916	22/10/1916
Operation(al) Order(s)	41st. Divisional Artillery Group Operation Order No. 33	23/10/1916	23/10/1916
Operation(al) Order(s)	41st. Divisional Artillery Group Operation Order No. 34	23/10/1916	23/10/1916
Operation(al) Order(s)	41st. Divisional Artillery Group Operation Order No. 36.	24/10/1916	24/10/1916
Miscellaneous	2nd Amendment To 41st Divisional Artillery Group Operation Order No. 36	25/10/1916	25/10/1916
Miscellaneous	Third Amendment to 41st. Divisional Artillery Group Operation Order No. 36	28/10/1916	28/10/1916

Operation(al) Order(s)	41st. Divisional Artillery Operation Order No. 35	29/10/1916	29/10/1916
Operation(al) Order(s)	41st. D.A.G. Operation Order No. 36	30/10/1916	30/10/1916
Miscellaneous	March Table		
Miscellaneous			
Heading	41st Div. R.A., H.Q., November, 1916		
Miscellaneous	Division Order No. 70 Appendix 11		
War Diary	Pommiers Redoubt	01/11/1916	01/11/1916
War Diary	Bonnay	02/11/1916	02/11/1916
War Diary	Villers Bolage	03/11/1916	03/11/1916
War Diary	Doullens	04/11/1916	04/11/1916
War Diary	Boubers Sur Canche	05/11/1916	05/11/1916
War Diary	Monchy Cayeux	06/11/1916	08/11/1916
War Diary	Lambres	09/11/1916	09/11/1916
War Diary	Staple	10/11/1916	10/11/1916
War Diary	Boeschepe	11/11/1916	12/11/1916
War Diary	Reninghelst	13/11/1916	30/11/1916
Miscellaneous	41st. Divisional Artillery Operation Order No. 37 Appendix I	29/10/1916	29/10/1916
Miscellaneous	Artillery, 30th Div. Appendix I	29/10/1916	29/10/1916
Miscellaneous	Fourth Army. No. QC/806 Vol	30/10/1916	30/10/1916
Miscellaneous	Fouth Army No QC/806 1 Anzac Corps.	31/10/1916	31/10/1916
Miscellaneous	Administrative Order Issued Under 1st Anzac Order No. 60	31/10/1916	31/10/1916
Operation(al) Order(s)	41st. D.A.G. Operation Order No. 38 Appendix II	30/10/1916	30/10/1916
Miscellaneous	March Table		
Operation(al) Order(s)	41st. Divl. Artillery March Order No. 2. Appendix 4	02/11/1916	02/11/1916
Miscellaneous	March Table		
Miscellaneous	IV Corps. "Q"	30/10/1916	30/10/1916
Miscellaneous	March Table Issued with March Order No. 2 App 5	03/11/1916	03/11/1916
Miscellaneous	March Table		
Operation(al) Order(s)	41st. Divl. Artillery March Order No. 3 App 6	03/11/1916	03/11/1916
Miscellaneous	March Table.		
Operation(al) Order(s)	Third Army Order No. 85 App 6	31/10/1916	31/10/1916
Miscellaneous	41st Divisional Artillery March Table.		
Miscellaneous	Divisional Artillery H.Q.-Boubers-sur-Canche.		
Map	Boubers Area		
Operation(al) Order(s)	41st. Divl Artillery March Order No.4 App 7	05/11/1916	05/11/1916
Miscellaneous	March Table		
Miscellaneous	41st. Divl. Artillery March Order No. 5 App 8	06/11/1916	06/11/1916
Miscellaneous	March Table		
Operation(al) Order(s)	41st. Divisional Artillery March Order No. 6 App 9	09/11/1916	09/11/1916
Miscellaneous	March Table		
Miscellaneous	Officer Commanding, 183, 187,190th. Bdes, D.A.C., & HQ. Divl. Train	09/11/1916	09/11/1916
Operation(al) Order(s)	41st Divisional Artillery Operation Order No. 1 app10	11/11/1914	11/11/1914
Operation(al) Order(s)	Amendment To 41st Division Order No. 60	10/11/1916	10/11/1916
Operation(al) Order(s)	41st Division Order No. 60 App 10	05/10/1916	05/10/1916
Miscellaneous	App 11 Enemy's Altillery File	16/11/1916	16/11/1916
Miscellaneous	41st. Divisional Artillery App II	14/11/1916	14/11/1916
Miscellaneous	41st Divisional Artillery Daily Operation Report. from 6 p.m. 15-11-16 to 6 p.m. 16-11-16. App 12	17/11/1916	17/11/1916
Miscellaneous	41st Divisional Artillery Daily Operation Report. from 6 p.m. 16.11.16 to 6 p.m. 17.11.16. App 13	16/11/1916	16/11/1916
Miscellaneous	41st. Divisional Artillery App 14	19/11/1916	19/11/1916
Miscellaneous	41st. Divisional Artillery App 15	20/11/1916	20/11/1916
Miscellaneous	41st. Divisional Artillery App 16	21/11/1916	21/11/1916

Miscellaneous	41st Divisional Artillery Operation Order No. 40 App 17	18/11/1916	18/11/1916
Miscellaneous			
Miscellaneous	41st Divisional Artillery Daily Operation Report from 6 p.m. 20-11-16 to 6 p.m. 21-11-16. App 18	21/11/1916	21/11/1916
Miscellaneous	General Summary	22/11/1916	22/11/1916
Miscellaneous	1st Divisional Artillery Daily Operation Report from 6 p.m. 21.11.16 to 6 p.m. 22.11.16. App 19	23/11/1916	23/11/1916
Miscellaneous	Weekly Summary of Operations App 19a	23/11/1916	23/11/1916
Miscellaneous	41st. Divisional Artillery Daily Operation Report from 6 p.m. 22.11.16 to 6 p.m. 23.11.16. App 20	23/11/1916	23/11/1916
Miscellaneous	Enemy's Artillery Fire.	24/11/1916	24/11/1916
Miscellaneous	41st. Divisional Artillery App 21	23/11/1918	23/11/1918
Miscellaneous	Enemy's Artillery Fire	25/11/1916	25/11/1916
Miscellaneous	41st. Divisional Artillery Daily Operation Report from 6 p.m. 24.11.16 to 6 p.m. 25.11.16. App 22	24/11/1916	24/11/1916
Miscellaneous	General Summary.	26/11/1916	26/11/1916
Miscellaneous	Re-organisation of Artillery Positions App 23	23/11/1916	23/11/1916
Miscellaneous	With reference to Re-organisation Preliminary Order circulated under our S 304, para 3 should be amended to read us follows:-	23/11/1916	23/11/1916
Miscellaneous	Reorganisation Preliminary Order.	23/11/1916	23/11/1916
Miscellaneous	41st. Divisional Artillery Daily Operation Report from 6 p.m. 25.11.16 to 6 p.m. 26.11.16. App 24		
Miscellaneous	Enemy's Artillery Fire	27/11/1916	27/11/1916
Operation(al) Order(s)	41st. Divisional Artillery Daily Operation Report from 6 p.m. 26.11.16 to 6 p.m. 27.11.16. App 25	26/11/1916	26/11/1916
Miscellaneous	Enemy's Artillery Fire	28/11/1916	28/11/1916
Miscellaneous	41st. Divisional Artillery Daily Operation Report from 6 p.m. 27.11.16 to 6 p.m. 28.11.16. App 26	27/11/1916	27/11/1916
Miscellaneous	General Summary	29/11/1916	29/11/1916
Operation(al) Order(s)	41st. Divisional Artillery Daily Operation Report from 6 p.m. 28.11.16 to 6 p.m. 29.11.16.App 27	28/11/1916	28/11/1916
Miscellaneous	Enemy's Artillery Fire.	30/11/1916	30/11/1916
Miscellaneous	41st Divisional Artillery Operation Order No. 42 App 28		
Miscellaneous	Schedule "A"		
Miscellaneous	Schedule B		
Operation(al) Order(s)	41st. Divisional Artillery Daily Operation Report from 6 p.m. 29.11.16 to 6 p.m. 30/11/16.App 29	29/11/1916	29/11/1916
Miscellaneous	General Summary	01/12/1916	01/12/1916
Miscellaneous	41st. Divisional Artillery App 29a	30/11/1916	30/11/1916
Heading	D.A.G. 3rd Echelon		
Heading	HQ R.A. 41 Div Vol 8		
War Diary	Reninghelst	01/12/1916	31/12/1916
Miscellaneous	41st. Divisional Artillery Daily Operation Report from 6 p.m. 2/12/16 to 6 p.m. 3/12/16. App 34	02/12/1916	02/12/1916
Miscellaneous	Enemy's Artillery Fire	04/12/1916	04/12/1916
Operation(al) Order(s)	41st. Divisional Artillery App 35	03/12/1916	03/12/1916
Miscellaneous	Enemy's Artillery Fire.	05/12/1916	05/12/1916
Miscellaneous	41st. Divisional Artillery Daily Operation Report from 6 p.m. 4.12.16 to 6 p.m. 5.12.16. App 36	04/12/1916	04/12/1916
Miscellaneous	41st. Divisional Artillery Daily Operation Report from 6 p.m. 5.12.16 to 6 p.m. 6.12.16. App 37	05/12/1916	05/12/1916
Miscellaneous	41st. Divisional Artillery Daily Operation Report from 6 p.m. 6.12.16 to 6 p.m. 7.12.16. App 38	06/12/1916	06/12/1916

Miscellaneous	General Summary.	08/12/1916	08/12/1916
Miscellaneous	41st. Divisional Artillery Daily Operation Report from 6 p.m. 7.12.16 to 6 p.m. 8.12.16. App 39	07/12/1916	07/12/1916
Miscellaneous	41st. Divisional Artillery Daily Operation Report from 6 p.m. 8.12.16 to 6 p.m. 9.12.16. App 40	08/12/1916	08/12/1916
Miscellaneous	Divisional Shoot Blister App 41	09/12/1916	09/12/1916
Miscellaneous	41st. Divisional Artillery Operation Order No. 43- Amendment (3). App 42		
Miscellaneous	41st. Divisional Artillery Operation Order No. 43- Amendment (2)	09/12/1916	09/12/1916
Miscellaneous	41st. Divisional Artillery Operation Order No. 43- Amendment.	07/12/1916	07/12/1916
Operation(al) Order(s)	41st Divisional Artillery Operation Order No. 43.	05/12/1916	05/12/1916
Miscellaneous	Appendix A. St Eloi Group		
Miscellaneous	Appendix B		
Miscellaneous	Appendix C Total Ammunition Expenditure.		
Miscellaneous	41st. Divisional Artillery Daily Operation Report from 6 p.m. 9.12.16 to 6 p.m. 10.12.16. App 43	09/12/1916	09/12/1916
Miscellaneous	Enemy's Artillery Fire	11/12/1916	11/12/1916
Miscellaneous	41st. Divisional Artillery Daily Operation Report from 6 p.m. 11.12.16 to 6 p.m. 12.12.16. App 44	11/12/1916	11/12/1916
Miscellaneous	General Summary	13/12/1916	13/12/1916
Miscellaneous	41st. Divisional Artillery Daily Operation Report from 6 p.m. 12.12.16 to 6 p.m. 13.12.16. App 46	12/12/1916	12/12/1916
Miscellaneous	Enemy's Artillery Fire	14/12/1916	14/12/1916
Operation(al) Order(s)	41st. Divisional Artillery Daily Operation Report from 6 p.m. 13.12.16 to 6 p.m. 14.12.16. App 46	13/12/1916	13/12/1916
Miscellaneous	App 47		
Miscellaneous	41st. Divisional Artillery Ry Daily Operation Report from 6 p.m. 14.12.16 to 6 p.m. 15.12.16. App 48	14/12/1916	14/12/1916
Miscellaneous	R.A. 41st Divn App 49	15/12/1916	15/12/1916
Operation(al) Order(s)	41st. Divisional Artillery. Operation Order No. 44	15/12/1916	15/12/1916
Miscellaneous		16/12/1916	16/12/1916
Operation(al) Order(s)	Xth Corps Artillery Operation Order No. 12	15/12/1916	15/12/1916
Miscellaneous	Appendix A. Bombardment of Hill 60 Area by Heavy and Field Howitzers and Trench Mortars on 16th Instant.		
Miscellaneous	Appendix B. Bombardment of Bluff Area by Heavy and Field Howitzers and Trench Mortars on 16th Instant.		
Miscellaneous	41st. Divisional Artillery App 50	15/12/1916	15/12/1916
Miscellaneous	41st. Divisional Artillery App 51	16/12/1916	16/12/1916
Miscellaneous	General Summary	18/12/1916	18/12/1916
Miscellaneous	App 52	15/12/1916	15/12/1916
Miscellaneous	Hostile T.M. Code App 53	18/12/1916	18/12/1916
Miscellaneous	41st. Divisional Artillery App 54		
Miscellaneous	General Summary	19/12/1916	19/12/1916
Miscellaneous	Daily Operation Report from 6 p.m. 18.12.16 to 6 p.m. 19.12.16. App 55	18/12/1916	18/12/1916
Miscellaneous	41st. Divisional Artillery App 56	19/12/1916	19/12/1916
Miscellaneous	41st. Divisional Artillery App 57	20/12/1916	20/12/1916
Miscellaneous	App 58 General Summary	23/12/1916	23/12/1916
Miscellaneous	41st. Divisional Artillery Daily Operation Report From 6 p.m. 21st to 6 p.m. 22nd Dec		
Miscellaneous	41st Divisional Artillery App 59	21/12/1916	21/12/1916
Miscellaneous	General Summary	24/12/1916	24/12/1916

Miscellaneous	41st. Divisional Artillery. Daily Operation Report From 6 p.m. 22nd. to 6 p.m. 23rd Dec. 1916.	22/12/1916	22/12/1916
Miscellaneous	41st. Divisional Artillery. App 61	25/12/1916	25/12/1916
Miscellaneous	Addenda To 41st Divisional Artillery operation Order No.45 App 62	23/12/1916	23/12/1916
Miscellaneous	41st Divisional Artillery Operation Order No. 45		
Miscellaneous	41st. Divisional Artillery App 63	23/12/1916	23/12/1916
Miscellaneous	General Summary.	26/12/1916	26/12/1916
Miscellaneous	Addenda to 41st Divisional Artillery Operation Order No. 46 Appendix 64	25/12/1916	25/12/1916
Miscellaneous	41st Divisional Artillery Operation Order No. 46	24/12/1916	24/12/1916
Miscellaneous	Appendix A.		
Miscellaneous	Appendix B.		
Miscellaneous	41st Divisional Artillery Operation Order No.47	23/12/1916	23/12/1916
Miscellaneous	41st Divisional Artillery Operation Order No. 48	27/12/1916	27/12/1916
Miscellaneous	41st. Divisional Artillery App 30	02/12/1916	02/12/1916
Miscellaneous	41st. Divisional Artillery App 31	01/12/1916	01/12/1916
Miscellaneous	General Summary	03/12/1916	03/12/1916
Miscellaneous	41st Divisional Artillery Operation Order No. 39	28/11/1916	28/11/1916
Miscellaneous	Schedule A.		
Miscellaneous	Schedule B St Eloi Group		
Miscellaneous	Sehedule Ammunition Expenditure.		
Map			
Heading	HQ.R.A. 41 Div Vol 8 Vol 8		

WO 95/2620 (3)
41 DIV.
Commander R A
May '16 — Dec '16

41ST DIVISION

C. R. A.

~~MAY 1916-JUN 1917~~

1916 MAY — 1916 DEC

Army Form C. 2118

WAR DIARY
or
INTELLIGENCE SUMMARY
(Erase heading not required.)

of 41st Div. Art. HQrs. from May 1916

Instructions regarding War Diaries and Intelligence Summaries are contained in F.S. Regs., Part II. and the Staff Manual respectively. Title Pages.

Place	Date	Hour	Summary of Events and Information	Remarks and references to Appendices
ALDERSHOT	4/5/16		Commenced move of 41st D.A. overseas – via SOUTHAMPTON – HAVRE – & by rail to concentration area in vicinity of MERRIS –	
MERRIS	5th to		Concentration completed by night of May 8th/9th.	
	8/5/16		Arrangements made for registering guns – & personnel to batteries of 9th Div. Art. in Sector N of ARMENTIERES. Detachment, specialists (signallers etc.) & officers were attached to units of 9th D.A. for instruction.	
MERRIS	9th – 6		Reorganisation of R.F.A. into brigades of 3 batteries & 1 Am. Col. Bty. arranged. Change to take effect from day of taking over line from 9th Div.	
MERRIS	26th		Reorganisation of Artillery Ammunition Cols. carried out. Three Divisions (2.) & 1 heavy (sect.in.) Trench Mortar Btys. formed. Command handed over. Lines at BERTHEN –	
			T.M.C. Lt. Langhorne, Afficis led by Lt. Cape R.A. –	
			NB. Great inconvenience, delay & some loss, trouble have been caused & hindrance to organisation of these T.M. Btys. in Officers & other ranks left behind as supplementary troops have been transferred to form new Btys.	

Army Form C. 2118

WAR DIARY of HQrs 41st Divisional
or
INTELLIGENCE SUMMARY Artillery for May 1916

(Erase heading not required.)

Place	Date	Hour	Summary of Events and Information	Remarks and references to Appendices
STEENWERCK	27th		HQrs 41st DA moved to STEENWERCK. Relief of 9th Divl Artly completed at 12 noon at which hour CRA 41st DA took over command. At the hour Bdgs assumed new nomenclature necessitated by reorganisation of Brigades. Guns of 9th DA were taken over in situ - 9th DA Tching over 41st DA guns at Wagon lines. Trench mortars 2" were not handed over. "A" Echelon DAC by order 2nd Corps remain at BORRE	great numerous cannot by impossibility of obtaining no. 14 Periscope.
do	28th		had construction not planned & commenced e.g. making new gun positions & OPs, & strengthening & repairing existing gun positions & OPs. Existing OPs very inadequate & many of them having been much knocked about by shell fire recently.	Cur.
do	29th		Tour of Right Group OPs with BGRA II Corps & Right Group Commander	Cur.
do	30th		- Left Group Bdgs & OPs -	Cur.
do	31st		Tour of Centre Group OPs & section of MTM Bdgs in Centre Group area. Various constructional work planned.	Cur.

(A). Weather throughout May on the whole good - country well dried up -
(B). Unit in Flanders. South N.Z. Division. NORTH 24th Division.

COMMANDING 41st DIVISIONAL ARTILLERY, BRIGADIER-GENERAL

RA 41 Div(3)

Army Form C. 2118

WAR DIARY
or
INTELLIGENCE SUMMARY

(Erase heading not required.)

of 41st Divl Artn H&rs for month of June 1916

Vol 2

Instructions regarding War Diaries and Intelligence Summaries are contained in F.S. Regs., Part II. and the Staff Manual respectively. Title Pages will be prepared in manuscript.

Place	Date	Hour	Summary of Events and Information	Remarks and references to Appendices
STEENWERCK	1/6/16		Special objectives successfully engaged with aeroplane cooperation no 7 Squadron RFC. Hostile artillery somewhat active - LE BIZET and vicinity receiving some attention. A great Observation Balloon of no 7 KBS broke away owing to high winds & travelled over German lines - both occupants (one of whom was Lt Dankeste 41st D.A) made successful parachute descents within our lines -	Cont. new OPs & Gun Emplacement - &
	2nd		Objectives successfully engaged with observation by no 7 Squadron RFC. Enemy activity normal	Cont. repairing & strengthening
	3rd		Some registration carried out. Hostile activity normal	existing ones. All new available
	4th		Hostile activity normal. We registered various points	in shooting
	5th		Shelled "White House" & "Red House" C 4 d 2 2 with good results. Enemy activity normal	Cont. DAC & 4o guns from
	6th		Little activity normal	last Park Deployed
	7th		normal	
	8th	3 pm	An emplacement with 11 Lyrid HA bombardment of enemy's trench at U 28 a 4 6. Shoot 36 1/10000 carried out - counterbomb at 3 pm & cleaning at 3.45 pm. Report is attached in Appendix "A"	Cont. 29
		10 pm	Fired 40 rounds 18 pdr shrapnel on trench U 28 a 4 6 in hope of catching working parties	

1875 Wt. W593/826 1,000,000 4/15 J.B.C. & A.   A.D.S.S./Forms/C.2118.

WAR DIARY or INTELLIGENCE SUMMARY

Army Form C. 2118 (2)

4/4th Div. Art. H.Qr.
for June 1916

Place	Date	Hour	Summary of Events and Information	Remarks and references to Appendices
STEENWERCK	June 9th		Enemy activity normal.	
"	10th		An enquiry then with 6" How. of II Corps Heavy Artillery bombarded hostile works between U.21.b.9.7 and U.22.a.0.9. Wire gun approaches on Kennenhofe were inspected. Bombardment was successful & considerable material damage done — vide report Appendix B attached — No 9 K.B.S. & no 7 Squadron RFC Co-operated.	Ans
"	11th		Enemy activity normal.	Ans
"	12th		4.5" How. of Left Group again engaged Enemy work between U.21.b.9.7 and U.22.a.0.9 with good result. 4.5" How. of Centre Group engaged S.W. corner of work U.28.d.4.6 which had not been seriously damaged by bombardment of 8/6/16 — Results obtained were satisfactory	Ans
"	13th		Some registration carried out. GRAND HAIE Fm. U.23.D.0.8 Shelled — Enemy activity normal.	Ans
"	14th		Normal	Ans
"	15th		Enemy shelled PLOEGSTEERT WOOD & vicinity — we in reen[?] bulk engaged hostile transport on WARNETON road knocking out two wagons and	30

Army Form C. 2118

WAR DIARY
or
INTELLIGENCE SUMMARY
(Erase heading not required.)

of 41st Divl Arty (3)
HARS

Place	Date	Hour	Summary of Events and Information	Remarks and references to Appendices
STEENWERCK	June 16th		Enemy's artillery somewhat active shelling PLOEGSTEERT WOOD & VILLAGE LAURENCE Fm. & The PLOEGSTEERT — ROMARIN ROAD.	
		11:30 pm	Our infantry gave gas alert. Shortly before midnight "gas alarm" — Infantry called for S.O.S. & guns at once responded. Gas came from over HILLS 63 (24th Divl front) in a dense white cloud passing over T 24 and T 30. Gas had a strong smell of Ammonia as well as Chlorine — Preventive measures taken with perfect success.	None
"	17th		Enemy shelled HYDE PARK CORNER C.19.B.5.8 and LE BIZET Church. Many horses in the wagon lines were effected by the gas of the previous night — As a rule nothing was noticeable till the horse had moved about — then severe coughing & choking set in — All horses eventually recovered in periods varying from 2 – 7 days. N.B. after gas horses should be kept as quiet as possible & not exercised or worked.	Ans
"	18th		Hostile shelling normal. Successfully registered various points with aeroplane observation. At 11:45 pm enemy discharged gas in small quantities — Infantry in trenches once called for S.O.S. which was at once forthcoming — On fire approached to cease gas cloud to left & it then rolled back over enemy lines	1 Ans

1875 Wt. W592/826 1,009,000 4/15 J.B.C. & A. A.D.S.S./Forms/C.2118.

WAR DIARY or INTELLIGENCE SUMMARY

Army Form C. 2118

Ham 4th Div. Arty.

32

Place	Date	Hour	Summary of Events and Information	Remarks and references to Appendices
STEENWERCK	June 19th	1.20	Enemy shelled ST YVES heavily. Hostile transport on WARNETON Road successfully engaged. In centre LE TOUQUET station, but ceased in retaliation.	Confidential Engaged
"	20th		Sector we bivouac's South shelled enemy's front line trenches.	cont.
"	21st		Neighbourhood of T.24 & PLOEGSTEERT VILLAGE heavily shelled. Gas alarm sounded at 11.30 pm but no gas attack eventuated.	Anl.
"	22nd		Normal.	
"	23rd		Successfully registered 2 hostile Bty/positions with KB. Balloon Observation. Wood of our PLOEGSTEERT troops was heavily shelled. Retaliation carried out by 5th HAG & Cdn How & 42nd DA.	Conf.
"	25th 24th		Normal. No aircraft engaged hostile this Balloons with new phosphorous bombs.	Conf.
"	24th 25th		Dgi:shaken. Carried out enemy shelled DE SPIERRE Fm and LE BIZET and front line trench from C4c77 to C4a1/2 2, the latter very heavily. At 10.30 pm a bright red light lasting 5 secs was seen high up in sky from STEENWERCK in direction of FLEURBAIX. Three hostile kite balloons brought down in flames by hos. squadron RFC	Anl.
"	26th		Normal.	
"	27th		Normal.	
"	28th		Little artillery somewhat active in whole Div't front.	Anl.
"	29th		PLOEGSTEERT Wood heavily shelled. During night of 28th/29th B/190 cooperated with 24th Div'n in a minor enterprise - Inf. Btty have previously cut wire for same - 24th DA reported wire cutting very satisfactory & enterprise successful.	Conf.

Army Form C. 2118

WAR DIARY
or
INTELLIGENCE SUMMARY 41st Divl Artly Hdqrs
(Erase heading not required.)

Place	Date	Hour	Summary of Events and Information	Remarks and references to Appendices
STEENWERCK	June 30th		41st D.A. in conjunction with X/41 Y/41 & Z/41 Btys M.T.M engaged the enemy with two in wire cutting on Divl front. This operation was in conjunction with a minor enterprise to be carried out later — Full report in WAR DIARY for July —	ant.

30/6/16

[signature]
CRA 41st Divn

War Diary Appendix "A"

Copy. No. 5.

Report on Bombardment of "Work" U 28 a 4.6 on 8.6.16
━━

1. From reports received up to date the bombardment as per programme would appear to have been satisfactorily carried out. Reports as to material damage done are somewhat conflicting, an aeroplane photograph will no doubt show any results obtained. Hostile retaliation was of a local nature, the following received most attention:-

   Trench 112, AYE STR. I, LANCH HILL, Fm. CONVENT and vicinity of LE GHEER.

   At 10 p.m. the "work" was subjected to a short burst of rapid fire, in the hopes of surprising working parties etc.

2. Detailed summary of reports as follows:-

   (a) RIGHT GROUP. Reports from F.O.O's. show fire to have been well distributed over the various objectives and correct for range and fuze.

   (b) CENTRE GROUP. Fire reported satisfactory.
       Major Hulton observing from trench 112 reported fire on "work" accurate - none of our rounds fell in trench 112. Observation from front line trench after bombardment shows one corner of "work" intact remainder "flattened out".

   (c) LEFT GROUP. Reports from F.O.O's. show shooting satisfactory - especially on LOPHOLE FARM on which many direct hits obtained.

   (d) Report from Observer No. 7 Squadron R.F.C. by wire and subsequent telephone conversation shows that in his opinion fire on the "work" was very accurate. The fire on the various other objectives he describes as "erratic" but told me that he only knew the map squares into which we were firing, not the actual objectives, and was under the impression all fire was intended for front line trenches.
       He had to fly low and our side of the line and observation was difficult.

   (e) No.9 K.B. Reports by phone that throughout operation shooting seemed accurate and range good. Only the first few rounds on the "work" could be observed. These he described as "very accurate" - after these rounds smoke prevented observation.

   (f) T.M.O. 41st Division, reports shooting of 2" T.M."as observed from front line trench not very successful." "Rifle mechanisms gave trouble and stopped two mortars firing full number of rounds." B.M.C. in visiting H.Q.T.M.A. 41st Division today to report in detail.

   Both No.7 Squadron R.F.C. and No.9 K.B.S. reported various hostile batteries active and these were effectively dealt with by 11th H.A.G. and II Corps Heavy Artillery.

Copy No.1 to 41st Division.
     2 to II Corps G.A.
     3 to II Corps H.A.
     4 FILE.
     5 FILE.

Comdg. 41st D.A.

10.6.16

Appendix "B"   COPY NO.

Report on Bombardment of hostile work
U.21.b.9.7. - U.22.a.0.9.
10-6-16.

(1) F.O.O. left group reports.

"Only general observation of the bombardment was possible. This was very effective - fire being chiefly concentrated on the trench junction at U.21.b.7½.5 and on the three fire trenches radiating from this point to a distance of about 100" along each.
(during last 10 minutes of bombardment I observed movement at FACTORY FARM. I switched one gun on to this, getting 7 direct hits out of ten rounds).
Generally the material effect on hostile front trench was good. Several breeches were made in it, deck boards etc., flying in the air.

(2) F.O.O. Centre Group reports.

"Shoot as a whole was fair. Fire seemed most concentrated on "left upper corner" of BIRDCAGE (i.e U. 1.b.9.7.) and the left .i.e. northern half of the trenches to be bombarded were not so well engaged.
Timber and tape flew all over the place.

(3) No. 9 K.B.S. reported shooting good.

(4) No 7 Squadron R.F.C. reported shooting accurate and parapet at U.21.b.9.8. damaged.

11-6-16.

Brigade Major
41st Divl. Artillery.

Copy No. 1 41st Divsn.
"   "   2 II Corps H.A.
2 copies   File.

Headquarters,
    41st. Division.

    Herewith War Diary for month of July. Duplicate forwarded direct to Records.

                                        [signature]
                                        Brigade Major,
                                           for Brigadier General,
                                        Commanding 41st.Divl: Artillery.

1.8.16
HHP

41 July (1)

Army Form C. 2118

WAR DIARY
or
INTELLIGENCE SUMMARY

HQrs 41st Divl. Arty.
for month July 1916 41 Dw CRA Vol 3

(Erase heading not required.)

Instructions regarding War Diaries and Intelligence Summaries are contained in F.S. Regs., Part II. and the Staff Manual respectively. Title Pages will be prepared in manuscript.

Place	Date	Hour	Summary of Events and Information	Remarks and references to Appendices
STEENWERCK	July 1st		During night June 30/July 1st a minor enterprise or raid on hostile trenches was carried out by 41st Divn. 41st Divl. Arty Co-operated – Detailed report programme etc in Appendix A attached.	Cont.
"	2nd		Quiet day.	Cont.
"	3rd		During night July 2/3 41st Divl. Arty selected roads in hostile area to shell fire – Detailed report – programme etc in Appendix "B" attached. Right Group Co-operated with N.Z. Division in a minor enterprise or raid with barrage fire etc	Cont.
"	4th		A quiet day	Cont.
"	5th		Very quiet day – carried out a little registration	Cont.
"	6th		A quiet day. 41st DA carried out wire cutting & bombardment etc as per attached programme to which is added report in detail Appendix C.	Cont.
"	7th		A quiet day – left group shelled & silenced two Trench Mortars	Cont. 36811
"	8th		Engaged & silenced 2 Heavy Btys. Centre & Left Groups wire cutting for raid on night 9/10 & 10/11 – Programme & detailed report for raid 9/10 See Appendix D attached	Cont.

1875   Wt. W593/826   1,000,000   4/15   J.B.C. & A.   A.D.S.S./Forms/C.2118.

Army Form C. 2118

WAR DIARY or INTELLIGENCE SUMMARY

HQrs 41st Divl Arty

(Erase heading not required.)

Month July

Place	Date	Hour	Summary of Events and Information	Remarks and references to Appendices
STEENWERCK	July 9th		From 8 am for about 3 hours D/189 was shelled with 5.9 & 4.2 shells. 10 OR wounded. 60 pdrs & 115 HAG engaged Btys suspected of silencing them. 4.5" Hows. A/189 about 6.30 pm fired at hostile Battery near LES ECLUSES – at 6.50 pm a fire broke out in LES ECLUSES, at 7 pm & at 7.20 pm there were two large explosions – At 7.40 pm centre & right front found heavy bursts of fire on the burning village. About 4 pm B/183 heavily shelled with 5.9. 4 direct hits on emplacements 1 emplacement receiving 2 direct hits – no casualties & no damage – except outer layer of earth on 1 emplacement cracked across. These emplacements had only been completed very recently. MGRA II Army visited Eastern Bty 41st D.A. During night of 9/10th a raid carried out with Artillery Support for which wire was cut on S.E. front – wire satisfactorily cut – See Appendix D.	Ans.
	10th		A quiet day – During night July 10/11 a raid with Artillery Support was carried out by 124th Infantry Bde see Appendix E attached – wire was reported satisfactorily cut	appx

37

WAR DIARY or **INTELLIGENCE SUMMARY** of 4/1st Div: Arty

Army Form C. 2118.

Month of July 1916

Place	Date	Hour	Summary of Events and Information	Remarks and references to Appendices
STEENWERCK	July 11th		Normal day. Some registration carried out. Enemy shelled LE BIZET, our guns retaliating on suspected Bty. All groups shells hostile support line the firm which artillery & machine gun fire was being brought on British aeroplane flying low	nil
	12th		Between 7.20 am and 10.30 am C/163 at T17 B95 was heavily shelled with 5.9" 1 Gun damaged – Captain Heysman & L/c Gibbs + 8 ORs wounded. Bty moved at night to T 24 c.1.9. Left Group cut wire etc in support of mine explosion 122nd Infantry as per Appendix F attached. Wire appeared to be successfully destroyed.	nil
	13th		A quiet day. Right group cut wire & gave support as per Appendix G to gunnery raid by 123rd Infantry Bde.	nil
	14th		A quiet day except for two hostile shelling of ST YVES about 11 am. Right Left & Centre Groups cut wire during day & neutralised support at night as per attached Appendix H to mine explosive 124th Infantry Bde. Trench mortars co-operated as per attached Appendix H.	nil
	15th		A normal day. Cut wire & gave Artillery Support to 124th Infantry Rifle raid as per attached Appendix I – hostile retaliation mild –	nil

34

Army Form C. 2118

WAR DIARY or INTELLIGENCE SUMMARY
(Erase heading not required.)

HQrs 41st Div¹ Art⁴

Month July 1916

Place	Date	Hour	Summary of Events and Information	Remarks and references to Appendices
STEENWERCK	July 16		Normal day. During night 16/17 July carried out a shoot on hostile villages & billets as per attached Appendix J. Hostile retaliation mild.	Encl.
	17th		A quiet day. Wirecutting carried out for "Stung Raid". MT. No co-operation.	Encl.
	18th		A normal day. A hostile aeroplane was seen & fired on rapidly at H 23 C 3/2.4 & fire was at once taken & ran on vicinity	Encl.
	19th		A quiet day. Wire cutting continued by Right & Left Centre Groups	Encl.
	20th		A quiet day	Encl.
	21st		Enemy shelled B & B very heavily with 15cm & 21cm during morning - doing no harm - otherwise a normal day	Encl.
	22nd		A normal day. Enemy artillery active & a slight extent on front back of front	Encl.
	23rd		A normal day. Right & Left Centre Groups wire cutting	Encl.
	24th		A quiet day. Right & Centre Groups wirecutting	Encl.
	25th		A quiet day. All groups wire cutting	Encl.
	26th		A quiet day. During night 26/27 July sting raids were carried out by 123 & 124 Inf. Bdes. Artillery support rendered in accordance with attached Appendix K by batteries from our own Div¹ A. in co-operation - MTMs - HTMs & 495 HAG to co-operate. All arrangements worked well. Wire successfully cut. All arranged operation was successfully carried out	39

WAR DIARY
or
INTELLIGENCE SUMMARY
(Erase heading not required.)

Army Form C. 2118

Place	Date	Hour	Summary of Events and Information	Remarks and references to Appendices
STEENWERCK	July 27th		A quiet day.	Aut
	28th		A normal day.	cut
	29th		A very quiet day - a few rounds 5.9 fired into NIEPPE	cut
	30th		A quiet day	cut
	31st		A quiet day - a few rounds 5.9 were fired into NIEPPE. 6" gun fired on LILLE in retaliation	cut

31/7/16

[signature] Brig. Gen.
CRA 4th Divn.

40

Appendix B. War Diary.

REPORT ON OPERATIONS NIGHT JULY 2/3

I. From 7.45 p.m., July 2nd. to 12 midnight July 2nd., 41st. Divisional Artillery subjected roads in enemy area to shell fire.

II. Detailed tasks, Ammunition allotted, and method of fire as per Appendix A attached.

III. Batteries opened fire at 7.45 p.m., as ordered. Centre Group batteries temporarily suspended fire between 7.50 p.m., and 9 p.m., owing to large number of hostile balloons up.

IV. II Corps H.A., and 11th. H.A.G. lent valuable assistance in Counter battery work.
No. 9 K.B.S. was of the utmost assistance in spotting hostile batteries active and directing counter battery fire on them. Their observations proved most accurate and I cannot speak too highly of the good work their Section did.

V.   Hostile Shelling   Retaliation

(a) Right Group (1) Trenches 98.99   —   B/189 & A/183 shelled enemy S.T.
                 (2) C.3.c.7.7½.   —   C/189 shelled BRICKFIELD U.30.c.
                                             and see counter battery work
                 (3) B/189 heavily shelled 5.9 and 4.2.
                                             See Counter battery work

(b) Centre   C/183   )
    Group   ROODEE (Gass)) Shelled consistently from 9 p.m., to
                     A/187   ) 12 midnight
                     C/187   ) Farm at A/187 burnt.
                     B/187   )

Infantry reported no activity.

(c) Left Group   C/189 received about 150 shells (4.2 and 5.9), otherwise retaliation mild and of a diffused nature.

VI. Casualties:-

    Major Multon   )
    2/Lieut. Easton) — Wounded

    1 Sergeant   — Killed

    10 Other ranks   — Wounded

VII. Damage to Guns   — Nil

VIII. Communications worked well, many wires cut by shell fire but were promptly mended, in this connection telephonists and linesmen deserve praise.
A/187 (heavily shelled and farm and outbuildings completely burnt) was dis with Group Headquarters throughout operation, but communication was maintained through C/187.

IX. In addition to general reports as to fall of our own shell -
Balloon   No.9 K.B.S., reported following:-
position
B.21.b.2.2.   (1) 8.43 p.m. Retaliation H.E. shell on farm at C.3.
                 (2) 9.0 p.m. Flashes of 4 guns at D.8.b.4.5. This Battery was engaged by 127th. H.B. (60 pdrs) and was not observed to fire again.
                 (3) 9.37 p.m. Three guns observed firing from hedge at

                U.24.d.2.4.
            at 9.57 D/190 (4.5 How) engaged this Battery
              9.58 1° Left and range.
              9.59 Dud
              10.1 Good burst and target
              10.6 Shrapnel rounds."To left & lift a little"
              10.10 Registration completed. Guns to distribute along hedge 1° at 15' interval.
              This Battery did not fire again. F.O.O. reported a direct hit.

(4) 8.55 p.m.   Two guns firing in front hedge and one in rear hedge at 0.25.d.2.3.(far north)

10.30 p.m.   Corroborated information received from 41st. D.A. that 15 c.m., battery was firing from C.6.b.3.6. This Battery was engaged and silenced in 4 rounds by D/187

Balloon position B.21.b.5.4.

10.59 p.m.   Flashes on Magnetic bearing 72°

11.10 p.m.   2 Searchlights, one MESSINES-WYTSCHAETE ridge - one on Magnetic bearing 178°

11.15-11.30 pm 1st. N.Z. trench line fighting.

ˣ11.40 p.m.   Searchlight on Magnetic bearing 153°

ˣ do. do.   Battery active. Magnetic bearing 164°

ˣ11.50 p.m.   Two Batteries active, bearings 99° & 106°

ˣ do. do.   Gun flashes Mag. bearing 140° & 154°

(ˣThese were repeated N.Z. Artillery.)

X. At 10.30 pm an aeroplane (hostile) passed over A/189 dropping 3 white lights.

[signature] Brig. Gen.
CRA 41st Divⁿ

~~Appendix A~~

RIGHT GROUP

The following shoot will ~~probably~~ take place on the night of July 2-3rd.

1. Batteries will fire on Cross Roads, Bridges, and search roads as detailed.

2. Fire should not be continuous but in short sharp bursts at irregular intervals from 7.45 p.m. to 12 midnight.

3. Number of rounds allowed per Battery 500 18 pr. Shrapnel.

4. 200 rounds of 4.5" How. H.E., may be used by D/189 for counter battery work during the operation.

5. **TARGETS**

A/183
(Road   C.6.a.0.3 to
(Cross Roads U.30.c.1½.6
(Bridges   C.5.a.3.3½
("   C.5.a.3½.5.

A/189
(Cross Roads C.11.c.7½.7½. and search
(Road back to C.11.d.8½.4
(Cross Roads C.11.c.8½.4.

B/189
(Cross Roads U.28.d.5.5. to U.29.c.0.1.
(and search road in direction of PONT
(ROUGE

C/189
(Bridge C.11.a.4½.1½., and search back
(to Cross roads C.11.a.8½.½.
(Cross Roads   C.11.b.3.9.
("   "   C.12.b.9.½.

Orders will be issued later whether this will take place tonight. The code word "GINGER" will be sent as signal to carry on.

Signal not to carry on will be "NO BARLEY WILL BE ISSUED"

Batteries detailed for N.Z. enterprise will give N.Z. enterprise preference, doing as much of the other task as possible.

PROGRAMME OF SHOOTS   NIGHT 2/3rd. July 1916.

CENTRE GROUP.

C/187   Road U.17.c.8.0.   U.17.b.3.7.

U.17.a.4.2.   to U.22.a.8.0

A/187   Road U.22.b.6.6.   U.17.c.8.0.   to

U.23.c.9.6. and

U.24.c.6.0.   U.30.b.4.7.   to

U.30.c.2.0.

B/187   Road U.23.c.9.6.   U.29.b.2.7. to U.30.b.1.6.

and roads leading from

U.23.c.9.6.   to U.28.b.9½.7½

U.29.b.2.7.   to U.29.a.5.1.

U.29.a.5.1.   to U.29.b.9½.7½

60^0 rounds a battery. 4^0 rounds each time - a burst evry 16 minutes.

Roads to be swept and searched with a large proportion of concentrated bursts on cross roads.

D/187 Counter batteries on U.23.c.9.6., U.23.c.9.2.,

U.30.a.5.3., V.19.c.4.5.

PROGRAMME OF SHOOTS for NIGHT 2/3rd. JULY

LEFT GROUP

Road	U.17.a.4.2.	to U.10.d.5½.2.	)	
X Roads	U.10.c.6.4		)	A/190
Road	U.12.c.3.0.	to U.11.d.4½.5.	)	
Road	U.10.c.4.8.	to U.10.d.6.9.	)	B/190
Road	U.4.a.7.7.		)	
Road	U.16.b.0.2½	to U.17.a.2.3½	)	
Road	U.16.b.8.9.	to U.11.c.6.5.	)	C/190
Road	U.16.b.0.7½	to U.16.b.8½.8½	)	
X Road	U.17.a.4.1½		)	B/183
Road	U.17.b.5.0.	to U.18.a.0.7.	)	

These will be fired in sharp bursts of 20 to 30 rounds at intervals of about 10 to 20 minutes.

REPORT on ARTILLERY OPERATION July 6th. and night
       July 6th/7th.

The shoot was successfully carried out last night, in accordance with programme.

In the evening commencing at 5 p.m., two batteries were engaged in cutting wire from U.15.b.1.5½. to U.15.a.9.6., and from U.15.d.8½.5 to U.15.d.9½.3½., the latter target being also engaged by two M.T.M's. Reports indicate that the wire was much damaged.

Between 10 p.m., and 10.5 p.m., the same two batteries carried out a short and sharp bombardment on the enemy's front line from U.15.b.4.5-U.15.a.9.6., and from U.15.d.8.7 - U.15.d.9½.3½.

Between 10.5 p.m., and 10.10 p.m., a barrage was put up on the following points:-

    S.T.   U.15.b.4.7. - U.15.b.0.8.
           U.15.b.4.5. - U.15.b.6.2.
           U.15.b.0.5½.- U.15.a.6½.7.
           U.16.c.2½.3½v U.16.c.2½.6.
           U.16.c.2.8.-U.16.c.1½.9.-U.15.d.9½.6½vU.15.b.
                                                           8½.0.

The bombardment was again re-opened between 10.10 p.m., and 10.15 p.m., on the front line trench from U.15.b.1.5½. - U.15.d.3½.3½.U.15.a.9.6 and from U.15.d.8½.5 -U.15.d.9½.3½., by 2 4.5" How. Batteries and 2 Sections of 18 prs.

The Centre and Right Group during the whole operation gave covering fire.

From 5.0 p.m., and 7.0 p.m., and 10 p.m.,- 10.30 p.m., the enemy retaliated firing 160 rounds (approx) of 10 c.m., and 7.7 c.m., into the neighbourhood of ST YVES, U.15.c.7.6., and the surrounding communication trenches. In the latter case a Heavy Trench Mortar was also used. This was at once engaged by three of our batteries and silenced.

No casualties were caused in the R.F.A., by their retaliation.

REPORT
on
WIRE CUTTING, Saturday JULY 8th., and
Artillery co-operation in raid night
JULY 9th/10th.

WIRE CUTTING - July 8th- carried out to satisfaction of Brigade Commanders and Infantry Concerned - Hostile retaliation on T.ms. and support trenches near ST YVES heavy.   Z/41 M.T.M. Battery carried out its task satisfactorily in spite of heavy shell fire.

Casualties: 1 O.R. killed.

Bombardment and barrage, night July 9th/10th. carried out as per programme - Wire appears to have been satisfactorily cut - Hostile retaliation very slight.

10.7.16

Cunynghame
Bh.Hth DA

Appendix. D.
War Diary

Secret

63

Herewith amended my S 449, viz Artillery Co-operation for 124th Infantry Brigade Minor Enterprise on July 8th. night 9/10
O.C. Left Group to arrange any further details with 124th Infantry Brigade.

                                                Brigade Major

6-7-17.   41st Divisional Artillery.

```
Copy No. 1  41st Division
 "   "   2  Left Group
 "   "   3   Centre  "
 "   "   4  T.M.G.
 "   "   5  124th Infantry Bde.
 "   "   6  Right Group  )
 "   "   7  183rd Bde.   )  For information.
122nd Inf. Bde.          )
Copy No. 9  123rd Inf.   )
```

K.R.A. 497

N.B.
To commence at 8.a.m. M.T.Ms to fire concurrently with B/190. O.C. Left Group to inform covering Bty times at which M.T.Ms. are firing.

WIRE CUTTING SATURDAY JULY 3rd

BATTERY	OBJECTIVE	Rounds per gun H.E.	Rounds per gun Shrapnel	T.M.	Total rounds H.E.	Total rounds Shrapnel	REMARKS
A/183 1 Sect.	U.15.d.9¾.5½ to U.15.d.9.4½¼.		150			300	
4 M.T.Ms	U.15.d.9¼.4. to U.15.d.9.4⅜½	75		300			
B/190 1 Sect.	U.15.b.1.5½ to U.15.c.8.6.		80			160	
C/187	U.21.b.8.6½ to U.21.b.8½.8½.		80			320	
A/190	To cover M.T.Ms.	15	15		60	60	
					60	60	
					300	840	

NOTE. Time of zero hour to be notified direct to Groups by 124th Infantry Brigade.

BOMBARDMENT Saturday July 8th *night July 9/10*

BATTERY	OBJECTIVE	Rds per gun H.E.	Shrapnl.	TOTAL ROUNDS M.T.M.	H.E.	Shrapnl.	REMARKS
C/190	U.15.b.1.5½ to U.15.a.9.6.	20			80	⎫ ⎬ ⎭	From 0.0 hours To 0.2" "
C/187	U.21.b.8.6½ to U.21.b.8½.8½	10			40		

BARRAGE JULY 8th *Barrage night July 9/10*

B/190 1 Sect.	U.15.d.8.6½ to U.15.d.9.7½	25	25			50	50
B/190 1 Sect.	U.15.d.9.7½ to U.16.c.½.7½	25	25			50	50	⎫ ⎬ ⎭ From 0.2' Hours To 0.22 "
A/190	U.16.c.½.7½ to U.16.c.3.4⅞	25	25			100	100
B/183 1 gun	U.16.c.3.4⅞ to U.16.c.2¼.3	25	25			25	25
B/183 3 guns	U.16.c.2.1½ to U.21.b.8½.9¼	25	25			75	75	⎫ ⎬ ⎭ From 0.2' hours To 0.22 "
C/190 4 guns	U.15.b.2.5. to U.15.b.6.2.	20	20			80	80
C/187 4 guns	U.21.b.8½.6½ to U.21.b.8½.9	20	20			80	80

19

BATTERY	OBJECTIVE	Rds per guns		TOTAL ROUNDS		REMARKS
		H.E.	Shrapnel	H.E.	Shpnl	
B/183 4 guns	U.15.d.9½.4.	5		20		From 0.25' hours to 0.27' hours
D/183	Counter battery work as active	40		160		During whole operation i.e. wire cutting july 8th and bombardment and barrage night July 8/9.
D/190		40		160		

	M.T.M	18-pr H.E.	18-pr Shpnl.	4.5" How.
TOTAL AMMUNITION	300	640	1300	320

War Diary Appendix E

Report on Artillery Support for 124th
Infantry Brigade Minor Enterprise,
night JULY 10/11th.

Wire cutting - bombardment and barrage were carried
out as per programme.

Hostile retaliation very slight and confined to
neighbourhood of Observation Posts.

Material damage   Nil
Casualties,   Nil

Communications worked well.

Wire was apparently satisfactorily cut.

An Artillery Officer was detailed as liaison officer with
OC Enterprise.
Communication was established between CoY Hdrs &
Arty Group Hdrs.

11.7.16

Bde Lt. D.A.

124th Infantry Brigade will carry out a raid on night July 10/11
41st Divisional Artillery will co-operate in accordance with
attached tables. Zero hour will be notified direct by
124th Infantry Brigade to groups concerned and this
Office.

                                                           Brigade Major

7-7-16.   41st Divisional Artillery

Copy No. 1 to 41st Divsn
"   "   2 " Left Group
"   "   3 " Centre Group
"   "   4 " 124th Inf. Bde.
"   "   5 " 122nd Inf. Bde.
"   "   6 " Right Grou)
"   "   7 " 123 Inf. Bde) for information

69

124th Infantry Brigade.

WIRECUTTING FOR ENTERPRISE JULY 10/11   S 454

BATTERY	POSITION	OBJECTIVE	rds per gun H.E. Shrap.	rds per gun Shrap.	TOTAL Rds. H.E.	TOTAL Rds. Shpnl.	REMARKS.
To be cut Saturday July 8th commencing 8 am.							
B.287 3 guns	U.15.X.3.2½ b	U.22.c.3½.4½ to U.22.c.4.2½	20	140	60	420	Range about 2400^x. Length of wire 80^x

NOTE.

(1) If wire is not cut to satisfaction of O.C. Bty and 124th Inf. Bde. by evening of 8th operations will be continued on Saturday July 9th Ammn. up to 10 rounds H.E., and 60 rounds Shpnl. per gun being used.

(2) If G.O.C., 124th Inf. Bde decides that he wishes wire at above points kept open by Artillery fire during night July 9/10, July 10/11 and up to midnight on night July 10/11, G.O.C., 124th Inf Bde. will arrange direct with O.C. Centre Group - who will use ammunition up to 60 rounds H.E. and 60 rounds Shrapnel per night.

(3) O.C. Left Group will keep wire open from U.15.a.9.6. to U.15.b.1.5½ and from U.21.b.8.6½ to U.21.b.8½.8½ open during nights July 8/9 July 9/10 and up to 12 midnight on night July 10/11 using up to 60 rounds H.E. and 60 rounds Shrapnel per night.

O.C. Left Group will inform 123rd Inf. Bde. and 124th Inf. Bde. times of firing.

70

Night JULY 10/11 BOMBARDMENT S 454

BATTERY	OBJECTIVE	Rds per gun. H.E.	Rds per gun. Shpnl.	TOTAL ROUNDS H.E.	TOTAL ROUNDS Shpnl.	REMARKS.
C/190 4 guns	U.15.b.1.5½ to U.15.a.9.6.	20		80		0.0. Hours to 0.2 "
B/183 4 guns	U.21.b.8.6½ to U.21.b.8½.8½.	20		80		

NIGHT JULY 10/11 BARRAGE From 0.2 hours to 0.22 hours

BATTERY	OBJECTIVE	Rds per gun. H.E.	Rds per gun. Shpnl.	TOTAL ROUNDS H.E.	TOTAL ROUNDS Shpnl.	REMARKS.
C/187 2 guns	U.21.b.7¾.1¼ to U.22.a.1.2¼	20	20	40	40	Length of barrage 180 yds 2¼ yds to 1 rounds
C/187 2 guns	U.22.c.3.6½ to U.22.c.3.7¼ to U.22.c.5¼.7¾	20	20	40	40	Length of barrage 160 yds 2 yds to 1 round
A/190 4 guns	U.22.c.6½.6¼ to U.22.c.7.1½	15	15	60	60	Length of barrage 250x $2\frac{1}{12}$ yds to 1 round
A/187 4 guns	U.28.a.3½.8½ to U.28.a.5¼.9¾ to U.22.c.5.1. to U.22.c.7.2.	20	20	80	80	Length of barrage 270x $1\frac{11}{16}$ yds to 1 round.

FINAL BOMBARDMENT   NIGHT JULY 10/11   0.22 to 0.25 hours

BATTERY	OBJECTIVE	rds per Gun H.E. Shrapnl.		TOTAL ROUNDS. H.E. Shpnl.		REMARKS.
B/183 4 guns	U.28.a.4.9.	10	10	40	40	
D/187 4 guns	Counter Btys as active	40		160 160 160		During whole operation i.e. wire cutting bombardment and ~~range~~ barrage
D/190 "						
D/183 "						

TOTAL AMMUNITION   Shrapnel 1040 }
                    H.E.   690 }
                    H.E.   480 4.5" How.

Appendix F. /22nd Inf Bde 12/13

Artillery Support for raid 122nd
Infantry Brigade night July 12/13th.

WIRE CUTTING JULY 12th

BATTERY	OBJECTIVE	Rounds per gun H.E.	Rounds per gun Shpnl.	TOTAL Rounds H.E.	TOTAL Rounds Shpnl.	REMARKS
B/183 1 section	U.15.a.7½.6¾ to U.15.a.9¾.6		200		400	
C/190	U.15.a.4.7. to U.15.a.6.x. 3.8½		150		600	DUD
2 T.Ms.	U.15.a.8.0. U.15.a.9.7.	20		40		DUD
B/190	U.15.b.6.2. U.15.b.8.1.		150		600	DUD By Day
A/190	Covering fire T.M.		40		160	Working in conjunction with T.M. Section
	Covering fire	20	20	40 80	80	
D/183	Counter Battery as active	40		160		
				280	1840	

War Diary

NOTE. No fire will br brought to bear from
U.15.a.5½.7¼ to U.15.b.0.5¼ from
- 0.15' to 0.0'

BOMBARDMENT (Casual) Night JULY 12/13th

Battery	OBJECTIVE	Rounds per gun H.E.	Rounds per gun Shpnl.	TOTAL ROUNDS H.E.	TOTAL ROUNDS Shprnl.	
D/183	U.15.a.4¼.9 to U.15.b.0.8	30		120		8 p.m. to 12.30 a.m.
D/190	U.15.b.0.8. to U.15.b.6.5.	30		120		8 p.m. to 12.30 a.m.
A/190	S.O.S. lines Hostile trenches front line	20	10	80	40	8 p.m. to 12.30 a.m.
C/190 1 Section	S.O.S. Hostile trenches front line	10.	10	20	20	8 p.m. to 12.30 a.m.
				240	60	
				280	1840	
		Brought forward		520	1900	

BARRAGE & BOMBARDMENT Night JULY 12/13th

BATTERY	OBJECTIVE	ROUNDS PER GUN H.E. Shpnl.		TOTAL ROUNDS H.E. SHPNL.		REMARKS
C/190 1 Section	U.15.a.2¾.9 to U.15.a.5¼.7½	10	10	20	20	
C/190 1 Section	U.15.a.6½.9 to U.15.b.0.8		20		40	
B/190 1 Gun	U.15.a.5½.½ to U.15.a.6½.9	10	10	10	10	0.0 to 0.2b'
B/190 3 guns	U.15.b.0.8 to U.15.b.2½.8 to U.15.b.2½.5½	10	10	30	30	
A/190 2 guns	U.15.b.2½.5¼ to U.15.b.5.4.	10	10	20	20	
A/190 2 guns	U.15.d.9.7. to U.15.d.7⅜.6¼	10	10	20 100 520	20 140 1900	
		Brought Forward		620	2040	

Appendix - G.

WIRE CUTTING 8 a.m. - 12 noon   12-7-16.

BATTERY	POSITION	OBJECTIVE	Rounds per gun H.E. Shpnl.		TOTAL ROUNDS H.E. Shrpnl.		REMARKS.
A/183	C.14.c.8.9.	C.4.d.1.5½ to C.4.d.2.4½ & C.4.d.2½.3½ to C.4.d.3½.2½	100	25	400	100	2 lanes 20X wide
B/189	C2a.5.5	LE TOUQUET SALIENT	40	25	160	100	
C/189	C.13.a.7.8	Point between U.28.a.5.6. & U.28.a.7.3½	40	25	160	100	

BARRAGE

TIME 0 - 0.83

A/183		C.4.d.4.6. to C.4.d.5.4.	80	20	320	80	
B/189		C.4.d.0.8. to C.4.d.2.6½ searching to C.4.d.4.6.	80	20	320	80	
C/189		C.4.d.4½.2.to C.4.d.5.1. searching to C.4.d.6.3. to C.4.d.5.4.	80	20	320	80	
D/189		Counter Bty as active	40		1680	540	160

TOTAL Ammn. 18-pr { H.E.   540
                  { Shpnl. 1680
             4.5   H.E.   160

S.170

Programme for night of 13 July 1916.

Objective	Ammunition per gun		Total		Remarks
	S.	H.E	S.	H.E	
A/183 ① C4d24 – C4d42½ and ② C4d46 – C4d54	42	15	168	60	Bombard ① P.M. 10.31 – 10.36 Stop 10.36 – 10.46 Bombard ② 10.46 – 10.51
B/189 ① C4d15 – C4d24 and ② C4d06 – C4d37	42	15	168	60	A/183 ② B/189 ② C/189 ② } 10.46 – 10.51 A/189 ① D/189 ①
C/189 ① C4d42 – C10b5.9 – C4d30. And ② C4d54½ – C4d72	42	15	168	60	resp. 10.51 – 10.56
A/189 (2 guns) ① C4d63 – C4d54½	42	15	84	30	Bombard ② at 10.31 except C/189 10.56 – 11.1 Remains on ②
			566 210 798		Total 1008
D/189 ① C4d37. C4d35 C4d54 C4d63.		30		120	Total 4.5 How.

The fire on legs in front of German trenches is being arranged by infantry own & previously your own trenches.

W.J. Pollie
Col.
Cmmg Right Group

13.7.16.

Appendix H.

ARTILLERY SUPPORT FOR AID of 124th INF. Bde. NIGHT JULY 13/14th

BATTERY	OBJECTIVE	Rds per gun H.E.	Shpnl.	TOTAL Rounds H.E.	Shpnl.	REMARKS.
Wire cutting during day JULY 13th						
4 M.T.Ms.	U.15.d.8.8½ to U.15.d.8½.9¼		75		300	Front of wire 25^X
B/190 4 guns	U.15.d.8½.9¼ to U.15.b.8.1.		200		800	Front of wire 75^X
C/190 4 guns	U.15.b.4.4½ to U.15.b.2½.5¼		100		400	"DuD" front of wire 75^X two lanes 10^X wide.
A/190 4 guns	U.15.d.9¾.3½ to U.15.d.8½.5		100		400	"DuD" front of wire 100^X two lanes 10^X wide.
C/183 4 guns	Covering fire for M.T.Ms.	25	75	100	300	
D/183 4 guns	Counter batteries as active	40		160		
D/190 4 guns	- do -	40		160		

NOTE. M.T.Ms to fire concurrently with B/190
       M.T.Ms to have a line to O.P pf C/183

TOTAL Ammunition   M.T.M   300
                   18-pr H.E. 100
                   "   Shpnl. 1900
                   4.5" How H.E. 320

BARRAGE FROM 0.0' to 0.15'

BATTERY	OBJECTIVE	ROUNDS PER GUN H.E.	ROUNDS PER GUN SHPNL	TOTAL ROUNDS H.E.	TOTAL ROUNDS SHPNL.	REMARKS
C/190 4 guns	U.15.b.0.5 to U.15.b.3½.5	5	15	20	60	i.e. 1 round to 1⅞ yds.
B/190 4 guns	U.15.b.5½.2½. to U.15.b.6.2¼ to U.15.b.9¾.3½	5	15	20	60	i.e. 1 round to 2½ yds in enfilade.
A/190 4 guns	U.16.c.1¾.8½ to U.15.d.8.6. to U.15.d.8½.5½.	5	20	20	80	i.e. 1 round to 2½ yds in enfilade.
C/183 4 guns	U.15.b.9¾.3½ to U.16.c.1¼.8½	5	25	20	100	i.e. 1 round to 2½ yds.
B/183 4 guns	U.21.b.9.7. to U.15.d.9½.0 bombardment of Front line trench	40		160		i.e 1/15 round per yard
	Brought forward			240	300	
				100	1900	
				340	2200	

TOTAL AMMN. 18-pr H.E. 340
18-pr Shpnl 2200
4.5" How. 320
M.T.M 300

NOTE.
There is no bombardment prior to raid. B.Cs. must therefore fire one or two rounds in evening on their barrage points to make sure of error for day.

78

SECRET C.R.A.
S 510.
No. 6.

WAR DIARY

(1) In connection with Minor Enterprise 124th Infantry Brigade night JULY 15/16, in order to mislead and inflict loss upon enemy.
Artillery support as per attached table will be given, <u>in addition</u> to that already arranged in my S 483 and S 507.

(2) Groups will arrange to synchronise watches with 124th Infantry Brigade and pass on time to batteries.

(3) Attention is called to note on page 2 i.e. that dose as per attached programme is repeated at - 2.0 hours.

[signature]
Brigade Major
41st Divisional Artillery.

14-7-16.

Copy No. 1 124th Inf. Bde.
"   "   2 Left Group
"   "   3 Centre "
"   "   4 41st Division.
"   "   5 FILE
"   "   6 WAR DIARY.

MINOR ENTERPRISE 124th Infantry Brigade Night JULY 15/16.

(In addition to BARRAGE from 0.0 to 0.25')

BATTERY	OBJECTIVE	Rounds per Gun H.E.	Rounds per Gun Shrap.	TOTAL AMN. H.E.	TOTAL AMN. SHRAP.	REMARKS.
C/190 4 guns	Hostile Support trenches immediately in rear of U.15.b.0.5. to U.15.b.3½.5.		15		60	From - 3.0' hours to - 2.55' hours
--do--	Hostile front line trench U.15.b.0.5. to U.15.b.3½.5.	15	5	60	20	From - 2.55' to - 2.50'
B/190 4 guns	U.15.b.5.2¼ to U.15.b.6.2½ to U.15.b.9½.3½.		15		60	)
A/190 4 guns	U.16.c.1½.8½ to U.15.d.8.6. to U.15.d.8.5½.	15		60		) From - 3.0') to - 2.55'
C/183 3 guns	U.15.b.9½.3½ to U.16.c.1½.6½.	20		60		)
B/190 4 guns	Hostile front line trench U.15.b.6.2¼ to U.15.b.8.0.	15	5	60	20	)
C/183 3 guns	Hostile front line trench U.15.b.8.0. to U.15.d.9.7½	15	5	45	15	) From - 2.55') to - 2.50'
A/190 4 guns	Hostile front line trench U.15.d.8½.5 to U.15.d.9½.3½	15	5	60	20	)
B/183	Hostile front line trench U.21.b.9.7. to U.15.d.9½.0	20	10	80	40	From - 3.0' to - 2.50'
				305	355	
				305	355	

N.B. Above will be repeated at - 2.0 hours
                                to - 1.50 "

Making total expenditure of ammunition in addition to that shown in my S 463 of 610 rounds 18-pr H.E.
                                                              710 "   "   Shrapnel.

Report on Operation of 14.7.16

Target.   U.15 d 8.8½   Wire Cutting
          to
          U 15 d 8½. 9¼

Three Mortars   No.1 manned by subsection X/41 in action
                                            about U15.c 9¾.4½
                No.2   "   "   "   Y/41 in action
                                            about U 15 d. ½.5.
                No.3   "   "   "   Z/41 in action
                                            about U 15 d ½.5

Commanded by 2/Lieut. G. Tilley. R.F.A.

Arrangements.

     Firing was done in series of 25 rounds per Mortar, each 25 being split up into groups of 5 on same line and range. Ranging was done at commencement of operation.

     The communication between O.P. and Battery was done by an orderly, telephone being proved useless on previous occasions, owing to line being broken near the guns by enemy's shelling after a short time.

Operation.

     Fire was opened about 9 A.M.

     The first series went off satisfactorily, each Mortar getting off 25 rounds.

     During second series No. 1 subsection was put out of action, owing to two hits being obtained by the enemy with 5·9's on main working trench in rear of gun pit, half burying three out of four of the gun team, and badly shaking them, while the passage between guns and bomb store was blocked up more or less. The other Guns finished their rounds although subject to very heavy retaliation with 4.2's, 5.9's, and a certain number of Trench Mortars.

Result.

As far as can be seen through a strong magnifying periscope, all wire has been stripped off the Knife rests comprising the enemy's wire, and the frames have been thrown about everywhere in disorder. Good observation was made difficult owing to the long grass among the enemy's wire.

Covering Fire

was poor, the covering Battery not having prepared in time to give much assistance to start with, though later on having accomplished the necessary switch, the Battery registered a supposed German Trench Mortar emplacement; and fired on that with apparent good results as the enemy's Trench Mortar was not very troublesome.

Retaliation

was heavy. 5.9's, 4.2's used in large numbers, apparently one Battery of each type firing, also some .77's and a few Trench Mortars.

Damage.

Casualties. To hospital, Nil, although one man was badly shaken.

Material. None reported at present. One emplacement damaged by a direct hit of 5.9" (see report above)

Rounds fired. 138.

15/7/16.

J. Longhouse. Capt R.F.A.
T.M.C. 41st Division

SECRET   Appendix I   C.R.A.
                                                        S 510.
FILE   No. 5

(1)   In connection with Minor Enterprise 124th Infantry Brigade
      night JULY 15/16, in order to mislead and inflict loss
      upon enemy.
      Artillery support as per attached table will be given, <u>in
      addition</u> to that already arranged in my S 483 and S 507.

(2)   Groups will arrange to synchronise watches with 124th Infantry
      Brigade and pass on time to batteries.

(3)   Attention is called to note on page 2 i.e. that dose as
      per attached programme is repeated at - 2.0 hours.

                                              [signature]
                                              Brigade Major
      14-7-16.   41st Divisional Artillery.

      Copy No. 1 124th Inf. Bde.
         "   " 2 Left Group
         "   " 3 Centre "
         "   " 4 41st Division.
         "   " 5 FILE
         "   " 6 WAR DIARY.

MINOR ENTERPRISE 124th Infantry Brigade. Night JULY 15/16.

(In addition to BARRAGE from 0.0 to 0.25')

BATTERY	OBJECTIVE	Rounds per Gun H.E.	Rounds per Gun Shrap.	TOTAL AMMN. H.E.	TOTAL AMMN. SHRAP.	REMARKS.
C/190 4 guns	Hostile Support trenches immediately in rear of U.15.c.0.5. to U.15.b.3½.5.		15		60	From - 3.0' hours to " - 2.55' hours
-do-	Hostile front line trench U.15.b.0.5. to U.15.b.3½.5.	15	5	60	20	From - 2.55' to " - 2.50'
B/190 4 guns	U.15.b.5.2½ to U.15.b.6.2½ to U.15.b.9½.3½.		15		60	
A/190 4 guns	U.16.c.1½.8½ to U.15.d.8.6. to U.15.d.8.5½.	15	15	60	60	From - 3.0' to " - 2.55'
C/183 3 guns	U.15.b.9½.3½ to U.1c.c.1½.8½.		20		60	
B/190 4 guns	Hostile front line trench U.15.b.6.2½ to U.15.b.8.0.	15	5	60	20	
C/183 3 guns	Hostile front line trench U.15.b.8.0. to U.15.d.9.7½	15	5	45	15	From - 2.55' to " - 2.50'
A/190 4 guns	Hostile front line trench U.15.d.8.5 to U.15.d.9½.3½	15	5	60	20	
B/183	Hostile front line trench U.21.b.9.7. to U.15.d.9½.0	20	10	80	40	From - 3.0' to-2.50'
				305	355	

N.B. Above will be repeated at - 2.0 hours
to - 1.50 "

Making total expenditure of ammunition in addition to that shown in my S 483 of 610 rounds 18-pr H.E.
" 710 " " Shrapnel.

84

ARTILLERY SUPPORT FOR AID of 124th INF. Bde. NIGHT JULY 13/14th

BATTERY	OBJECTIVE	Rds per gun H.E.	Shpnl.	TOTAL Rounds H.E.	Shpnl.	REMARKS.
Wire cutting during day JULY 13th						
4 M.T.Ms.	U.15.d.8.8½ to U.15.d.8½.9¼		75		300	Front of wire 25x
B/190 4 guns	U.15.d.8⅝.9½ to U.15.b.8.1.		200		800	Front of wire 75x
C/190 4 guns	U.15.b.4.4½ to U.15.b.2½.5⅝		100		400	"DuD" front of wire 75x two lanes 10x wide.
A/190 4 guns	U.15.d.9¾.3½ to U.15.d.8½.5		100		400	"DuD" front of wire 100x two lanes 10x wide.
C/183 4 guns	Covering fire for M.T.Ms.	25	75	100	300	
D/183 4 guns	Counter batteries as active	40		160		
D/190 4 guns	- do -	40		160		

NOTE. M.T.Ms to fire concurrently with B/190
M.T.Ms to have a line to O.P pf C/183

TOTAL Ammunition M.T.M   300
                  18-pr H.E. 100
                  "   Shpnl. 1900
                  4.5" How
                       H.E. 320

BARRAGE FROM 0.0' to 0.25'

BATTERY	OBJECTIVE	ROUNDS PER GUN H.E.	SHRAPNL.	TOTAL ROUNDS H.E.	SHRAPNL.	REMARKS.
C/190 4 guns	U.15.b.0.5. to U.15.b.3.5.	10	40	40	160	i.e. 1 round to 1¾ yds.
B/190 4 guns	U.15.b.5½.2½ to U.15.b.6.2½ U.15.b.6½.3½.	10	40	40	160	i.e 1 round to 2½ yds in enfilade
A/190 4 Guns	U.15.c.1½.8½ to U.15.d.8.6. U.15.d.8½.5½	10	40	40	160	i.e. 1 round to 2½ yds in enfilade
C/183 4 guns	U.15.b.9½.3½ to U.16.c.1½.8½	10	40	40	160	i.e. 1 round to 2½ yds
B/183 4 guns	U.21.b.9.7. to U.15.d.9½.0 bombardment of Front line trench	60	10	240	40	i.e. 1 1/15 1 round per yard.
	Brought forward			400 100 500	680 1900 2580	

TOTAL AMMUNITION 18-pr H.E. 500
                      " Spnl. 2580
                      4.5" How. 320
                      M.T.M.   300

NOTE. There is no bombardment prior to raid. B.Cs. must therefore fire one or two rounds in evening on their barrage points to make sure of error for day.

SECRET   CRA/SA90   COPY NO. 4

FILE.

Appendix J
87

(1) "Town" shoot as per attached will be carried out on night of JULY ~~15/16~~th. 16/17 ˣ

(2) The utmost secrecy will be maintained in connection with this shoot to prevent any possibility of leakage to the enemy.

(3) No reference whatsoever to this shoot must be made by telephone. All instructions in regard to same being given verbally or in writing.

(4) Group Commanders will inform G.O.C., Infantry Brigades and T.M.Btys that "41st Divl. Arty. will engage certain targets behind hostile front line between the hours of 9.0 p.m. and 10.30 p.m. night JULY 15/16th and that retaliation may be expected."

(5) Group Commanders will assemble their B.Cs and personally give them their instructions.

Battery Commanders will issue no orders until last possible moment before shoot takes place.

ˣ See my T2 of 13-7-16

Brigade Major
41st Divisional Artillery.

13-7-16.

Copy No. 1 Right Group
" " 2 Centre "
" " 3 Left "
" " 4 FILE.

S E C R E T.

TOWN SHOOT

WARNETON. including LA BASSE VILLE (for batteries that cannot reach WARNETON, only) under Officer Commanding Left Group.

A. B. C/190., B. C./183., B.A.C./187   32 18-prs
D/190   D/183,   D/187.   12 4.5" Hows.
----

per 18-pr gun   30 Shrap.   10 H.E.   960   320
Per 4.5" How.   20 H.E.   -   240

TARGET A from U.17.d.2.5. along road to U.17.b.8.4.
TARGET B   U.12.c.5.2.   "   "   " U.12.d.9.9½.

TARGET A is allotted to A.B.C. 187.
TARGET B "   "   " Remainder   O/C Left Group will notify
                                  exact target allotted to
                                  D/187 to O/C Centre Group.

Fired at the most rapid rate, commencing 9.33 p.m.

LES ECLUSES under O/C Right Group

A (1 Sec.) B.C/189., A/183   14 18-prs
D/189 Howr.   4 4.5 Hows.

Per 18-pr   30 Sh.   10 H.E.   420   140
Per 4.5" How.   20 H.E.   80

Target enclosed in following pin points :-

        U.30.d.7.2.
        U.30.d.8.2.
        C.6.b.9.7½.
        C.6.b.6½.7.

Fired at the most rapid rate commencing 9.51 p.m.

PONT ROUGE

(1 Sec.) A.B.C/189., A/183., A.B.C/187., A/190., B/183 34 18-prs

D/189., D/187   8 4.5" Hows.

Per 18-pr.	30 Sh.	10 H.E.	1020	340
Per 4.5" How.		20		160

Target enclosed in following pin points :-

        U.29.b.1.8½.
        U.29.b.7½.5½.
        U.29.b.6.3.
        U.29.b.4.3.

Divided as follows :-

RIGHT GROUP
       All houses to the South and East of contour 15 including BRIDGE. Allotment to batteries by O/C Right Group.

CENTRE GROUP
       All houses to South and East of U.29.b.2.7. up to contour 15 Allotment to batteries by O/C. Centre Group.

A/190 and B/183
       Remainder of target. Allotment to batteries by O/C Left Group.

Fired at the most rapid rate commencing at 10.11 p.m.

Total Ammunition required :-

18-pr 2,400 Sh.   800 H.E.

4.5 How.   480 H.E.

Date to be fixed and notified later.

                                                        Brigade Major

13-7-16.   41st Divisional Artillery.

Headquarters,
41st. Division

REPORT ON OPERATIONS of Night
July 26th/27th.

(1) **Right Group** in support 123rd. Infantry Brigade reports:-

guns fired as per table

hostile retaliation very slight

no material damage)
and no casualties) from hostile fire

D/187 had 2 prematures - one of which blew back killing
                                      1 other rank
                            wounding 3 other ranks

Communication with Liaison Officer with O.C. enterprise worked throughout satisfactorily.

Barrage ceased at 12.32 a.m., on order from O.C. Enterprise

(2) **Centre Group** in support 124th. Infantry Brigade reports:-

Guns fired as per table.

Immediately guns opened enemy retaliated on front and support line trenches near 112 113 and 114.

Hostile retaliation on Batteries very slight.

No material damage

No casualties

Communication with liaison Officer with O.C. Enterprise worked perfectly throughout and was used by Infantry to send messages to Battalion and Brigade Headquarters as their line was for some time "dis"

Liaison Officer was told by some of raiding party

    (a) that wire was well cut

    (b) that trench was not very badly damaged and that dug-outs were on a level with the ground.

    (c) that on approach of raiding party 4 red rockets were sent up by a German Officer from enemy front trench

Barrage ceased 1.4 a.m., on order from O.C. Enterprise.

(3) **Left Group**

Batteries fired as per table.

Hostile retaliation very slight

No casualties and no material damage.

(4) **49th. Heavy Group, R.G.A.**

Co-operated firing as per table and engaging in addition certain hostile Batteries reported active by "Flash Spotters"

Retaliation on Batteries - nil

Casualties and material damage - nil.

(5) H.T.Ms. and M.T.Ms., fired as per programme.

1 O.R. wounded.

[signature] Brigadier General,
Commanding 41st. Divisional Artillery

27.7.16

HHP

S 585

COPY NO. 14

Herewith tables shewing Arty. co-operation for strong raids to be carried out on Wednesday JULY 26th.

(1) Wirecutting will commence at once and continue till completed to satisfaction of O.C. Groups and O.C. Raids.

(2) Heavy Artillery will carry out necessary registration at once, arranging direct for necessary assistance with No. 9 K.B.S. and No. 7 Squadron R.F.C.

(3) Centre Group will use for these operations:-

    2 guns A/190
    2 guns D/183

The 2 4.5" Hows. will be moved to position selected by O.C. Centre Group.

Right Group will use :-

    2 guns C/190) under Lt. Ellison
    2 " C/183)

    2 " D/183
moved to positions selected by O.C. Right Group.

All guns to move at 12 midnight 25th and register on 26th not otherwise disclosing their positions
Where position have insufficient or now protection, deep shelter pits 2 ft. wide will be dug for detachments. No over head cover need be provided for these pits. Also similar pits for ammunition.

(4) O/C Heavy Group will notify this office when he intends to register so that T.Ms. can ~~kxxxxxxxxx~~ co-operate in wire cutting under cover of their fire.

(5) Group Commanders will make arrangements to notify T.Ms assisting their groups when to commence, and will also give such covering fire as is possible with 18-pr to 160 rounds per group and 4.5" How 40 rounds per group.

    2 T.Ms will assist Centre Group and 2 T.Ms. Right Group

(6) Dud wire cuts to be commenced as arranged by Group Comdrs.

(7) Groups will report to this office when wire is cut.

(8) Acknowledge.

22-7-16.
                                            Brigade Major
                                        41st Divl. Artillery.

Copy No.			Copy No.		
"	"	1 41st Divsn	"	"	7 Centre Group
"	"	2 II Corps H.A.	"	"	8 Left "
"	"	3 122 Inf Bde.	"	"	9 T.M.C.
"	"	4 123 " "	"	"	10 190 Bde
"	"	5 124th Inf. Bde.	"	"	11 49th Hvy. Group
"	"	6 Right Group	"	"	12 FILE
			"	"	13 Spare

583/F

SECRET

Copy No. 13

AMENDMENT to S 583

Please amend my S.583, as follows:-

RIGHT GROUP.

(1) Bombardment -1.0 hours to 0.0 hours
    2 M.T.Ms. Front line trench from
        C.4.d.2.4½.to C.4.d.3¼.3.

(2) Bombardment -1.0 hours to 0.10' hours
    should now read
    Bombardment -1.0 hours to ~~0.10'~~ hours
                           0.0

(3) Add:-

    Bombardment 0.0 hours to 0.10' hours
    4 4.5" Hows. C.4.d.3¾.6 to C.4.d.6½.3.
    1 4.5" How.   C.4.d.6¼.2¾
    1 4.5" How.   C.10.b.5.6. to C.10.b.4½.4.
    1 6"   How.   C.4.d.3¾.6. to C.4.d.4½.4½.
    1 6"   How.   C.4.d.4½.4½.to C.4.d.6½.3.

(4) Barrage by Howitzer 0.10' hours to time of exit of
                                raiding party.
    1. 4.5" How. Machine Gun at C.4.a.7½.4½.
    should now read
    1 4.5" How. C.5.a.3.3½.

N.B. Above all apply to programme for Right Group, i.e.,
      in support of 123rd. Infantry Brigade raid.

Acknowledge.

                                    Brigade Major,
24.7.16   41st.Divisional Artillery.
HHP

No.1 41st.Division
No.2. Right Group
No.3. Centre Group
No.4. Left Group
No.5. 190th.Brigade, R.F.A.
No.6. T.M.C.,
No.7. 122nd.Infantry Brigade
No.8. 123rd.Infantry Brigade
No.9. 124th.Infantry Brigade
No.10. 49th.H.A.C.
No.11. II Corps.H.A
No.12 FILE
No.13 Spare.

Army Form C. 2118

WAR DIARY
or
INTELLIGENCE SUMMARY
(Erase heading not required.)

of 41st Div! Art. HQrs Vol 4
Month of August 1916

Place	Date	Hour	Summary of Events and Information	Remarks and references to Appendices
STEENWOORDE	Aug 17		A quiet day	Cont.
	18		A quiet day	Cont.
	19		A quiet day	Cont.
	20		A quiet day. During night 19/20 1 Sect of each Bty 41st DA relieved by 1 Sect 23rd DA - Sections 41st DA relieved being withdrawn to wagon lines for night & proceeding on morning of 20th to billets in IX Corps Reserve area near EECKE.	Cont.
	21		A quiet day. During night 20/21 Remainder 41st DA Btys relieved by Remtr 23rd D.A. Btys - Btys 41st DA proceeding to wagon lines & thence on morning of 21st to billets in IX Corps Reserve Area near EECKE. At 10 am Comm and handed from CRA 41st Div to CRA 23rd Div. HQrs 41st Div proceeding to EECKE	Cont.
	22		During night 22/23 Aug - Day Aug 23 - & night 23/24 Aug. 41st DA Intrained at BAILLEUL WEST & main & GOEDWAERSVELDE Stations & proceeded to X Corps Area HQRS at PONT REMY. By 11 am. 25.8.16 all units 41st DA reported in billets. Detraining having taken place at ABBEYVILLE, PONT REMY & LONG PRÉ LES CORPS SAINTS.	Cont.
PONT REMY	23 24 25			

1875 Wt. W593/826 1,000,000 4/15 J.B.C. & A. A.D.S.S./Forms/C. 2118.

Army Form C. 2118

WAR DIARY
or
INTELLIGENCE SUMMARY of H&rs 41st Divl Arty
(Erase heading not required.)

Instructions regarding War Diaries and Intelligence Summaries are contained in F. S. Regs., Part II. and the Staff Manual respectively. Title Pages will be prepared in manuscript.

Place	Date	Hour	Summary of Events and Information	Remarks and references to Appendices
PONT REMY	Aug 26		Continued training of all units 41st D.A.	And
	27		do	and
	28		do	and
	29		do	and
	30		do	and
	31		do	and

H. Mackinnon Brig. Gen. commdg
41st Divl Artly

31/8/16

Army Form C. 2118

WAR DIARY
or
INTELLIGENCE SUMMARY

(Erase heading not required.)

Vol 5

of 41st Divl Artly Hqrs
Month of September 1916

Place	Date	Hour	Summary of Events and Information	Remarks and references to Appendices
PONT REMY	Sept 1st		On night 1st/2nd 41st Divl Arty accompanied by HQ. 41st Divl Train	
ARGOEUVES	2nd		ASC marched in accordance with attached orders Appendix A to billets WEST OF AMIENS. HQ 41st DA being established at ARGOEUVES	nil
RISEMONT	3rd		On night Sept 2nd/3rd 41st Divl Arty with HQ Co 41st Divl Train marched to billets bivouac immediately WEST of DERNANCOURT in accordance with attached orders Appendix B. 41st Divl Arty Hqs being established at RISEMONT 5.30 a.m. 3rd Sept.	nil
"	4th		Reconnoitred positions for 183 & 187 Bdes RFA near S.16.d & S.22.d (LONGUEVAL 1/10000) near LONGUEVAL	nil
"	5th		183rd & 187th Bdes RFA commenced preparation of positions. Reconnoitred positions for 189 & 190 Bdes RFA near Sqre. S.9.d. S.10.c & S.10.d NORTH & EAST of BAZENTIN-LE-GRAND	nil
"	6th		189 & 190 commenced preparation of positions. Some difficulty in obtaining sufficient material.	nil
BELLEVUE Fm	7th		During day of Sept 7th & night Sept 6/7 41st DA moved up into action in accordance with attached Appendix "D" HQrs 41st DA being established at BELLEVUE Fm N28.d5 12 noon Sept 7th	nil

WAR DIARY or INTELLIGENCE SUMMARY

Army Form C. 2118

Place	Date	Hour	Summary of Events and Information	Remarks and references to Appendices
BELLEVUE Fm	Sept 7th		Uu til 41st Divn take over portion of line 41st DA remained XVth Corps Artillery. Approximate zone of 41st DA 600 yds on either side LONGUEVAL – FLERS Road. Brigades continued to dig in. Arm't Dumps established & manned. All Brigades reported in position by 7 pm Sept 7th.	
"	8th		CRA visited Bdys 189 & 190 Bdes. All Batteries to have digging in selected positions. Arm't supply as per attached Appendix E	cont.
"	9th		Batteries commenced registration & continued digging in	cont.
"	10th		Registration continued. Officers of 21st DA proceeded to Bdys.	cont.
"	11th		From 12 noon 41st DA took over close defence of portion of line into Appendix F. Position of Bdys 21st DA to cover same zone as 41st DA commenced by 41st DA	cont.
"	12th		At noon 12th. The preliminary bombardment commenced in accordance with Appendix G (xthorta RA O – O – 410 & 41st DA O no 8) C/190 attached Appendix H to be under Corp for attached Appendix H	cont.
"	13th		Position in any bombardment continues as per Appendix G. Night 13/14 Bdy. 21st DA got into position, left group 21st DA approximately close to 189 & 190 Bdes 41st DA – Right group 21st DA close to 163 & 187 Bdes RFA	A.C.

WAR DIARY
INTELLIGENCE SUMMARY 41st Divl. Artl. HQrs.

(Erase heading not required.)

Army Form C. 2118

Place	Date	Hour	Summary of Events and Information	Remarks and references to Appendices
~~Sept 15~~ BELLEVUE Fm	14th		Preliminary bombardment continues - All Btys 21st DA remain position & carry out registration - a quiet day.	Cont
"	15th		Attack commences. 41st Divl Arty Group (41st & 21st DAs) act as laid down in attached Appendix I.	
		7.12 am	Infantry reported in 1st line	
		7.28 am	F.O.Os sent forward	
		7.54 am	122nd Inf Bde have SWITCH TRENCH	
		8.31 am	95th Bde report Infantry advancing on FLERS - F.O.Os. sent forward	
		8.10 am	Hostile shelling on Btys slight	
		9.12 am	1. 106th "D" pound Bty left group 21st DA ordered to advance	
		9.33 am	2. Remaining "D" pound Btys left group 21st DA ordered to advance	
		9.45 am	D pound Btys right group McDA ordered to advance	
		9.58 am	Major Lewis 183 + 167 Bdes ordered forward to MAMETZ	
		10.1 am	Tanks ordered to proceed to reach Btys not moving & await orders	
		10.12 am	183rd RFA report "second objective taken, Infantry fighting in outskirts of FLERS - Hostile barrage	
		10.20 am	NORTH edge of DELVILLE Wood. Situation + all Btys	
		10.17 am	C/189 only 2 guns in action	
		10.30 am	Report from Lt Lancaster RFA - we hold SOUTH of FLERS and trench T.1.C.8.2."	
		10.50 am	Major Wickham reports we hold all FLERS	

WAR DIARY or INTELLIGENCE SUMMARY

Army Form C. 2118

(4)

Place	Date	Hour	Summary of Events and Information	Remarks and references to Appendices
BELLEVUE FM Cont.	Sept 15	9.40 am	F.O.O. via Major Wickham report "We are well into FLERS - one Tank there also"	
		11.1 am	1 Bty of 167 Bde RFA from Creeping barrage ordered forward to join remnant of 167 Bde.	
		11.30 am	From 7=DA Enemy massing at N25 d 4.2. XV=Corps HA informed.	
		11.30 am	183rd Bde report little or no hostile shelling of Batys.	
		11.50 am	Tank seen advancing between FLERS and GUEUDECOURT	
		11.58 am	B/95 ordered forward	
		10.am delayed	95th Bde RFO report our troops pouring into FLERS - hostile supports advancing W & NW of GUEUDECOURT	
		10.35 am	Delayed Liaison Officer reports our troops well into FLERS & hostile supports on both flanks.	
		12.45 pm	All Bdes ordered to push forward observation to ensure forward liaison Officers & Infantry. Bdes + to act on situation demands.	
		12.10	F.O.O. reports "NZ Bty coming into action near me at T1c24. Our infantry digging themselves in along front of FLERS TRENCH M46 S6B & T1a. This line not heavily shelled - but small hostile barrage in front of it. Our supports moving up to this line. Enemy barrage seen the hollow FLERS which is being shelled"	
		12.40	F.O.O. reports "a 2"d NZ Bty coming into action near T1c24 - 1 Tank has returned from FLERS - Can see no sign of a Counter attack".	
		1.15	183 Bde report "Bn of nd Bde Right flank advanced 12.15 pm"	
		1.30	Major Wickham reports:- "1 Bn enemy troops massing 1000 x N of FLERS - 15" Buffs HA informed 1.15 pm" "Reinforcements continually pouring along road M30C5.2 to M34B9.6 XV° Corps HA informed.	

WAR DIARY or INTELLIGENCE SUMMARY

Army Form C. 2118

41st Divl. Artly. H.Qrs.

Place	Date	Hour	Summary of Events and Information	Remarks and references to Appendices
BELLEVUE Fm	Sept 15	p.m. 1.50	FLERS heavily shelled - within 300 x in village. 95 Bde RFA HQrs HONEY-ALM CHURCH	
		2.6	Reinforcements moving E + NE of GUEUDECOURT	
		2.10	Parties of men seen at M35.B at 12.20 (delayed)	
		2.27	F.O.O. reports at 12.25 p.m. "FLERS village was captured - Boche had heavy casualties + its left flank was exposed - So withdrew. Our front line is now FLERS TRENCH + support line SWITCH TRENCH - Highest point QUADRES TRENCH is a strong point. One tank been advancing to GUEUDECOURT - The tank which stopped this side of FLERS is returning".	
		2.55	At 1.50 barrage on FLERS RIDGE and HIGH WOOD slackening.	
		3.12	190 Bty which have not moved are putting barrage about 700 x NORTH of FLERS at 2.55 p.m.	
		3. pm	At 2 pm 2 Btys 21st DA reported in action about SUN Central.	
		3.30	Our infantry in Box + Cox - all Brigades informed.	
		3.30	C/96 moved to join 95 Bde RFA Remaining Battery 187 to join Colonel Hoods group in 187 Bde.	

Army Form C. 2118

WAR DIARY
or
INTELLIGENCE SUMMARY
(Erase heading not required.)

41st Divl. Arty. HQrs.

Place	Date	Hour	Summary of Events and Information	Remarks and references to Appendices
BELLEVUE Fm	Sept 15th	4 P.M.	All Btys. ordered to "cut wire in GIRD TRENCH by tonight — 4.5 How'rs ordered to deal with Trenches & OPs as far as safe — Gas shell to be used on points where roads cross OPs both advance & during night.	
		4.12	Hostile guns at N26.d.5.4 again written turned on to genl. Heavies informed.	
		5.0	Hostile Howrs firing from direction of LE SARS	
		8.30	Orders to B/187 to advance not received.	
		9.A	All Brigades ordered to carry out inform night firing on GIRD LINE AND WESTERN portion of GUEUDECOURT and on any known gun positions. Order repeated by phone through 183 Bde RFA	
		10.18	B + C Btys 187 Bde not having moved — 187 Bde ordered to have Btys in action in advanced position by 5 am 16th Sept.	
"	Sept 16th	1.15 am	190 Bde RFA with A/189 + D/189 under O.C. 190 Bde ordered to advance to positions SOUTH of FLERS & in vicinity of SGd.	
		1.35 am	Report that "A" wht/w DAC arrived in new position 11 pm Sept 15th	
		9.20 am	O4. B. to harness the ready to move	
		12.50 p.m	183.? Bde report Btys less C/183 entrained	

1375 W.. W593/826 1,000,000 4/15 J.B.C. & A. A.D.S.S./Forms/C. 2118.

Army Form C. 2118

WAR DIARY
or
INTELLIGENCE SUMMARY   41st D.A. H&AN
(Erase heading not required.)

Place	Date	Hour	Summary of Events and Information	Remarks and references to Appendices
BELLEVUE Fm	Sept 15	1.30 pm	C/190 and D/9B came to be employed under OC Cavalry Rly Amn Pk & report to Commander 41st DA	
		1.45	Attack on GIRD TRENCH reported failed — enemy barrage very heavy. Orders for barrage received to all Bties.	
		1.50	7 Dials wired to 169 Bde.	
		2.7	C/190 placed under orders of 169 Bde.	
		2.5	Orders re barrage etc for attack at 6.25 pm received to all Bties.	
		7.15	Heavy firing & red lights reports SE of GUEUDECOURT	
		9 pm	Attack noted for 6.25 pm having apparently failed (or not materialised) all Bties ordered to stop barrage	
		10.20	Orders re night firing issued	
		11.10	169 Bde ordered to reconnoitre positions about S5c + 2	
			183 — — — — — — S6a + b + M36d	
			Rifle group 21st DA — — — — N31c. T1 & T.1c	
		11.50	189 ordered to advance Composite Bty (B + C/189) to most forward position vacated by 190 Bde RFA	aul

WAR DIARY
or
INTELLIGENCE SUMMARY
(Erase heading not required.)

41st D.A. H&rs

Army Form C. 2118

(8)

Place	Date	Hour	Summary of Events and Information	Remarks and references to Appendices
BELLEVUE Fm	17th	12.30 am	Orders for bombardment & wire cutting on 17th received from Bde.	Sept 17th Weather very wet
		10.20	189 Composite Bty in action in position vacated by 190 Bde.	
		1.5 pm	Instructions from XV Corps re Amm allotment.	
		4.30	Amm allotment for night received	
		4.25	183 & 94 Bde intend to advance	
		8.45	183 and 95 Bde intend to reach Schattich afterwards from in FLERS to wirecutting.	Ard.
		10.30	Orders re day & night firing from all Bdes.	
	18th		During night Sept 16/17 41st Divᵈ (less 41st DA) relieved by 55th Divᵗ Weather very wet. Continued normal day & night firing & improvement of position. Supply of Ammn very difficult - whole country axle deep in mud. Hars 41st DA moved at 6 pm to POMMIERS REDOUT	Ard.
POMMIERS	19th		Continued normal day & night firing - Weather very wet - Ammn supply almost impossible	Ard.
"	20th		" " " " " " " "	Ard.
"	21st		" " " " " " " "	Ard.
"	22nd		Weather improved - normal day -	Ard.

Army Form C. 2118

(9)

WAR DIARY
or
INTELLIGENCE SUMMARY 41st D.A. H.Qrs

(Erase heading not required.)

Place	Date Sept	Hour	Summary of Events and Information	Remarks and references to Appendices
POMMIERS	23rd		Normal day. Weather fine & country drying up well - horse lines somewhat worn out.	cont
"	24th		Bombardment commenced in accordance with orders attached & proceeded normally - Hostile shelling normal - Weather fine but very thick mist in early morning -	cont
"	25th		Bombardment continued till 12.35 pm a few rounds attached.	
		12.35 pm	At 12.35 pm (zero hour) Barrage as counter as a per 41st DA OO 17 & Appendices - Infantry commenced assault	
		1.3 pm	Aeroplane reports infantry our GIRD TRENCH	
		1.22	CUBIC FOO reports "1.9 pm Infantry in GIRD TRENCH - at 1.10 pm infantry at FACTORY CORNER - at 1.13 pm Red flare at N26 c 45".	
		1.31	LINNET FOO reports "Infantry moving over crest to left of GUEUDECOURT"	
		1.45	21st Div. reported hung up in GIRD TRENCH from junction of GIRD TRENCH and N33 c00	
		1.55	Flares seen at N26 c 46 & N26 c 63	
		2.5	1.90 reports heavy barrage on FLERS	
		2.6	Balloon hostile which brought down.	
		1.58	Red flare high ground 300x WEST of GUEUDECOURT	
		2.10	Red flares at N25 B 88 & FACTORY CORNER at 1.25 pm. Our Suffolk moving up & right of GUEUDECOURT	

Army Form C. 2118

WAR DIARY
or
INTELLIGENCE SUMMARY
(Erase heading not required.)

A/2nd Div¹ R.A. HQrs

(10)

Place	Date	Hour	Summary of Events and Information	Remarks and references to Appendices
POMMIERS	25th Sept	2.28	190-Bde F.O.O. reports "at 2.3 pm our Infantry can be seen consolidating GIRD SUPPORT at N26C58. No enemy movement visible N of FACTORY CORNER"	
		2.35	At 1.5 pm our Infantry advancing on trench W. WEST corner of GUEUDECOURT.	
		2.45	Our Infantry report they are in GIRD TRENCH & in touch on right with 110 Inf. Bde 21st Divs.	
		2.52	21st Divs reports they are in S.W. corner of GUEUDECOURT	
		2.55	Two large fires in FLERS. Enemy appear to be massing WEST of GUEUDECOURT	
		3.5	95th Bde R.F.A reports "large numbers of enemy retreating along LIGNY TILLY road about N16a29. Red Flares in GUEUDECOURT — Our Infantry consolidating FACTORY CORNER.	
		3.30	94th Bde R.F.A. observed barrage 1 15pdr B.E, to S.E of FLERS	
		3.40	190 Bde R.F.A reports "Infantry hold FACTORY CORNER. Hostile barrage in FLERS & GUEUDECOURT diminishing. Machine gun fire from LES BOEUFS. 9/90 Dispersed parties of enemy at N20B75. No signs of counter attack. Large bodies of our infantry advancing parallel to left coy of GUEUDECOURT.	
		4.16	Barrage reduced to 1 round per gun per 6 minutes	
		4.30	Cavalry reported moving along LONGUEVAL — FLERS road.	

Army Form C. 2118

WAR DIARY
or
INTELLIGENCE SUMMARY   41st D.A. H&rs

(Erase heading not required.)

Place	Date	Hour	Summary of Events and Information	Remarks and references to Appendices
PONIVILLERS	25	4.50	55th Divn 1G1. Cavalry hill advance by WEST side of GUEUDECOURT — Head of C.ant h.W NE of FLERS	
			Barrage expedited in accordance. All Bdes learned to watch situation & support Cavalry	
		5.10	94th Bde RFA report M.G and N7b&y 1 holding up 21st Divn. 7th Dn informed	
		5.30	Heavy enfilading attack on Cavalry — It Winfield tells that C.oxt. moved up to between FLERS & GUEUDECOURT to then withdraw.	
		7 pm	Orders issued re night firing — 500 barrage etc & to commence harassing early Sept 26 on GIRD LINE north of SUNKEN ROAD.	
		8 pm	Rept of 94th Bde last report movet of troops to remain in its present position.	
		9 pm	Situation in GUEUDECOURT very obscure — but almost certain that 21st Divn has troops in village. Earlier in day but have since had to withdraw	
		9.5 pm	183 Bde ordered to move Counter Bn into FLERS for his entering.	
	26th	5.30 am	B/183 which secured gun in action in FLERS	
"		7.40 am	Heavy Barrage on GUEUDECOURT	
			Situation in GUEUDECOURT still somewhat obscure.	

Army Form C. 2118

(12)

WAR DIARY
or
INTELLIGENCE SUMMARY
(Erase heading not required.)

41st Divl Arty HQrs

Instructions regarding War Diaries and Intelligence Summaries are contained in F.S. Regs., Part II. and the Staff Manual respectively. Title Pages will be prepared in manuscript.

Place	Date Sept	Hour	Summary of Events and Information	Remarks and references to Appendices
POMMIERS	26th	9.5 am	Wire cutting continuing — orders for normal day firing issued.	
		9.25	Enemy seen at N14d.7.1. & very heavy hostile barrage. All roads under F. barrage. 95 Bde RFA & dead HIGNY TILLOY road.	
		10.15	Situation — 55th Divn front normal — on 21st Divn front objecting down — hostile barrage almost ceased.	
		11.5	55th G Report Strong point Construction & movement at N20D.1.0 — all R.Bn heard.	
		11.20	Various conflicting reports re movement of troops and cavalry.	
		4.20 b	Local counter attack on FACTORY CORNER driven by m. gun fire.	
		4.30	Counter attack by 2 Battalions from N14d dispersed by our gun fire before it could materialise.	
		4.50 4.7 5.50	Various conflicting reports re cavalry.	
		7 pm	Situation :— 55th Divn holds line of front objective of 25th forming with NZ Divn on left and 21st Divn on right who now hold all GUEUDECOURT + GIRD TRENCH. LES BOEUFS, MORVAL TIEPVAL in British hands. — COMBLES in French hands.	
		7.15pm	Orders for night firing issued — also 41st DA 20 to 18 2e Combardment showing for 27th Sept.	

Army Form C. 2118

WAR DIARY
or
INTELLIGENCE SUMMARY

(Erase heading not required.)

41st D.A. H.Qrs

Instructions regarding War Diaries and Intelligence Summaries are contained in F.S. Regs., Part II. and the Staff Manual respectively. Title Pages will be prepared in manuscript.

Place	Date Sept	Hour	Summary of Events and Information	Remarks and references to Appendices
POMMIERS	27	11.45 a.m.	D.A. O.P reports North Bty in action O.2.0.a - XVI Corps H.A informed	
		11.55	Huns observed working in trench in N.9 central & N.10. Bty of Artillery moving E.7 & 5° on road in N.9. Engaged & henced 7.0	
		p.m. 12.5	95½ Batt took effect - line in N.9.d just east of road not cut - 189 Bde & 95°. Bde take it on	
		12.10	Infantry report all ready to line no obstacle. Good lanes through it, wire not completely destroyed.	
		1.20	Huns reported lying out in rear of GIRD SUPPORT. Ground scanned.	
		1.20	Continuous movement seen in N.3, N.6, N.9 - Heavies told.	
		1.35	M.Gs traffic in BAPAUME - TRANSLOY Rd - Heavies told.	
		1.55	2.0.0. Huns retire from N.14d to N.8d - Engaged with success.	
		1.58.	Wire reported now all cut.	
		2.25.	Our infantry advancing rapidly with little opposition.	
		2.35.	Fire reported in D/189. Three gun pits burnt out - 3 guns out of action wheels carriage, & sights damaged - 1 casualty only as at time guns were looking & drivers. Fire caused by high shell fire	
		2.36	Infantry passed our wire without hindrance.	
		2.37	Infantry advancing steadily from FACTORY CORNER - Huns retiring towards LIGNY TILLY	
		2.55	GIRD TRENCH Taken - Infantry advancing on GIRD SUPPORT	

WAR DIARY
or
INTELLIGENCE SUMMARY
(Erase heading not required.)

Army Form C. 2118

41st D.A. HQrs.

Place	Date Sept.	Hour p.m.	Summary of Events and Information	Remarks and references to Appendices
POMMIERS	27	3.12	Cubit report:—	
			(1) Enemy retreating at his South of TILLOY ROAD at N8 a 1.7 — Heavier told	
			(2) Our infantry have gained their objective	
			(3) Our troops digging in	
			(4) Heavy hostile barrels on font of behind our infantry but is now slackening	
		3.20	D.A.O.P. reports hostile Btys active along 130 contour between MLLE AUX POIS & ROEQUIGNY — Heavies, etc	
		3.34	Huns retiring in Orgs	
		3.50	N9c & N8d full of Huns. Huns retiring (about 1 Coy) in N7 d 8.0 — Heavier barrage — & support by our guns.	
		4 pm	Enemy observers at N14 B 73 — Engaged	
		4 pm	14th D.A. report counter attack on N.Z. front — Our Btys told to assist — but no confirmation of this attack can be obtained.	
		4 pm to 4.15 pm	Conflicting reports as to enemy retiring & advancing in front of 65th Divn Btys sweep & search Huns observed with Lead ground about N20 a & N9 B. This ground clear.	
			C/190 get good effect against bodies in open moving from N8 & N9 to N13 d N14 c d	
		4.28	Counter attn at about 500 strong reported in N9. N10 — B/190 engages with success.	
		4.28	94th Bde ordered to advance at dusk 1 18 pdr Bty to S6 B 74. 1 How Bty to T 1 a 1/2.7.	
		4.30	14th DA report enemy in N8 & N13 — Engaged	
		4.40	95th Bde deals with Huns in N14	
		4.45	DA O.P. reports all quiet on our front. No movement can be seen	

Army Form C. 2118

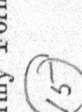

WAR DIARY
or
INTELLIGENCE SUMMARY 4/15 D.A.H.Arz.
(Erase heading not required.)

Instructions regarding War Diaries and Intelligence Summaries are contained in F. S. Regs., Part II. and the Staff Manual respectively. Title Pages will be prepared in manuscript.

Place	Date Sept	Hour a.m.	Summary of Events and Information	Remarks and references to Appendices
PONNIERS	27	5.5	G.S.F. Bde report:—	
			(1) TILL TRENCH full of enemy & much movement along it.	
			(2) The advance from FACTORY CORNER met with no opposition — Huns retired from N.19 central — bolts in front of our infantry —	
			(3) Infantry in sight of attack have eaten up so far behind barrage	
			(4) On whole front small parties of enemy retiring	
			(5) Have seen small party enemy advanced from TILL TRENCH.	
			(6) Observed turn on LESARS - BAPAUME road & in BEAULENCOURT CHURCH — Heavies told.	
			(7) Hostile balloon looks loose — occupants descending in parachutes.	
		5.15	All Bdes noticed Kitchen barrage.	
		5.25	B/90 report heavy movement in Felix hill redan from Nq. N10 & N3 towards N13 central & engaging them with machine guns.	
		5.10	CHEW report " Tramtrack West of BAPAUME about H.26" — Heavies told.	
			" HAV Bty got into troops advancing in line N13d & N14a & stopped them.	
		5.35	Counter attack about N.19 B reported — Engaged by 189, 190 & 95 Bdes.	
		5.45	55th Divn. report "Huns many S.9 & H and lying out in N.13 central & sunken road N.13 d & 3. Road reached with Hows. & open ground with 18 pdrs.	
		6 pm	All quiet on our front.	
		6.20	Night barrage arranged with 7E & 14E D.A.	

Army Form C. 2118

WAR DIARY
or
INTELLIGENCE SUMMARY
(Erase heading not required.)

Place	Date Sept	Hour am	Summary of Events and Information	Remarks and references to Appendices
POMMIERS	27-	6.50	95th Bde report that when our Infantry advanced to the attack the enemy used a packet breaking into 4 red stars.	
		7.45	Liaison Officer at 2nd Aus Div HQrs reports :— Our Infantry consolidating — Some shell fire — Our Casualties not heavy — many Hun dead & a few prisoners — Enemy reported massing in N20A & in trench at N20C3b	
		8.20	Orders issued to Stop barrage — Night firing to slow time — XVI Corps "Prisoners Report" copy hereto helping him "SEVEN DIALS" — FACTORY CORNER are to be believed tonight — All Bdes informed to attend to any special alteration to sustain barrage.	
		10.30	All Bdes warned re patrols going out.	
			General. Night 27/28. Quiet. Intense interest to bring in normal day firing on Sept 28th. Information from prisoner shows that the enemy hostile movement reported during the day Sept 27th was the enemy attempting a daylight relief — only 1 Co got through & that suffered heavily. Infantry report enemy heavy troop & left of attack gained objective without a casualty. Hostile aeroplane dropped bombs in POMMIERS near about 11 pm. Killing 60 or 70 horses of a 47th Bty —	Cont.

WAR DIARY or INTELLIGENCE SUMMARY

Army Form C. 2118

HQ 41st D.A.

(Erase heading not required.)

Instructions regarding War Diaries and Intelligence Summaries are contained in F. S. Regs., Part II. and the Staff Manual respectively. Title Pages will be prepared in manuscript.

Place	Date	Hour	Summary of Events and Information	Remarks and references to Appendices
POMMERS	28		Night 27/28 quiet. A quiet day.	Ant
"	29		A quiet day. During night 28/29 123rd Inf Bde attacked 21st Div. relieved 104 Inf Bde of 35th Div. 55th Div'n left the line.	Ant
"	30		XVth Corps Artillery rearranged. Right Group now consisting of 41st Div. 30th Infantry Gp. Sth D.A's under CRA 41st Div'n.	
			A quiet night – a day.	
			Anti-tank defence 41st D.A. to No 19. Order moved & reorganising to be more complete by noon. Left 30th.	Ane
			Change of gone complete by noon. Left 30th.	
			General Remarks.	
			Experience contains this essential that HQ DA should be able to repeat to Bde HQs. Every operation on a purely RA line.	
			Provide supply light Railways for forward supply should be for his forward much lower than tends have many casualties & men & heavy not unnecessary in state of knocked.	
			Reinforcement. Sonisjon gunners should be kept separate from tent up definitely earmarked to How Btys.	
			Refer Felegion of all such are required.	Signature CRA 41st D.A. Whittington Brig. Genl. CRA 41st DA

Appendix A   CRA
                     ――――
                     SM 420

41st. Divisional Artillery

Operation Order No. 3

1. 41st. Divisional Artillery will march during night September 1st/2nd. to billets WEST of AMIENS in accordance with attached March Table.

2. 41st. Divisional Artillery will remain in billets during day September 2nd., and continue march on night September 2nd/3rd. under orders to be issued later

3. Units should at once send forward billeting parties of one Officer per Brigade or D.A.C., and 1 N.C.O. per Battery or Section D.A.C.
   O/C., 189 Brigade, R.F.A., will leave accommodation for H.Q., Co. 41st. Divisional Train, A.S.C., (approximate strength = 1 Battery) and for Headquarters 41st. Divisional Artillery in ARGOEUVES.
   O/C., 187th. Brigade, R.F.A., will arrange billets for T.M.C., and X/41, Y/41, Z/41, and V/41 T.M. Batteries at AILLY (approximate strength 9 Officers and 146 Other ranks).

4. Refilling point to-morrow, September 2nd. CHURCH at AILLY - SUR - SOMME at 10 a.m.

5. All units will halt for ten minutes at ten minutes before each hour. There will be a halt of 1 hour's duration, commencing at 9.50 p.m., till 10.50 p.m., at which hour march will be resumed (the ten minutes' halt at ten minutes before the hour in this case, being omitted)

6. Brigades will arrange to fetch Guns from I.O.M. Workshop at HANGEST-SUR-SOMME. Limbers and teams to be at I.O.M., Workshop at 6 p.m., to-day and proceed thence to their respective Billets via CROUY and PICQUIGNY. Those billeting NORTH of RIVER cross at PICQUIGNY and proceed via LA CHAUSSEE etc.

7. All units will send orderlies to 41st. Divisional Artillery Head quarters at ARGOEUVES at 9.a.m., 12 noon, and 4 p.m., on September 2nd.

8. All chalk-marks on billets will be obliterated and billets will be left clean. Units will be responsible that these orders are carried out.

                                    Brigade Major,
                                    41st. Divisional Artillery.

1.9.16
HHP.
No.1 183rd. Brigade R.F.A.,
No.2 187th.   "   "
No.3 189th.   "   "
No.4 190th.   "   "
No.5 "A" Echelon, D.A.C.
No.6 "B" Echelon, D.A.C.
No.7 T.M.C. 41st. D...
No.8 41st. D...
No.9 ....
No.10 ....

Appendix B

SECRET   Ref AMIENS Sheet 17

41st. DIVISIONAL ARTILLERY
OPERATION ORDER No. 4.

I. On night Sept. 2nd/3rd. 41st. Divisional Artillery, accompanied by H.Q., Co. 41st. Divisional Train, A.S.C., will march to the neighbourhood of DERNANCOURT, in accordance with attached March Table, where they will bivouac.

II. ½ mile interval will be maintained between Brigades, ¼ mile interval between Batteries and Sections of D.A.C.

Connecting files must be maintained between Brigades Batteries, D.A.C., etc., to ensure that above intervals are carefully preserved.

When head of column reaches DERNANCOURT, units must halt without closing up.

III. (a) Rate of March 3 miles per hour.

(b) 10 minutes halt at 10 minutes before each hour

(c) halt of 1 hour's duration from 11.50 p.m., to 12.50 a.m., at which hour march recommences (the 10 minute halt at 12.50 a.m., being omitted)

IV. Guides will meet Brigades etc., at Cross roads 1¼ miles N.W. of DERNANCOURT D.12.d.8.6. (Sheet 62 d)

V. Officer Commanding HQ., Co. 41st. Divisional Train A.S.C., will, on arrival, report to Officer Commanding M.T. at BUIRE.

VI. 41st. Divisional Artillery Headquarters will be at West end of RIBEMONT. Brigades, D.A.C., and T.M.C. will send orderlies to 41st. Divisional Artillery Headquarters immediately on arrival to report, and also at 9 a.m., 12 noon and 8 p.m., daily.

BRIGADE MAJOR,
41st. Divisional Artillery.

10.15 am
2.9.16
HHP
No.1 183rd. Brigade,
No.2 187th. Brigade,
No.3 189th. Brigade,
No.4 190th. Brigade
No.5 D.A.C.,
No.6 T.M.C.,
No.7 H.Q.Co., 41st. Divisional Tarin, A.S.C.,
No.8 41st. Division,
No.9)
" 10) SPARE.
" 11)
" 12)

MARCH TABLE

Ref.Map Amiens Sheet 17 and Sheet 62D,

UNIT	Starting Point	Time Head of Unit passes starting point.	ROUTE
Headquarters 41st.Divl.Artillery	CHURCH at LONGPRE	8.30 p.m.	AMIENS - QUERRIEUX - Cross Roads 1½ miles N.W. of DERNANCOURT D.12.d.8.8. - DERNANCOURT
190th.Brigade,R.F.A.	"	8.40 p.m.	Ditto.
189th.Brigade,R.F.A.	"	9.20 p.m.	Ditto.
H.Q., Co.41st.Divl. Train A.S.C.	"	9.55 p.m.	Ditto
187th.Brigade,R.F.A.	"	10.10 p.m.	to starting point via ST.SAUVEUR & ARGOEUVES, and as above.
183rd.Brigade,R.F.A.	"	10.50 p.m.	Ditto.
41st.D.A.C.	"	11.30 p.m.	Ditto
T.M.Batteries	Billets	5. 0p.m.	per Motor Lorry via AMIENS QUERRIEUX and as above.

41st DIV.
R.A., H.Q.
October, 1916

WAR DIARY or INTELLIGENCE SUMMARY of 41st Divl Arty

Army Form C. 2118

Vol 6

Place	Date October	Hour	Summary of Events and Information	Remarks and references to Appendices
POMMIERS	1st		IVth Army continued the attack – 41st D.A. Group (41st D.G. & 5th (Ind) D.A.C.) co-operating in accordance with Appendix A attached.	
			B/187 Bty remained under orders from Bty Group XVth Corps H.A.	
			2 18pdr Btys from 187 & 189 Bdes were detailed to assist attack by III Corps with Appendix B.	
			41st DA.G. carried out programme as ordered – barrage finally ceasing at 7.15 p.m. When night firing was resumed.	
			Operation successful – N.Z. Divn gaining its objective. 21st Divn advanced patrols some 600 yds but these patrols were withdrawn at dusk.	
			Observation was bad owing to haze.	
			Hostile shelling on Bty's light.	
			Night Oct 1/2 183 Bde advanced registering guns & new positions in FLERS.	Oct.
	2nd		A quiet day.	
			New hostile trenches left under fire to prevent but weather very bad to permit main becoming a bog.	
			Night Oct 2/3. Remainder of Btys 183 Bde moved into new positions with orders to remain silent till next offensive.	
			190 Bde advanced registering guns from new position about M36B.	Oct.

WAR DIARY or INTELLIGENCE SUMMARY

Army Form C. 2118

(Erase heading not required.) HQ 41st DA

Place	Date	Hour	Summary of Events and Information	Remarks and references to Appendices
POMMIERS	3		A quiet day – 183rd Bde in new position – weather wet.	
"	4		A quiet day – weather very wet. Ammunition supply exceedingly difficult – roads practically impassable.	
"	5		Quiet day, weather very bad	
"	6		Strong wind considerably drying up roads. At 3.15 pm bombardment of attack on F commenced in accordance with Appendix C attached.	
"	7th		Bombardment continued from 7.45 am to zero – 183 Bde RFA joining in. Observation good – weather cold leaving to wet in afternoon. Hostile shelling on Bty posns slight – in front line very heavy.	
		1.45pm	Barrage & attack commenced in accordance with Appendix D attached – programme was carried out in 4th orders.	
			Throughout the afternoon somewhat conflicting reports were received from all sources as to progress of the attack –	
		9.30pm	Situation as follows – Left & centre of 12th Divn practically in original trenches, attack failed owing to very heavy hostile barrage & machine gun fire from N.20 central approx. Right attack of 12th Divn progressed better but only succeeded in establishing string posts from about N.27.B to N.27.W to original line about NE corner of GUEUDECOURT	

WAR DIARY or INTELLIGENCE SUMMARY

(Erase heading not required.) 41st Divl Artl HQrs.

Army Form C. 2118

(3)

Place	Date Oct	Hour	Summary of Events and Information	Remarks and references to Appendices
POMMIERS	7th		20th Divn on right obtained greater part of objective — 41st Divn — left established a line about 200 yds in front of objective — Advanced part of a good resistance being put up by 6th Bavarian Divn — Infantry main line from heavy command before attack — & prisoners stated they were reforming attack at 1.45 pm. This looks as if Huns had got information as to zero hour. — A quiet night — country again impassable.	Ack
	8th		A quiet day — wet & visibility very bad. Gentle shelling on B/ys not close — but very heavy shelling on front line — 5th DA B/ys ordered to withdraw during night 8/9 Oct & proceed to LA NEUVILLE on arrival at which place they come under command of CRA 5th Divn. 3 men relieved to cover gap left by 5th DA.	Ack
	9th		A quiet day. A slow methodical bombardment of both hr dn continued	Ack
	10th		Slow bombardment continue - 62nd Bde RFA (Colonel Myrue DSO) 12th DA (3 18pdr Btys & 1 4.5 How Bty) joined 41st Dvy & received priorities rations by 5th DA about 17a 27. 17a 55 of a new position at SBC. Guides & assistance supplied by 41st & 30th DAs. Above 2e 3 men SK embodied in 41st DA oo no 24 zero for bombardment revised at 5 pm & attached in Appendix E.	Ack

Army Form C. 2118

WAR DIARY
or
INTELLIGENCE SUMMARY

(Erase heading not required.) 41st DA HQrs.

Place	Date Hour	Summary of Events and Information	Remarks and references to Appendices
POMMIERS	11th	Bombardment continued vide Appendix E. 6.4th Bde 12th DA (2.6pm 15pdr BP) joined 41st DAG into action right bat 11/12 in S5d (approx). Order to arrange for attack out rot round after change of arrangements from higher authority.	
POMMIERS	12th	Attack commenced at 2.5 p.m. 41st DAG cooperating as per Attached Appendix F. Enemy barrage somewhat late in starting and then very heavy on GUEUDECOURT behind Brit front	
	2.30 pm	British aeroplane brought down near FLERS	
	3.7 pm	Own infantry seen advancing. Situation very obscure till about 4.50 pm - visibility bad + fumes obscured by smoke + dust	
	4.50 pm	Situation "Right Brigade gained 2nd objective + is in touch with left Bde. On right no touch with 6th Div."	
	5 —	Quiet in front - hostile shelling slight - some prisoners coming in. Sent say 1st line taken. Easily + full of German dead.	
	5.30 pm	Situation "Right Brigade apparently driven back on 1st objective"	
	5.33 pm	he again bangs on BACON Trench + to the East along 2nd objective	
	5.35 pm	Prisoner of 92nd Hanoverian Regt. captured by Durhams had no news of the Brandenburg Division + he said German losses were very severe	

WAR DIARY or INTELLIGENCE SUMMARY

Army Form C. 2118

HQrs 41st DA

(5)

Place	Date Oct	Hour	Summary of Events and Information	Remarks and references to Appendices
POMMIERS	12th	6.5pm	Situation apparently home in 2nd objective – Barrage placed on 2nd objective. How rate of fire reduced. 1/181 Bde moved to head road from North of HORSENNOF to LIGNY TILLOY.	
		6.20pm	30E DA Barrage brought back to 150 yds in front of 1st objective	
		7.10pm	Whole barrage placed 150 yds in front of 1st objective	
		8.20pm	Situation finally as follows:– Left Brigade back in original line – Right Brigade holding 1st objective as far west as N.20.d.4.6. Normal night firing resumed. S.O.S line 150 yds in front of above line. Orders to shift of 12½ DA Bdys by 29th DA Bdys to finishing zones. A quiet day. Raining & muddy. normal day firing. BGs of 147 & 15 Bdes 29th DA proceeded to Bdy positions of 62 & 64 Bdes RFA.	Ant. Ant.
	13th			
	14th		Ghost bombardment carried out as per attached Appendix G – in addition normal day & night firing. A.C. & D Bdys 163 Bde withdrawn from FLERS position owing to heavy shelling & positions about S.6.d.3.2. prepared. 15E Bde RHA & 147 Bde RFA 29th DA completed relief of 62 & 64 Bdes RFA. 12E DA on night 14/15th Oct.	Ant.
	15th		HQrs 41st DA & 185 Bde & 15E Bde RHA & 63rd Div on right as per Appendix H attached & carried out bombardments as per Appendix I.	Ceek

Army Form C. 2118

WAR DIARY
or
INTELLIGENCE SUMMARY

(Erase heading not required.)

H/Q 1st D.A. HQrs

Place	Date Oct	Hour	Summary of Events and Information	Remarks and references to Appendices
POZIERES	16th		A fine day. Observation good - wire cutting carried out. Bombardment as per attached appendix #J.185 Retp A.C.D. withdrawn to position near S.6.d. owing to h'enemy shelling. Hostile intermittent hy artie -	See
"	17th		A fine day - frost at night. Bombardment carried out as per attached Table K.	Cont.
"	18th a.m. 3.40		Attack commenced - Hun barrage opened 2 or 3 minutes later - Too much trench hostile. Shelling throughout morning & night.	
	5.45		148 Bde intercepted infantry message which stated 3 Cos in GREASE Trench.	
	6.0		FACE Trois left Co. gained objective - Right Co held up by concealed wire. Barrage main trained on BAYONET TRENCH from N20a65 to the WEST with occasional bursts of intense fire. Reinforced by 1 gun 190 Bde	
	6.40		189 Bde ordered to block BAYONET TRENCH at N20 b 65 with 1 section assisted by 1 gun 190 Bde	
	7.10		Liaison Officer FACE gives situation as :— Left Brigade. 3 right Cos held up by wire in shallow trench close in front of BAYONET TRENCH - Left Co. gained objective but was bombed out. Left Brigade went to original trench & holding new trench N20c38 - N20c89 Right Brigade holds GREASE TRENCH from N20d79 - N21c17 & one Co in HILT TRENCH about N20d65	

Army Form C. 2118

WAR DIARY
or
INTELLIGENCE SUMMARY

(Erase heading not required.) HQ 41st DA

Place	Date	Hour	Summary of Events and Information	Remarks and references to Appendices
PONNIERS		7.40	Barrage stopped - Artillery Action:-	
	30th		DA & 147 Bde maintain a slow rate of fire on hostile barrage line left flank Trenching SOUTH to about N20a82 & over GREASE TRENCH	
			41st DA & 15th Bde brought slow rate of fire both Howrs & 18pdrs onto BAYONET TRENCH as far EAST as N20d 27- All dead ground being searched & special attention paid to rallying from LIGNY TILLOY to N20B. FACE informed of above.	
		8.25	Right Bde held GREASE trench up E & including strong point at N20B 6.0	
			Right Bde reported bombing down - 15th Bde moved to come from Left of Right Bde attention BACON TRENCH & took over	
		10.0	BAYONET TRENCH and took over attention BACON TRENCH + took over. Barrages etc as per attached Appendix L.	
	19th		A quiet day - 29th Divi relieves 12th Divi on night 19/20. Weather very wet -	
	20th		Weather very wet - harassed day & night firing - heavy hostile shelling on Bdys.	90
	21st		informed fire & frag: heavy hostile shelling on Bdys.	
	22nd		fire & frag: a quiet day.	
	23rd		Very thick fog in morning. Heavy bombard. SOUTH END BAYONET TRENCH. Bombardment from 2.5 Bde commences bringing fire to no 35 attacks.	

Army Form C. 2118

WAR DIARY
or
INTELLIGENCE SUMMARY

(Erase heading not required.) HQrs 41st D.A.

Instructions regarding War Diaries and Intelligence Summaries are contained in F.S. Regs., Part II. and the Staff Manual respectively. Title Pages will be prepared in manuscript.

2747
SP
91

Place	Date	Hour	Summary of Events and Information	Remarks and references to Appendices
POMMIERS	24th		Weather very wet - Operations postponed	Cont.
	25th		A quiet day - incessant rain - country a quagmire - roads impassable	Cont.
	26th		Weather too bad for active operations - normal day & night firing	Cont.
	27th		Do	Cont.
	28th		Do Operations postponed to 31st Oct	Cont.
	29th		Do	Cont.
	30th		Do Operations postponed to Nov 12th	Cont.
	31st		On night Oct 30/31 and Oct 31/Nov 1, 41st DA relieved by sections by 2nd Australian DA. Guns & Amn being handed over owing to impossibility of withdrawing guns in the mud. Relief withdrawn to wagon lines - to march on Nov 1st to BONNAY area.	

Signature: [signed] Br General R.A.
Comdg 41st D.A.

SECRET

I. If tactical position permits, 21st D.A. will be withdrawn on nights Oct. 13/14 and 14/15th.

II. 12th D.A. will take the place of 21st D.A. - and the group at present known as 21st D.A. Group will become 12th D.A. Group.

III. On same dates 29th D.A. will come into the line - 2 Brigades 29th D.A., joining 41st D.A.G., in lieu of the two Brigades 12th D.A., at present in 41st D.A.G.

IV. Communications, orders registrations, airphotos, maps, etc., and all dumped ammunition will be handed over by 62nd & 64th Bdes., to Bdes., 29th D.A.

V. D.As. will retain their own guns and Howitzers.

VI. From 12 noon on 13th Oct. D/190 will come under orders of XVth Corps Counter Battery Group for Counter Battery work. From this hour D/189 will take over zone of D/190 in addition to its own zone.

VII. On night 13/14th Oct.

1 Sect. per battery of 62nd & 64th Bdes R.F.A., with B.Cs and Bde Commanders will be relieved by 1 section per Bty B.Cs and Bde. Comdrs of 147th and 15 (less Howr Bty) Bdes 29th D.A. Sections 29th D.A. will carry out registration on Oct.14th.

On night Oct. 14/15th

Remainder of Btys 62nd & 64th Bdes will be relieved by remainder of Btys of 147th Bdes (less Howr Bty 15th Bde.) Detail of relief to be arranged between O.Cs 62nd & 64th Bdes and O.Cs 147 and 15th Bdes respectively.

VIII. Command will pass from O.Cs 62nd & 64th Bdes to Os.C 147th & 15th Bdes on completion if relief of first sections on night Oct. 13/14th.

IX. The two 18-pr Btys EAST of FLERS - LONGUEVAL and the How. Bty of 62nd Bde will be relieved by the 147th Bde. R.F.A.

The two 18-pr Btys 64th Bde & the 18-pr Bty 62nd Bde WEST of the FLERS - LONGUEVAL road will be relieved the 15th Bde R.F.A.

X. Zones of 147 & 15th Bdes will be :-

147th Bde. R.F.A.
(a) Right Boundary   N.20.d.2.0 - N.15.c.0.0, - N.3.d.1.0
(b) Left   "   N.20.c.9.0 - N.14.d.5½.0 - N.3.c.7.0

15th Bde. R.F.A.
(a) Right Boundary line in X (b)
(d) Left   "   N.20.c.6.4. - N.20.a.8.0 - N.8.d.5.0. to N.3.c.0.0.

N.B. 183rd Bde Right boundary will become line in X (d)

147th Bde.   2 18-prs   10th and 97th
              1 Howr.   D/147.

15th Bde. R.H.A.   B.L.Y.

At 10 a.m. Oct. 13th.

~~Representatives 29th D.A., Btys arrive POMMIERS.~~
~~Guides to meet~~

Howitzer Bty of 147th Bde. R.F.A., will cover whole zone of
147th Bde and and 15th Bde.
Above adjustment of zones will take effect from 6 p.m. Oct.
15th.

XI Hqrs 147th Bde R.F.A., will take over HQrs of 62nd Bde
    "   15th " R.H.A.   "   "   "   "   64th Bde.

Wagon lines of 62nd and 64th Bdes will not move.
147th Bde and 15th Bde will select their own wagons
(suggested S.28.a., S.28.b., S.22.c. or S.22.d.)

XII Representatives from each battery of 62nd and 64th Bdes will
     meet representatives of 147th and 15th Bdes at 41st D.A.
     Hqrs POMMIERS REDOUBT at 10 a.m. Oct. 13th.

XIII A portion of 29th D.A.C. will join 41st D.A.G., abd will be
     located near 41st D.A.G. Dump. Guide will meet representative
     of 29th D.A.C. as in para XII.

XIV Completion of relief will be notified to this office and
     co-ordinates of battery positions as soon after relief as possibe,

XV   ACKNOWLEDGE.

                                                              Brigade Major

12-10-16.   41st Divisional Artillery Group

XV Corps H.A.,
"   "   R.A.
12th D.A.,
29th D.A. (4 copies)
30th D.A. (5 Copies)
64th Bde
62nd "
183   "
187th "
189   "
190   "
41st D.A.C.,
5 spare
12th Divsn.

S E C R E T.   Appendix A   Ref. Sheet 57.c.S.W. 1/20,000.

41st Divisional Artillery Operation Order No.20.

1. Fourth Army in conjunction with Reserve Army continues the attack on October 1st.

2. XVth Corps takes part as under :-
   (a) The New Zealand Division will capture the enemy trenches from M.24.b.05 to REDOUBT at M.23.b.74 inclusive and establish a line through N.19.a.55 - M.24.b.75 - M.24.b.05 - M.23.b.74 connecting with III Corps on left.
   (b) 21st Division will proceed as in para. 8.

3. The attack will be carried out at zero hour which will be 3.15pm October 1st.

4. The attack will be preceded by a bombardment of the enemy's defences in front of the whole XVth Corps front commencing at 7.am. and continuing till one hour after zero by the Heavy Artillery.

5. There will be no intense fire before zero.

6. At zero hour there will be an intense artillery barrage on the enemy's defences opposite that part of the Corps front from which no attack is being launched.
   Advantage will be taken of this barrage to gain ground to the front with a view to future operations.

7. Flares will be lit on capturing the objective; also at 5.pm. and 6.pm. October 1st, and at 7.am. on October 2nd. Yellow flares will be used.

8. The G.O.C. 21st Division proposes to advance patrols as under :-
   (1) from about N.20.c.65 to N.20.Central.
   (2) three patrols from N.E. edge of GUEUDECOURT to trench N.21.c.1 to N.27.a.9.7½.

9. 41st D.A. Group will put up barrages as under to cover the advance of the patrols and their consolidation of strong points in their objectives.
   (a) Creeping barrage.
       (1) From zero hour to 2 minutes after zero
           N.27.a.8.5½ - N.21.c.0.4½ - N.20.d.6½.2½ - N.19.b.4.5.
       (2) At 2 minutes after zero creeps at 50 yards per minute to a line :-
           N.21.d.22 - N.21.c.38 - N.20.b.06 - N.19.b.4½.7. and remains until further orders.

   (b) Stationary barrage.
       (1) From zero to 4 minutes after zero
           N.27.a.9.7½ - N.21.c.1½.6 - N.20.b.20 - N.19.b.5.8½.
       (2) At 4 minutes after zero barrage advances by lifts of 100 yards per minute to a line
           N.21.d.57 - N.21.a.24 - N.14.d.60 - N.13.d.50 and remains till 1 hour 30 minutes after zero.
       (3) At 1 hour and 30 minutes after zero stationary barrages searches backwards and forwards to a line 400 yards North of line in para. (3) by lifts of 50 yards until further orders. para 9(b)(2)

   Rates of fire for creeping and stationary barrages :-
   From zero to 5 minutes after zero - 3 rounds per gun per minute.
   From 5 minutes after zero to 25 minutes after zero -
        1 round per gun per minute.
   From 25 minutes after zero to 45 minutes after zero -
        1 round per gun per two minutes.
   From 45 minutes after zero to 1 hour and 5 minutes after zero -
        1 round per gun per 4 minutes.

-2-

9.   (b) contd.

    From 1 hour 5 minutes after zero till stop -
        1 round per gun per 6 minutes or bursts
        of fire equivalent to that rate.

10.   The creeping barrage will be entirely 18-pdr shrapnel, of which 30% should burst on graze.
The stationary barrage will be 75% H.E.
50% of the 18-pdr batteries will be employed on the creeping barrage.
50% of the 18-pdr batteries on the standing barrage.

    Groups and Brigades will be responsible for barrages in their own zones.

11.   Counter battery work will be actively carried on.

12.   4.5" Hows. will deal with any active hostile batteries within range, search all dead ground beyond most distant line of standing barrage and take advantage of any fleeting opportunities in their own zones. Special attention will be paid to sunken roads.
    (a) in N.21.b. and N.15.d.
    (b) LIGNY TILLOY - Factory Road North of N.13.d.55.

13.   41st Divisional Artillery O.P. in SWITCH TRENCH will be manned by 187th Brigade from daylight till 6.pm. October 1st.

14.   183rd and 187th Brigades will each detail one 18-pdr Battery and the 30th D.A. two 18-pdr batteries from stationary barrage to take advantage of fleeting opportunities. Remaining batteries of stationary barrage sweeping at an increased rate to cover gaps left.

15.   The times in the above order are normal GREENWICH time.
    The change from Summer time to normal GREENWICH time takes place at 1.am. on 1st October at which hour watches will be put back one hour, i.e., to 12 midnight.

16.   Acknowledge by wire.

Issued 9.30.pm.   Major, R.A.,
30-9-1916.   Brigade Major, 41st Divnl. Artillery.

Copy to:-
    XV Corps H.A.   30th D.A. (7 copies).
    XV Corps R.A.   183rd Bde. (5 copies).
    41st Divn.   187th "   "
    21st   "   189th "   "
    N.Z. Divn.   190th "   "
    Guards "   41st D.A.C.
    14th D.A.   T.M.C. 41st Divn.
    20th D.A.   4 spare.

"A" Form.
MESSAGES AND SIGNALS.
Army Form C. 2121.

TO: 41" DA

Sender's Number.	Day of Month	In reply to Number	AAA
CA 439	30.9.16		

Following programme for two batteries of 18 pr of your ~~division~~ group in support of III Corps ~~batties~~ is forwarded for compliance

(a) Time 10.7am to 10.14 am

Objective Trench M23a 3½ 0 6 — M22b 3½. 0

Rate of fire Rapid

(b) Time Zero to 7 min after Zero

Objective as in (a)

Rate of fire Rapid

"A" Form.
MESSAGES AND SIGNALS.
Army Form C. 2121.

| Prefix...Code...m. | Words | Charge | This message is on a/c of: | Recd. at...m. |
| Office of Origin and Service Instructions. | Sent At...m. To... By... | | ...Service. (Signature of "Franking Officer.") | Date... From... By... |

TO { (2) }

| Sender's Number. | Day of Month | In reply to Number | AAA |
| CA 439 | | | |

(C) At 7 minutes after zero fire will be lifted back 50 yards at a time in a N.E direction to the road from M 23 a 6.8. to M 17 c 35 where the fire will remain till 0.30 and then cease

N.B (1) The period of rapid fire at noon is cancelled

(2) Rapid fire is considered as 2 rounds per gun per minute

(2) Acknowledge

From 15th Corps Artillery
Place
Time 10.35 pm

SECRET.

Appendix. C.

41st Divisional Artillery Group Operation Order No.22.

1. The XVth Corps will on October 5th attack.

   The trenches running round the East and North of GEUDECOURT from our junction with the XIV Corps.
   BAYONET Trench (N.20.Central - N.13.Central) and off shoots N.20.a.3.9 to N.19.b.8.9 and N.13.d.5.3 to N.13.d.2.3.
   LUISENHOF Farm (N.13.d.7.9).
   LIME Trench (N.13.b.8.0 - N.13.c.6.8 - N.13.c.2.8).
   GIRD Trench from M.24.b.0.4 to M.17.b.95.10.
   GIRD Support from M.24.b.6.6 to M.18.a.15.20.
   and various small trenches in M.18 and M.24 and establish themselves on a line running approximately N.21.b.6.0 - N.14.b.5.5 - N.13.b.7.1 - M.18.a.15.20. This latter will include taking BACON Trench (N.20.b.9.6 - N.14.d.4.2) and the portion of BARLEY Trench which lies West of N.15.a.3.1.

2. The bombardment will commence at 3.15.pm. on October 4th and continue till 5.15.pm.
   From 5.15.pm. October 4th until 7.45.am. on October 5th firing will be continued at reduced rates and from that hour until zero at the same rate as on the afternoon of October 4th.
   There will be no intense fire before zero.
   Commanders of 18-pdr batteries must be warned to be careful as on the 1st October the increase of 18-pdr fire was very noticeable 2 or 3 minutes before zero.

3. (a) The G.O.C. Heavy Artillery is arranging the bombardment of trench system in para. 1 as also villages of LE BARQUE, LIGNY-THILLOY and TILLOY.
   (b) The 41st D.A. Group will bombard the trenches in their zones with 4.5" howitzer and 18-pdrs using H.E. principally for this purpose.
   During bombardment the ground on both sides of the trenches for 400 or 500 yards will be searched in case the enemy withdraws.
   Any wire that may be in their zones will also be cut and night firing used to prevent repair.
   (c) The usual fire to prevent movement will also be carried on by day and by night.

4. ~~At night only half the 4.5" howitzer batteries need be firing at the same time, but the fire must be distributed throughout the whole of the trenches for moral effect.~~

5. Rates of fire -
   4.5"Hows. from 6.30.am. to 3.15.pm.   100 rounds per battery.
              3.15.pm. to 5.15.pm.   160   "   "   "
   Night firing - 5.15.pm. to 7.45.am.
   D/183 and D/150 will not take part in the night bombardment.
   4.5"How. batteries will fire 20 rounds per battery per hour.
   18-pdrs from 6.30.am. to 3.15.pm. will fire 40 rounds a gun.
          "   3.15.pm. to 5.15.pm. 30 rounds per gun.
          "   5.15.pm. 4th October to 7.45.am. 5th October
               90 rounds per gun.
   183rd Brigade will not fire until 7.45.am. 5th.
   On 5th October all 4.5"Hows. will fire 20 rounds per gun per hour from 7.45.am. until zero.
   All 18-pdrs will fire 30 rounds per gun between 7.45.am. and
                                                         Zero.

6.

O.O.22.   -2-

5̶6̶. 	Usual counter battery work will be carried out.

6̶7̶. 	Orders for lifts and Field Artillery barrages will be issued separately.

7̶8̶. 	Acknowledge.

[signature]

Major, R.A.,
3-10-1916.   Brigade Major, 41st Divisional Artillery Group.

  Copies to :- 41st D.A. 2.
         30th D.A. 2.
         183rd Bde. 5.
         187th Bde. 5.
         189th Bde. 5.
         190th Bde. 5.
         148th Bde. 5.
         149th Bde. 5.
         150th Bde. 4.
         27th Bde. 5.
         41st D.A.C. 1.
         30th D.A.C. 1.
         5th D.A.C. 1.
         30th Sig.Sec.1.
         41st " " 1.

SECRET

AMENDMENT to 41st. DIVISIONAL ARTILLERY
GROUP OPERATION ORDER NO.23.

Delete para 3 (d) From "At 27" to "and ceases" and substitute:-

3 (d) At 27 minutes after zero hour standing barrage WEST of N.14.a.0½.3½. (i.e., 189th., 190th., and 187th. Brigades, R.F.A) and 34 minutes after zero standing barrage EAST of N.14.a.8½.3½, searches back 400 yards at 100 yards a minute and ceases.

5.10.16
HHP

Appendix D

SECRET.   1.   Refs. Map 57.c.S.W.1.
                       1/10,000

41st DIVISIONAL ARTILLERY GROUP OPERATION ORDER No. 23.

In continuation of 41st Divisional Artillery Group Operation Order No.22 :-

1. At zero hour on October 7th 12th Division will attack, the 41st Division on left and 20th Division on right attacking also. The 41st Divisional Artillery Group will cooperate with (a) a creeping barrage, and (b) a standing barrage.

2. Creeping barrage (50% 18 pdrs. in action) entirely 18 pdr. shrapnel.
   (a). Zero to 2 minutes after zero on line :- N.13.d.2½.2 to N.20.a.7.2 to N.20.d.4.2½ to N.21.c.0.2¼ to N.27.a.6.8 to N.27.b.1.7.
   (b). At two minutes after zero, advances by 50 yards a minute to line :- N.13.d.5.7½ to N.14.c.3½.5 to N.20.b.2½.3 to N.21.d.5.2½ and remains till 20 minutes after zero.
   (c). At 20 minutes after zero advances by 50 yards a minute to line :- N.13.b.6.6½ to N.15.a.1.4 to N.21.b.9½.1 and remains till further orders.

RATES OF FIRE.

From zero to 2 mins. after zero	2 rnds. per gun per min.
From 2 mins. after zero to 7 mins. after zero	3 " " " " "
" 7 " " " " " 20 " " "	2 " " " " "
" 20 " " " " " 45 " " "	1½ " " " " "
" 45 " " " " " 65 " " "	1 " " " " "
" 65 " " " " " 85 " " "	1 " " " " " 2 mins.
" 85 " " " " onwards	1 " " " " 4 "

3. Standing barrage. Remainder 18 pdrs. in action firing 50% shrapnel 50% H.E.
   (a). From zero to 2 minutes after zero -
   41st and 5th D.A. on BAYONET TRENCH.
   From zero to one minute after zero -
   30th D.A. on trench N.20.d.8.4 - N.21.c.0.4 - N.21.c.7.0 - N.27.a.9.9 RAINBOW TRENCH.

   (b). At 2 minutes after zero 41st and 5th D.A's and
   at 1 " " " 30th D.A. lift by 100 yards a minute to line :-
   N.13.d.5.9¾ to BACON TRENCH, along BACON TRENCH to N.21.d.8.4 and remains till 20 minutes after zero.

   (c). At 20 minutes after zero barrage advances 100 yards a minute to line :-
   N.13.b.6.7 - BARLEY TRENCH to N.15.d.4.8 along trench to N.15.d.7.0 to N.22.a.2.6 and remains till 27 minutes after zero.

   (d) At 27 minutes after zero standing barrage searches back 400 yards at 100 yards a minute and ceases.
   N.B. 30th D.A. and 189th Brigade, R.F.A. will detail 18 pdr. Battery each from standing barrage to take advantage of fleeting opportunities, the gaps left in the standing barrage being made good by remaining batteries of standing barrage.

Rates of fire for standing barrage :-

From zero to 3 mins. after zero	3 rounds per gun per min.
3 mins. after zero to 20 mins. after zero	2 " " " " "
20 " " " " 2530 " " "	1 " " " " "
25 " " " " 3234 " " "	3 " " " " "
34 " " " " 38 " " "	1

4. On cessation of standing barrage, standing barrage batteries will be employed as follows :-

30th D.A. will maintain a barrage on :-
(a) Road from N.21.7.8 to N.15.b.5.1,
(b) BREAD TRENCH from N.21.b.9.7 to N.15.b.0.5
(c) BARLEY TRENCH from N.15.c.9.9 eastwards.

5th D.A. will maintain a barrage on :-
(a) Road junction at N.9.d.7.3.And search at frequent intervals,
(b) Valley from about N.15.central to N.8.central.

41st D.A. will frequently search villages of LIGNY TILLOY and TILLOY: all dead ground and all possible hostile approaches in their zone.

Rate of fire equivalent to 1 round per gun per 3 minutes for 1 hour, slackening thereafter to 1 round per gun per 4 minutes.

5. 4.5" Hows. will from zero onwards bombard all trenches in advance of standing barrage. After cessation of standing barrage they will deal with all sunken roads, roads and trench junctions communications and villages in advance of final line of creeping barrage.

Rate of fire equivalent to 1 round per gun per 6 minutes.

6. Zero hour will be notified.

7. Watches willbe synchronised at 9 a.m.

8. All batteries will have dumped near guns at zero hour :-
450 rounds 18pdr. per gun.
350 "   4.5" How. per gun.

9. 41st D.A. O.P. will be manned by 187th Brigade, R.F.A from one hour before zero.

10. Exact objectives of Infantry will be found in 12th Division O.O. No.113 attached.

11. The infantry will indicate their positions by means of yellow flares which will be lit on reaching each objective, also at 4 pm. and 5 pm. on October 7th and at 7 am. on October 8th.

12. Maps will be issued showing barrages and the two objectives of the Infantry.

13. ACKNOWLEDGE.

Major,
5-10-1916.   Brigade Major, 41st Div'nl. Artillery Group.

COPIES TO :- XV Corps R.A.   XV Corps H.A.   41st D.A.C.
             41st Div.   Div.(4 Copies)   T.M.C. 41st Dn.
             30th D.A.(20 Copies) 185 Bde.(5 Copies)   41st D.A.Signals.
             21st D.A.   187 "   "   Spare 4.
             20th D.A.   189 "   "
                                   190 "   "

S E C R E T.   Ref. Sheet 57 c.S.W.
                1/20,000.

Appendix E.

41st Divisional Artillery Group Operation Order No. 24.

I. The following will be bombarded by Field and Heavy Artillery and will be attacked on October 12th by 12th Division -

(a) Trenches EAST and NORTH of GUEUDECOURT from dividing line with XIVth Corps to N 20 Central.
(b) BAYONET TRENCH N 20 Central to N 14 c 20 to N 13 d 53.
(c) BACON TRENCH N 20 b 96 to N 14 d 42.
(d) SCABBARD TRENCH N 20 a 2½ 9½ to N 19 b 89.
(e) LIME TRENCH from N 13 b 9.½ to N 13 b 6.0
(f) LUISEN TRENCH (SOUTH of LUISENHOF Farm) N 14 c 17 to N 13 d 8.6 to N 13 d 66.
(g) LUISENHOF FARM.

II. Special attention will be paid to :-
BAYONET TRENCH about N 20 Central.

III. Any other trenches near the objectives and any known machine gun emplacements (e.g. N 20 d 4.6 N 21 b 6.3½ N 20 b 7.0. Old gun pits at N 20 d 2.2) dugouts, etc. will also be bombarded - Liaison officers must inform Brigades of any such points known to the Infantry.

IV. The bombardment will commence at 7 a.m. on October 11th and continue till 5 p.m.
From 5 p.m. October 11th to 7 a.m. October 12th it will continue at a reduced rate.
At 7 a.m. October 12th it will quicken up and continue till zero.
The bombardment will be a steady continuous one and will be distributed over the whole of the objectives.

V. The 41st Divisional Artillery Group will -
(a) Assist in the bombardment of the objectives in para. I and will search the ground in front of and behind the hostile trenches at frequent intervals.
(b) Search the villages and approaches in its zone and be especially careful to prevent work and movement by night.

VI. The following special bombardments with 18-pdrs. using H.E. only will be carried out :-
(a) Trenches EAST and NORTH of GUEUDECOURT as far NORTH as N 20 Central in RAINBOW and as far EAST as N 21 c 70.
~~October 11th - 9 a.m. to 9.10 a.m. and 2 p.m. to 2.15 p.m.~~
[12.30. 12.45] October 12th -11 a.m. to 11.20 a.m. and 3.30pm to 3.45 p.m.
(b) BAYONET TRENCH from N 20 Central to N 13 d 5.3 and SCABBARD TRENCH.
~~Oct. 11th - 10.30 a.m. to 10.40 a.m. and 1 p.m. to 1.15 pm.~~
Oct. 12th - 9 a.m. to 9.20 a.m. and 12 noon to 12.15 p.m.
(c) Trench just SOUTH of LUISENHOF Farm (LUISEN TRENCH), LUISENHOF Farm, LIME TRENCH EAST of the road, BACON TRENCH.
OCT. 11th - 11.15 a.m. to 11.25 a.m. and 4 p.m. to 4.15 pm.
Oct. 12th - 11.30 a.m. to 11.50 a.m. and 2.30 p.m. to 2.45pm.
                                        12.15   12.30

These special bombardments will be at the rate of 1 round per gun per minute.
Os.C. Brigades and Groups will use 1 gun for every 20 yards of trench to be bombarded in the special bombardment.
If on Octr. 12th the times selected come within 30 minutes of or after zero - Os.C. Brigades and Groups will select earlier hours (notifying this office). **These special bombardments must finish half an hour before zero.**

2.

VII. On October 11th there will be a "Chinese" bombardment :-

<u>At 3.15 pm.</u> all Howitzers will lift off all objectives, except LIME TRENCH, LUISEN TRENCH and LUISENHOF FARM, on to BARLEY TRENCH and the villages of THILLOY, LIGNY TILLOY, LE BARQUE and BAPAUME.

<u>At 3.15 pm.</u> all 18-pdrs. barrage will commence along the whole line on the hostile trenches on the line:- SCABBARD TRENCH up to junction with BAYONET TRENCH thence East down BAYONET TRENCH - RAINBOW TRENCH as far east as N.21.c.7.0.

<u>At 3.20 pm.</u> the barrage will creep back at 50 yards per minute.

<u>At 3.25 pm.</u> both Howitzers and 18-pdrs. will lift back to the front trenches (i.e. original barrage line) and continue till 3.35 pm.

<u>At 3.35 pm.</u> the barrage ceases and normal firing is resumed.

Rate of fire for 18-pdrs. during "Chinese" bombardment 2 rounds per gun per minute.

VIII. O.Cs. Brigades and Groups will be responsible for bombardments and barrage in their own zones.

IX. Rates of fire for bombardment (except where special rates are detailed i.e. paras. VI and VII) :-

4.5" Hows. (October 11th 50 rounds per Battery per hour.
(Night Oct.11/12. 50 rounds per Battery per hour.
(October 12th 60 rounds per battery per hour.

18-pdrs. as required - i.e. the utmost limit of Ammunition supply, aiming at 15 rounds per gun per hour.

<u>N.B.</u> 18-pdrs Batteries will have 650 rounds and 4.5" How. Batteries 450 rounds per gun near the guns at zero on October 12th.

X. Orders for barrages for the attack on October 12th will be issued later.

XI. Zero will be notified later.

XII. Division on our left will attack on October 12th also.

XIII. Every endeavour must be made to obtain direct observation or, if direct is impossible, to utilise the services of No.4. K.B.S., and to locate any new trenches or work.

New work should at once be reported to this office.

During the bombardment Brigade Commanders will arrange through Liaison Officers to have every Battery ranged by salvo or some distinctive method of fire accurately on a line 150 yards in front of the Infantry front line and report these pin points to this office at 8 pm. October 11th.

XIV. Watches will be synchronised at 9 am. on October 11th.

XV. On night October 10/11, 62nd Brigade R.F.A., 12th Divisional Artillery (Col. Wynne D.S.O.) comes into action and joins 41st Divisional Artillery Group.

62nd Brigade R.F.A. will carry out registration on October 11th assisted by Officers detailed from 41st and 30th Divisional Artilleries.

These Officers will remain with 12th Divisional Artillery Batteries till registration is completed and will assist in every possible way.

From 7 am. October 12th, 12th Divisional Artillery will be responsible for zone lately covered by 5th Divisional Artillery.

From this hour zones will be :-

(a).

3.

(a). <u>41st Divisional Artillery</u>. From left divisional boundary to line N.20.c.5.0. to N.20.a.9½.½. to N.9.a.0.2. to N.3.c.3.0.
(b). <u>62nd Brigade, 12th Divisional Artillery</u>. From line in (a) to a line N.20.d.2.0. to N.20.d.7.9½. to N.9.c.6.0. to N.3.d.1.0.
(c). <u>30th Divisional Artillery</u>. From line in (b) to Right Divisional boundary.

From 7 am. October 12th, 41st Divisional Artillery Brigades will be responsible for their original zones as shown in 41st Divisional Artillery Order No.19 of 29-9-16. para. VI.
N.B. From 7 am. on October 12th, 62nd Brigade R.F.A. will carry out the uncompleted portion of operations shown in this order in their own zone, and will be responsible in all ways for their own zone.

Up to 7 am. October 12th, 62nd Brigade R.F.A. will only carry out registration etc.: 41st and 30th Divisional Artilleries being responsible for and carrying out all operations on the whole 41st Divisional Artillery Group zone.

XVI. 62nd Brigade R.F.A. will from 7 am. October 12th find 1 Liaison Officer (Subaltern) at Headquarters Right Battalion Left Infantry Brigade.

XVII. ACKNOWLEDGE.

C M Longmore
Major R.A.

10-10-16.   Brigade Major, 41st Divisional Artillery.

<u>Copies to</u> :-
    XV Corps R.A.
    12th Div. (4 copies).
    21st D.A.G.
    20th D.A.G.
    30th D.A. (20 copies).
    62nd Brigade R.F.A. (5 copies)
  183rd Brigade (5 copies).
  187th Brigade (5 copies).
  189th Brigade (5 copies).
  190th Brigade (5 copies).
    30th D.A.C.
    41st D.A.C.
    T.M.C. 41st Div.
    Spare 8.

S E C R E T.　　　　　　　　　　　　　　　　　　　Ref. Sheet 57 c.S.W.
　　　　　　　　　　　　　　　　　　　　　　　　　　1/20,000.

41st Divisional Artillery Group Operation Order No. 24.

I. The following will be bombarded by Field and Heavy Artillery and will be attacked on October 12th by 12th Division -

- (a) Trenches EAST and NORTH of GUEUDECOURT from dividing line with XIVth Corps to N 20 Central.
- (b) BAYONET TRENCH N 20 Central to N 14 c 20 to N 13 d 53.
- (c) BACON TRENCH N 20 b 96 to N 14 d 42.
- (d) SCABBARD TRENCH N 20 a 2½ 9¼ to N 19 b 89.
- (e) LIME TRENCH from N 13 b 9.½ to N 13 b 6.0
- (f) LUISEN TRENCH (SOUTH of LUISENHOF Farm) N 14 c 17 to N 13 d 8.6 to N 13 d 66.
- (g) LUISENHOF FARM.

II. Special attention will be paid to :-
　　BAYONET TRENCH about N 20 Central.

III. Any other trenches near the objectives and any known machine gun emplacements (e.g. N 20 d 4.6　N 21 b 6.3½　N 20 b 7.0. Old gun pits at N 20 d 2.2) dugouts, etc. will also be bombarded - Liai officers must inform Brigades of any such points known to the Infantry.

IV. The bombardment will commence at 7 a.m. on October 11th and continue till 5 p.m.
　　From 5 p.m. October 11th to 7 a.m. October 12th it will continue at a reduced rate.
　　At 7 a.m. October 12th it will quicken up and continue till zero.
　　The bombardment will be a steady continuous one and will be distributed over the whole of the objectives.

V. The 41st Divisional Artillery Group will -
- (a) Assist in the bombardment of the objectives in para. I and will search the ground in front of and behind the hostile trenches at frequent intervals.
- (b) Search the villages and approaches in its zone and be especially careful to prevent work and movement by night.

VI. The following special bombardments with 18-pdrs. using H.E. only will be carried out:-
- (a) Trenches EAST and NORTH of GUEUDECOURT as far NORTH as N 20 Central in RAINBOW and as far EAST as N 21 c 70.
  October 11th - 9 a.m. to 9.10 a.m. and 2 p.m. to 2.15 p.m.
  October 12th -11 a.m. to 11.20a.m. and 3.30pm to 3.45 p.m.
- (b) BAYONET TRENCH from N 20 Central to N 13 d 5.3 and SCABBARD TRENCH.
  Oct. 11th - 10.30 a.m. to 10.40 a.m. and 1 p.m. to 1.15 p
  Oct. 12th - 9 a.m. to 9.20 a.m. and 12 noon to 12.15 p.m.
- (c) Trench just SOUTH of LUISENHOF Farm (LUISEN TRENCH), LUISENHOF Farm, LIME TRENCH EAST of the road, BACON TRENC
  OCT.11th - 11.15 a.m. to 11.25 a.m. and 4.p.m. to 4.15 pm
  Oct.12th - 11.30 a.m. to 11.50 a.m. and 2.30 p.m. to 2.45

　　These special bombardments will be at the rate of 1 round per gun per minute.
　　Os.C. Brigades and Groups will use 1 gun for every 20 yards of trench to be bombarded in the special bombardment.
　　If on Octr. 12th the times selected come within 30 minutes of or are after zero - Os.C. Brigades and Groups will select earlier hours (notifying this office). <u>These special bombardments must finish half an hour before zero.</u>

VII. On October 11th there will be a "Chinese" bombardment :-

<u>At 3.15 pm.</u> all Howitzers will lift off all objectives, except LIME TRENCH, LUISEN TRENCH and LUISENHOF FARM, on to BARLEY TRENCH and the villages of THILLOY, LIGNY TILLOY, LE BARQUE and BAPAUME.

<u>At 3.15 pm.</u> all 18-pdrs. barrage will commence along the whole line on the hostile trenches on the line:- SCABBARD TRENCH up to junction with BAYONET TRENCH thence East down BAYONET TRENCH - RAINBOW TRENCH as far east as N.21.c.7.0.

<u>At 3.20 pm.</u> the barrage will creep back at 50 yards per minute.

<u>At 3.25 pm.</u> both Howitzers and 18-pdrs. will lift back to the front trenches (i.e. original barrage line) and continue till 3.35 pm.

<u>At 3.35 pm.</u> the barrage ceases and normal firing is resumed.

Rate of fire for 18-pdrs. during "Chinese" bombardment 2 rounds per gun per minute.

VIII. O.Cs. Brigades and Groups will be responsible for bombardments and barrage in their own zones.

IX. Rates of fire for bombardment (except where special rates are detailed i.e. paras. VI and VII) :-

4.5" Hows. (October 11th 50 rounds per Battery per hour.
(Night Oct.11/12. 50 rounds per Battery per hour.
(October 12th 60 rounds per battery per hour.

18-pdrs. as required - i.e. the utmost limit of Ammunition supply, aiming at 15 rounds per gun per hour.

<u>N.B.</u> 18-pdrs Batteries will have 650 rounds and 4.5" How. Batteries 450 rounds per gun near the guns at zero on October 12th.

X. Orders for barrages for the attack on October 12th will be issued later.

XI. Zero will be notified later.

XII. Division on our left will attack on October 12th also.

XIII. Every endeavour must be made to obtain direct observation or, if direct is impossible, to utilise the services of No.4. K.B.S., and to locate any new trenches or work.

New work should at once be reported to this office.

During the bombardment Brigade Commanders will arrange through Liaison Officers to have every Battery ranged by salvo or some distinctive method of fire accurately on a line 150 yards in front of the Infantry front line and report these pin points to this office at 8 pm. October 11th.

XIV. Watches will be synchronised at 9 am. on October 11th.

XV. On night October 10/11, 62nd Brigade R.F.A., 12th Divisional Artillery (Col. Wynne D.S.O.) comes into action and joins 41st Divisional Artillery Group.

62nd Brigade R.F.A. will carry out registration on October 11th assisted by Officers detailed from 41st and 30th Divisional Artilleries.

These Officers will remain with 12th Divisional Artillery Batteries till registration is completed and will assist in every possible way.

From 7 am. October 12th, 12th Divisional Artillery will be responsible for zone lately covered by 5th Divisional Artillery.

From this hour zones will be :-

(a).

(a). 41st Divisional Artillery. From left divisional boundary to line N.20.c.5.0. to N.20.a.9½.½. to N.9.a.0.2. to N.3.c.3.0.
(b). 62nd Brigade, 12th Divisional Artillery. From line in (a) to a line N.20.d.2.0. to N.20.d.7.9½. to N.9.c.6.0. to N.3.d.1.
(c). 30th Divisional Artillery. From line in (b) to Right Divisional boundary.

    From 7 am. October 12th, 41st Divisional Artillery Brigade will be responsible for their original zones as shown in 41st Divisional Artillery Order No.19 of 29-9-16. para. VI.

N.B. From 7 am. on October 12th, 62nd Brigade R.F.A. will carry out the uncompleted portion of operations shown in this order in their own zone, and will be responsible in all ways for their own zone.

    Up to 7 am. October 12th, 62nd Brigade R.F.A. will only carry out registration etc.: 41st and 30th Divisional Artilleries being responsible for and carrying out all operations on the whole 41st Divisional Artillery Group zone.

XVI. 62nd Brigade R.F.A. will from 7 am. October 12th find 1 Liaison Officer (Subaltern) at Headquarters Right Battalion Left Infantry Brigade.

XVII. ACKNOWLEDGE.

                                                                  Major R.A.

10-10-16.   Brigade Major, 41st Divisional Artillery.

Copies to :-
        XV Corps R.A.
        12th Div. (4 copies).
        21st D.A.G.
        20th D.A.G.
        30th D.A. (20 copies).
        62nd Brigade R.F.A. (5 copies).
        183rd Brigade (5 copies).
        187th Brigade (5 copies).
        189th Brigade (5 copies).
        190th Brigade (5 copies).
        30th D.A.C.
        41st D.A.C.
        T.M.C. 41st Div.
        Spare 8.

"A" Form.
MESSAGES AND SIGNALS.
Army Form C. 2121.

Prefix............Code............m. | Words | Charge | This message is on a/c of: | Recd. at............m.
Office of Origin and Service Instructions. | | Sent | | Date............
Secret | At............m. | | **374** | From............
By D.R | To............ | | Service. | By............
| By............ | | (Signature of "Franking Officer.") |

TO { 21st Divl Arty Group
     41st Divl Arty Group
     Heavy Artillery

Sender's Number: CA488
Day of Month: 11
In reply to Number:
AAA

Reference	XV	CORPS	ARTILLERY	Operation
Orders	no	54	and	55
Zero	Hour	will	be	at
2.5 pm	to-morrow	October	12th	aaa
This	Hour	will	not	be
communicated	sooner	than	is	necessary
and	then	only	to	those
whom	it	immediately	concerns.	In
no	case	should	it	be
communicated	by	telephone	aaa	Ack

Recd 9.20 pm
Ackd 9.25 pm
W.S.B 11/10/16

From: XV CORPS Arty
Place:
Time: 7.35 pm

(Z) J.R Harrison Major SO RA XV Corps
Signature of Addressor or person authorised to telegraph in his name.

"A" Form.
MESSAGES AND SIGNALS.

Army Form C.2121 (in pads of 100).
No. of Message ....

Prefix .... Code .... m.	Words	Charge	This message is on a/c of:	Recd. at .... m.
Office of Origin and Service Instructions.				Date ....
....	Sent		........................Service.	From ....
....	At .... m.			
	To			
	By		(Signature of "Franking Officer.")	By ....

| TO | WREN |
| | 12 DIV (G) |

| Sender's Number. | Day of Month. | In reply to Number. | |
| T 6 | 13 11 | | AAA |

Ref AIR DA G order no 25 of Today para VIII AAA D Bty WREN will from twenty minutes after zero to twenty nine minutes after zero deal with LIME TRENCH N13b 6½ x to N13b 9 1 AAA Rate of fire as rapid as possible AAA At twenty nine minutes after zero D WREN will proceed as laid down in para VIII AAA Attenborough

From 41 DA
Place
Time   6.15 pm

The above may be forwarded as now corrected.

(Z) *Cuthinpund*

Censor.   Signature of Addressor or person authorised to telegraph in his name.

* This line should be erased if not required.

750,000. W 2186-M509. H. W. & V., Ld. 6/16.

SECRET.   G.X./291.

375

12th Signals.	C.R.E.
C.R.A., Right Group.	5th Northants.
35th I.B.	A.D.M.S.
36th I.B.	A.P.M.
88th I.B.	O.C., Troop. R. Wiltshire Yeomanry.

---

1. Reference 12th Division Order No.116 dated 10/10/16.

2. (a). ZERO hour will be at <u>2.5. p.m.</u> tomorrow, October 12th.

   (b). This hour will not be communicated sooner than is necessary, and then only to those whom it immediately concerns.
In no case should it be communicated by telephone.

3. Please acknowledge by wire.

                                                   Major,
                                                 General Staff,

9.20.p.m.   12th Division.
11th October, 1916.

Appendix F

AMENDMENTS to
41st DIVISIONAL ARTILLERY GROUP OPERATION ORDER NO.25.

I. In paragraph V. (a) (b) and (c) delete rates of fire and substitute
"from zero to 6 minutes after zero 4 rounds per gun per minute"
"from 6 minutes after zero to 30 minutes after zero 3 rounds per gun per minute".

II. Delete paragraph VII and substitute
From zero to 20 minutes after zero if wind is favourable 4.5" Howitzers will establish a gas barrage on the area
N 20 b 17 - N 14 d 64 - N 14 a 24 - N 13 d 68 - N 20 b 17. *(amended)*
All Howitzer batteries in 41st D.A.G. will distribute along the line N 13 d 68 - N 20 b 17 and search and sweep whole area.
Fire must be as rapid as possible, 4 rounds per gun per minute being aimed at.
If wind is unfavourable there will be no gas barrage and 4.5" Howitzers will from zero hour deal with objectives shown in 41st Divisional Artillery Group Operation Order No.25 paragraph VIII.

N.B. A code message will be sent from this office to all Brigades 1 hour before zero as to whether gas barrage will take place or not.
"VIOLETS" meaning gas barrage will take place.
"RUPERT" meaning no gas barrage.

Sent 12.30 p.m.

Major R.A.,

11-10-16.   Brigade Major, 41st Divisional Arty. Group.

Copies to :-
    XV Corps R.A.
    12th Div. (4 copies).
    21st D.A.G.
    20th D.A.G.
    30th D.A. (20 copies).
    62nd Brigade R.F.A. (5 copies).
    64th   "   "   3   "
    183rd   "   "   5   "
    187th   "   "   5   "
    189th   "   "   5   "
    190th   "   "   5   "
    30th D.A.C.
    41st D.A.C.
    T.M.C. 41st Div.
    Spare 8.

Further amendment

1 sect Hows on for barrage 0.0 to 0.20
1 ———————— 1st objective 0.0 to 0.5
1 ———————— gas barrage 0.5 to 0.20

and

SECRET.   Reference Map GUEUDECOURT 57cS.W.1
                                         1/10,000.

         41st Divisional Artillery Group Operation Order No.25.

I.   The FOURTH Army will continue the attack on October 12th,
at zero hour.
         The VI French Army will attack also.

II.   The XV Corps attacks with 12th Division on right and 30th
Division on left.
         The 18th Brigade, 6th Division, attacks on right of 12th
Division.

III. The 41st Divisional Artillery Group will act as below.
      Note. All ground EAST of a line N.27.a.3½.8½ to N.21.c.61.
             to N.21.c.8½.4. to N.21.b.6.5½ and South of a line
             N.21.b.6.5½ to Corps boundary at N.22.a.6.0 will be
             dealt with by 6th Division. On no account will 41st
             D.A.G. bring any fire into this area.

IV.   The 18-pdr. Barrage will be formed in depth by all 18-pdr.
batteries, except 64th Brigade which is allotted special tasks.

      (a) Each Battery will allot half its guns to the line of
          the first objective i.e. BAYONET TRENCH and RAINBOW
          TRENCH (N.13.d.63 - N.20.a.66 - N.20.d.35 - N.20.d.56½-
          N.21.c. 6.1)
      N.B. In the case of four gun batteries with three guns only
           in action, two guns will be allotted to the first
           objective.
           These guns will open at zero and continue on this target
           till 6 minutes after zero.
      (b) From zero to 2 minutes after zero remaining 18-pdrs.
          will fire on the line
             N.13.d.50 - N 20 a 3½.4 - N 20 d ½.3½ - N 21 c
             0.1½ - N 27 a 3½.9
          (shown as AAAA' in attached map).
          At 2 minutes after zero they will advance 50 yards a
          minute to line of first objective, arriving there
          approximately at 4 minutes after zero, and will
          continue on this line until 6 minutes after zero.
      (c) At 6 minutes after zero, all 18-pdrs. will advance
          50 yards a minute to the line :-
          N 13 d 67 - N 14 c 34 - N 14 c 5.2½ - N 20 b 50 -
          N 21 c 8½.4 (shown BBBB' on attached map), 150 yards
          beyond the first objective arriving at 9 minutes after
          zero and remain on this line till 23 minutes after zero,
          except :-
          At 12 minutes after zero
                190th Brigade will detail 1-18pdr. battery to fire
                on LUISENHOF FARM N 13 d 7.8½.
                189th Brigade will detail 1-18pdr. battery to fire
                on LUISEN TRENCH N.13 d 8½.6 - N.14 c 2.7.
                62nd Brigade will detail 1-18pdr. battery to fire on
                BACON TRENCH N 14 d 52 - N 20 b 9.6.
                30th D.A. will detail 1-18pdr. battery to fire on
                Sunken Road N 21 b 7.8½ - N 15 d 7.9.
          From 12 minutes after zero remaining batteries
          sweeping to cover gaps left by batteries turned on
          to special targets.

2.

(d) At 23 minutes after zero barrage advances 50 yards a minute to line :-
N 13 b 75 - N 14 a 1.4 - N 14 d 65 - N 21 a 1½.8½ - N 21 b 4½.2. (shown CCCC' on map).
The batteries of 190, 189, 62 Brigades and 30th D.A. detailed for special targets in IV (c) will accompany the lift as the barrage reaches their special targets. All batteries remain on this line till 38 minutes after zero.

(e) At 38 minutes after zero 50% of the 18-pdr. batteries will deal within their own zones with tasks as under searching 100 yards in front and rear of the trenches named and sweeping 50 yards on either side of the road.
BREAD TRENCH
BARLEY " WEST of N 16 c 5.8
Road from N 13 b 7.5 - N 7 d 9.9
and continue on these tasks till further orders.

(f) From 38 minutes after zero until 1 hour after zero 50% of the 18-pdr. batteries remain on line CCCC' searching continually to a depth of 200 yards.
At 1 hour after zero these batteries re-inforce batteries on special tasks in IV (e).

V. Rates of fire and ammunition for 18 pdr. batteries :-
(a) Guns on line AAAA' shrapnel only
~~Zero to 2 minutes after zero 2 rounds per gun per minute.~~
~~2 minutes after zero to 4 minutes after zero 3 rounds per gun per minute.~~
~~4 minutes after zero to 6 minutes after zero 4 rounds per gun per minute.~~

(b) Guns on 1st objective
Zero to 2 minutes after zero H.E. only.
~~2 minutes after zero to 6 minutes after zero Shrapnel~~ only.
Rates of fire :-
~~Zero to 2 minutes after zero 2 rounds per gun per minute.~~
~~2 minutes after zero to 4 minutes after zero 3 rounds per gun per minute.~~
~~4 minutes after zero to 6 minutes after zero 4 rounds per gun per minute.~~

(c) At 6 minutes after zero all guns go forward with Shrapnel only, rate of fire from 6 minutes after zero to 30 minutes after zero - 3 rounds per gun per minute.

(d) From 12 minutes after zero to 24 minutes after zero all guns on special targets will use H.E. only, changing to Shrapnel only at 24 minutes after zero.

(e) From 30 minutes after zero to 1 hour after zero all guns on barrage use Shrapnel only.
Guns turning on to special targets change to 50% H.E.
Rates of fire.
From 30 minutes after zero to 1 hour after zero 1 round per gun per minute.
From 1 hour after zero to 1 hour 30 minutes after zero 1 round per gun per 2 minutes.
From 1 hour 30 minutes after zero till stop 1 round per gun per 4 minutes.

VI. 64th Brigade R.F.A. will deal with tasks :-
(a) From zero to 20 minutes after zero
Left Battery. BACON TRENCH (N 14 d 52 - N 20 b 9.6).
Right Battery. Sunken Road N 21 b 6½.8 - N 15 d 6.9
and N 15 d 2.5 - N 15 d 4.9
using H.E. only. Rate of fire 2 rounds per gun per minute.
(b).

(b) At 20 minutes after zero
Left Battery lifts to TICK TRENCH (N 8 c 67 - N 8 d 66).
Right Battery continues on targets as in VI (a)
using 50% H.E.
Rates of fire.
20 minutes after zero to 1 hour after zero 1 round per gun per minute.
1 hour after zero to 1 hour 30 minutes after zero 1 round per gun per 2 minutes.
1 hour 30 minutes after zero to "Stop" 1 round per gun per 4 minutes.
N.B. Left battery on TICK TRENCH will search 200 yards in front and rear.
Right battery will sweep 50 yards on either side of roads.

VII. 4.5" Howitzers.
At 1 minute before zero all 4.5" Howitzers will form a Gas shell barrage on
(a) the line PPPP' (N 13 d 6.8½ - N 14 c 3½.6 - N 20 b 7.0 - N 21 c 9½.5½)

or (b) the line
Sunken Road N 21 b 78 - N 15 d 78 thence WEST along BARLEY TRENCH to Divisional Boundary at N 7.d 8.3½.
Rates of fire.
From 1 minute before zero to 4 minutes after zero - 2 rounds per gun per minute.
From 4 minutes after zero till all gas shell are used up - 1 round per gun per minute.
If gas barrage commences on line in (a) it will lift back, 41st D.A. batteries and 62nd Brigade battery at 100 yards per minute and 30th D.A. batteries at 125 yards per minute, to line in (b) at 4 minutes after zero.
If gas barrage commences on line in (b) there will be no lift.
N.B. Whether gas barrage commences on line in (a) or (b) depends on the wind.
A code message will be sent from this office to all Brigades at 1 hour before zero
"RANGE" meaning begin on line in (a)
"CROPS" " " " " " (b)

VIII. On conclusion of the gas barrage Howitzers batteries will be allotted tasks as follows :-
30th D.A. -
1 battery all trenches and Sunken roads in N 15 d.
2 batteries all valleys and approaches in 30th D.A. zone North of a line drawn through N 14, N 15, N 16, Centrals.
12th D.A. Howitzer battery -
Sunk road N 8 b 6.2 - N 9 c 5.6 and valley within 200 yards radius all round.
183) Valley from N 8 Central - N 15 a 6.8 inclusive of TICK
187) TRENCH to 187.
190 THILLOY and all approaches South.
189 Sunk Road from N 7 d 7.0 - N 7 b 95.40 and LIGNY THILLOY within Div area.

IX. Fleeting opportunities may be dealt with after 38 minutes after zero by any battery on BARLEY TRENCH LINE by order of Brigade Commander or on request through LIAISON Officer. Remaining guns will sweep to cover gap.
All Divisional Artillery will drop rates of fire to 4 rounds per gun per hour for 1 hour before zero, to rest detachments and make ready.

X.

4.

X. 187th Brigade R.F.A. will man the Divisional O.P. from 1 hour before zero - at which hour telephonic communication must be established with this Headquarters.

XI. Infantry will light yellow flares on reaching their objective and at 7 am. October 13th.

XII. Watches will be synchronised at 9 am. October 12th.

XIII. ACKNOWLEDGE by wire.

                                                  Major R.A.,

11-10-16.   Brigade Major, 41st Divisional Arty. Group.

Copies to :-
- XV Corps R.A.
- 12th Div. (4 copies).
- 21st D.A.G.
- 20th D.A.G.
- 30th D.A. (20 copies).
- 62nd Brigade R.F.A. (5 copies).
- 64th   "   "   3   "
- 183rd   "   "   5   "
- 187th   "   "   5   "
- 190th   "   "   5   "
- 30th D.A.C.
- 41st D.A.C.
- T.M.C. 41st Div.
- Spare 8.

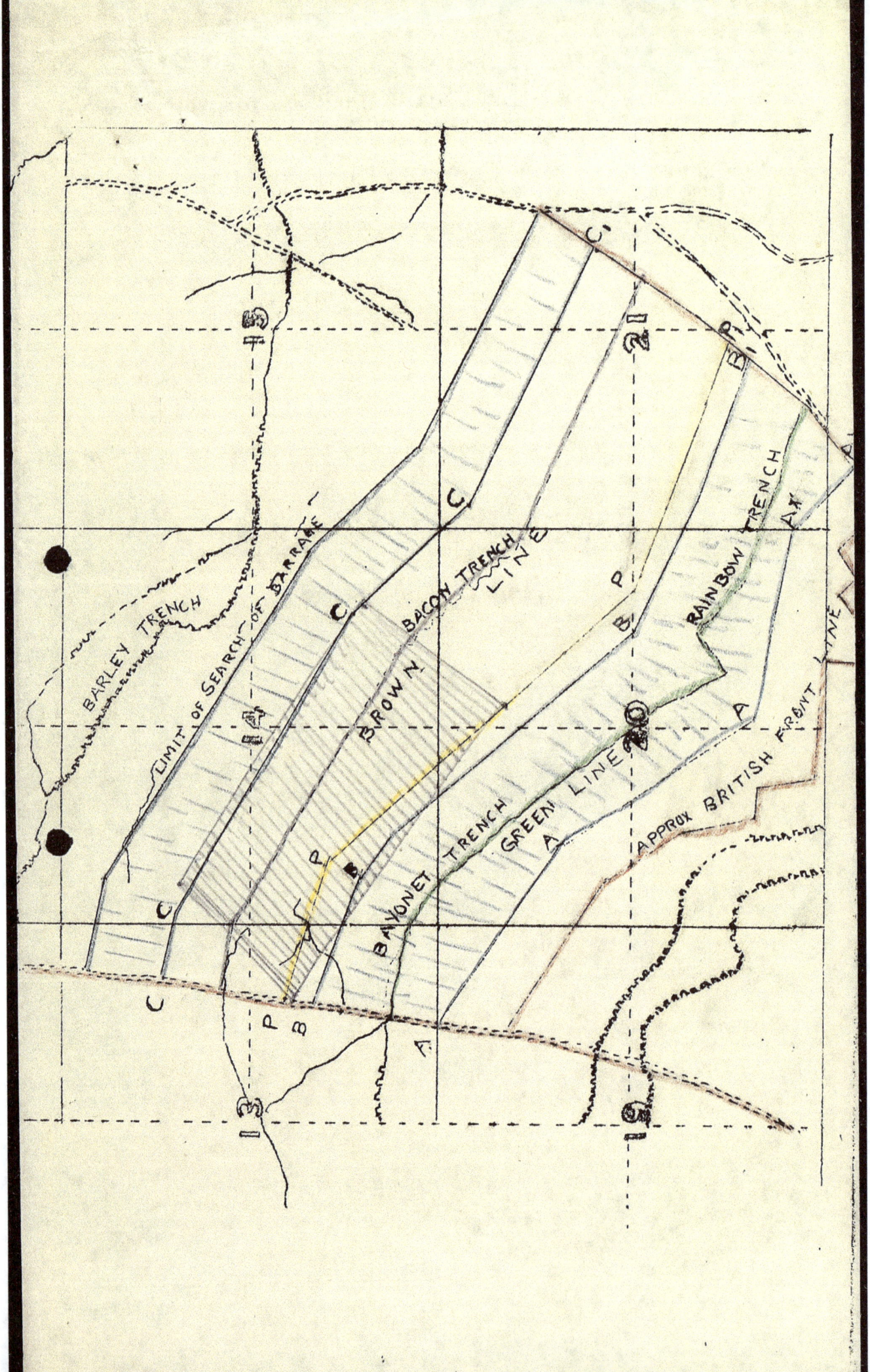

SECRET. Ref. Map GUEUDECOURT
1/10,000.

41st Divisional Artillery Group Operation Order No.26.

I. The following short bombardment will be carried out on October 14th by the Heavy Artillery :-
   (a) N.20.d.2.6½ to N.20.a.7.2. (BAYONET TRENCH)
   (b) N.20.a.3.8½ to N.13.d.7.2. (BAYONET TRENCH)

   (a) Commences 1 pm. and lasts 50 minutes.
   (b)   "   2.15 pm. and lasts 50 minutes.

II. All 18-pdrs. and 4.5" Hows. of 30th D.A. and 15th and 147th Brigades will take part in (a) the 18-pdrs. using H.E. only.
   Rates of fire :-
       30th D.A. 18-pdrs and 4.5" Hows. 1 round per gun per minute.

       15th and 147th Brigades 18-pdrs. and 4.5" Hows.
       1 round per gun per 2 minutes.

III. All 18-pdrs and 4.5" Hows. 41st D.A. (less 183 Brigade R.F.A.) and 15th and 147th Brigades will take part in (b) the 18-pdrs. using H.E. only.
   Rates of fire :-
       41st D.A. 18-pdrs. and 4.5" Hows. 1 round per gun per minute.
       15th and 147th Brigades 18-pdrs. and 4.5" Hows
       1 round per gun per 2 minutes.
   The 18-pdrs. besides firing on the trench will search as far south as the S.O.S. line and 400 yards North of the trench.

IV. Every endeavour must be made to register both 18-pdrs. and Hows. on the trench in the morning.
       30th D.A. will allot portions of (a) to their own Brigades.
       41st D.A. Brigades will each take 1/3rd of (b) in the order 187 Brigade, 190 Brigade, 189 Brigade from the right.
       15th and 147th Brigades will distribute their fire along the whole of (a) and similarly along the whole of (b).
       N.B. B. and D. Batteries 183 Brigade R.F.A. will fire on zone of 189 Brigade at same rates if feasible in opinion of O.C. 183 Brigade R.F.A.

V. ACKNOWLEDGE by wire.

                                                Major R.A.

13-10-16.   Brigade Major, 41st Divisional Arty. Group.

Copies to :-
       XV Corps R.A.   15th Brigade R.H.A. 4 copies.
       30 D.A.   20 copies.   41st D.A.C.
       183 Brigade 5 copies.   20th D.A.
       187   "   5   "   21st D.A.
       189   "   5   "   12th Div. G. 4 copies.
       190   "   5   "   147 Brigade 4 copies.
                                  5 spare.

Appendix. H

SECRET. Ref. Map. Sheet 57.c.S.W.
1/20,000.

41st Divisional Artillery Group Operation Order No.27.

I. On 15th October the 18th Infantry Brigade will assault and capture :-
   (1) That part of MILD TRENCH still in the enemy's hands from about N.21.d.1½.4 to its junction with CLOUDY TRENCH at about N.21.d.9.5.
   (2) The enemy trench from N.21.c.8.5. to N.21.d.2.7.
   (3) That part of CLOUDY TRENCH not already in our possession.

II. The 18th Infy. Bde. will establish itself at N.21.b.5½.0 (where a strong point will be constructed), with a defensive flank running South-West from that point.

III. Zero hour for the above assault will be at 5-35 am. on 15th instant.

IV. The 41st D.A.G. will co-operate with
   (a) a creeping barrage at zero along the whole of the 12th Division front - on the line :-
       N.13.d.4.2. - N.20.a.4.4. - N.20.c.9.6. - N.20.d.4½.9.- N.21.c.2.5. - N.21.d.0.7.
   (b) At 5 seconds after zero barrage creeps forward 50 yards a minute to line :-
       LIME TRENCH (N.13.b.7.1 to N.13.b.9½.1) to BACON TRENCH (N.14.d.4.2. to N.20.b.9.6) thence to N.21.b.6.5.
   (c) Barrage remains on this line till further orders.
   30th D.A. will detail 1-18 pdr.battery to form a standing barrage from zero to stop, from N.21.b.0.5 - N.21.b.1.7 and 1-4.5" How. Battery to search SUNKEN ROAD from N.21.b.7.8. - N.15.d.7.3. and 1-4.5" How. Battery to search Road from N.20.b.7.0. - N.20.b.9.2. from zero onwards.

V. All 18-pdrs. in action will be employed, Brigades being responsible for barrage in their own zone.
   18-pdrs will fire Shrapnel from zero to 30 minutes after zero, then H.E. till stop.
   Rates of fire :-
   Zero to 5 minutes after zero 3 rounds per gun per minute.
   5 minutes after zero to 15 minutes after zero 2 rounds per gun per minute.
   15 minutes after zero to 45 minutes after zero 1 round per gun per minute.
   45 minutes after zero to stop 1 round per gun per 4 minutes.
   N.B. Right Brigade 30th D.A. will conform up to 15 minutes after zero to rate of fire laid down in 20th D.A.G. O.O. No.

VI. Brigades 41st D.A. will when creeping barrage has advanced 150 yards beyond BAYONET TRENCH drop 1-18 pdr.battery per Brigade back into BAYONET TRENCH firing 50% H.E. and 50% Shrapnel. These batteries will sweep to cover BAYONET TRENCH in 41st D.A. zone at same rates of fire as laid down for creeping barrage and will remain on BAYONET TRENCH till 1 hour after zero - when they will cease fire.
   Remaining 18-pdr. batteries 41st D.A. will sweep to cover gaps in creeping barrage.

VII.

VII. 4.5" Hows. will continue normal day firing during the operation and should take advantage of any fleeting opportunities.

VIII. Watches will be synchronised at 10 pm. tonight.

IX. ACKNOWLEDGE.

[signature]

Major R.A.

14-10-16.   Brigade Major, 41st Divisional Artillery Group.

Copies to :-

      20th D.A.
      6th Div.
      12th Div.
      30th D.A. (20 copies)
      41st D.A. (30 ").
      XV Corps R.A.
      12th D.A.

SECRET *Appendix I* Reference GUEUDECOURT 57 c.S.W.1.

41st. DIVISIONAL ARTILLERY OPERATION ORDER No.28.

1. On October 15th. following bombardments will be carried out by the Heavy Artillery:-
   (a) BAYONET TRENCH from N.20 central inclusive to SCABBARD TRENCH inclusive.
   (b) LUISEN TRENCH, LUISENHOF FARM, and LIME TRENCH, East of N.13.b.7.1.

   (a) will be bombarded from 1 p.m., to 1.50 p.m.

   (b) "   "   "   "   3.20 p.m., to 4.10 p.m.

2. 41st.Divisional Artillery Group will join in these bombardments as under:-

   <u>30th. Divl:Artillery</u> two 4.5" How. Batteries and six 18 pdr. Batteries take part in (a)

   <u>41st. Divl:Artillery</u> two 4.5" How. Batteries and six 18 pdr. Batteries take part in (b)

   D/189 (1 Section on LUISENHOF FARM
         (1   "   " portion of LIME TRENCH

   D/190 LUISEN TRENCH

   2 18 pdr. Batteries 187th.Brigade on LUISEN TRENCH
                       189th.Brigade
   1 18 pdr.Battery/ LUISENHOF FARM

   1 18 pdr. Battery 190th.Brigade - portion of LIME TRENCH.

   2 18 pdr. Batteries 15th. Brigade, R.H.A., distributed in depth over whole of (b)

3. 18 pdrs. will use H.E. only and will search 500 yards beyond and about 200 yards on either side of the targets (in case of (a) if safe.

4. Rate of fire for 18 pdr. and 4.5" Hows:-

   1 round per gun per minute.

5. Batteries, not already registered on these targets, must endeavour to register in the morning.

6. ACKNOWLEDGE

14th.Oct.1916
HHP
XVth.Corps, R.A.
12th.Division
12th.Divisional Artillery
20th.Divisional Artillery
30th.Divisional Artillery (20 copies)
41st.Divisional Artillery (30 copies)
3 Spare.

Brigade Major
41st.Divisional Artillery.

Appendix J.

SECRET.   Ref. Map GUEUDECOURT 1/10,000.

41st Divisional Artillery Group Operation Order No.29.

I. On October 15th and 16th Heavy Artillery will carry out following bombardments :-
   (a) BAYONET TRENCH from N.13.d.5.3. to N.14.c.0.2. on October 15th from 11-15 pm to 12-15 am October 16th.
   (b) BAYONET TRENCH from N.20.d.2.6. to SCABBARD TRENCH October 16th 10-20 am to 11-20 am.
   (c) LIME TRENCH East of the LIGNY TILLOY Road BACON TRENCH and BARLEY TRENCH from N.15.a. 2.1 to N.14.b.4.6.
       October 16th 4 pm to 5 pm.

II. 189 Brigade will detail 2-18 pdr. batteries, and
    190 Brigade will detail 1-4.5" How Battery and 1-18 pdr. battery
       to join in bombardment (a).

    187 Brigade will detail 1-4.5" How. battery and 3-18 pdr. batteries,
    183 Brigade will detail 1-18 pdr. battery,
    15th Brigade will detail 2-18 pdr. batteries,
    30th D.A. will detail 1-4.5" How. battery (D/149)
       to join in (b).

    30th D.A. will detail 6-18 pdr. batteries and 2-4.5" How. batteries to join in (c).
    147, 149, and 150 Brigades will find the 18 pdrs., and 147 and 148 the 4.5" Hows.
    147 How. on BACON Trench and 148 How. on BARLEY Trench.
    18 pdrs. will fire H.E. taking as far as possible portions of targets in their own zones and searching 500 yards or as far as is safe on either side of the targets.
    4.5" Hows. will be distributed along the whole of each target.

    Rate of fire for 4.5" Hows. and 18 pdrs. 1 round per gun per minute.

    ACKNOWLEDGE.

                                                Major R.A.
15-10-16.   Brigade Major, 41st Divisional Arty. Group.

Copies to :-
    HHP.
    XV Corps R.A.
    12th Div.
    12th D.A.
    20th D.A.
    30th D.A. (20 copies).
    41st D.A. (30 "   ).
    3 spare.

SECRET.   Ref. Map GUEUDECOURT
                                                1/10,000.

    41st Divisional Artillery Group Operation Order No. 30.
    ------- --------

I. Heavy Artillery will carry out following bombardments on
October 17th and 18th :-
    (a) Trench from N.21.c.2.9. to N.20.b.0.7 and road junction
        at N.20.d.6½.9½
        October 17th 5 am. to 5-50 am.
    (b) LIME TRENCH west of LIGNY TILLOY Road and LUISEN trench
        October 17th 9-30 am. to 10-20 am.
    (c) BAYONET TRENCH from N.20.d.2.7. to N.20.a.5½.6.
        October 17th 4-35 pm. to 5-25 pm.
    (d) BAYONET TRENCH from N.20.a.4.8. to N.13.d.5.3. SCABBARD
        TRENCH LUISEN TRENCH and LUISENHOF Farm.
        October 18th 12-40 am. to 1-30 am.

II. 41st D.A.G. will co-operate as under :-
    (1) 30th D.A. will detail 2-4.5" How. Batteries and 6-18 pdr.
        batteries to take part in (a).
    (2) 189 Brigade R.F.A. will detail 1-4.5" How Battery and
        3-18 pdr. batteries to take part in (b).
    (3) 147 Brigade will detail 1-4.5" How. battery and 1-18 pdr.
        battery.
        15th Bde. R.H.A. will detail 2-18 pdr. batteries.
        187 Brigade will detail 1-4.5" How. battery and 2-18 pdr.
        batteries.
        183 Brigade will detail 1-18 pdr. battery
        to take part in (c).
    (4) 187 Brigade will detail 1-18 pdr. battery
        189 Brigade will detail 2-18 pdr. batteries and 1-4.5"
        How. battery.
        190 Brigade will detail 3-18 pdr. batteries and 1-4.5"
        How. battery
        to take part in (d).

III. 18 pdrs. will as far as possible shoot in their own zones
using H.E. only.
     4.5" How. will be distributed over whole target.
     18 pdrs. will, where safe, search 400 yards on either side
of targets.

ACKNOWLEDGE

                                              Major R.A.

16-10-16.   Brigade Major, 41st Divisional Artillery Group.

Copies to :-
        XV Corps R.A.
        30 D.A. (20 copies)
        12 Div.
        20 D.A.
        12 D.A.
        41 D.A. (30 copies).

Appendix - 1

AMENDMENT to 41st D.A.G. Order No. 31.
APPENDIX "A"

SECRET.

1. Para I (3) add.

   At 15 minutes after zero
   189th Bde (less 1 Bty) and 190 Bde will concentrate on
   BAYONET TRENCH from N.20 a 6 5 to N.20 a.3.8. searching
   100 yds SOUTH of this line and 200 yds NORTH of it until
   further orders.

   One Bty 189 Bde. will remain on BAYONET TRENCH and from
   N.20.a.3.8. to N.13.d.5.3 sweeping to cover the whole of
   this portion.

2. Para IV (a) delete "all guns 189 and 190 Bdes" and
   substitute "one Bty 189 Bde" (the remainder of 189 Bdes.
   act as above in para I.

3. ACKNOWLEDGE.

                                              Brigade Major
17-10-16.   41st Divl. Arty Group.

12th Divsn. G
189 Bde (5 copies)
190 "   "   "
6 Spare.

S E C R E T. Ref.Map GUEUDECOURT 1/10,000.

41st Divisional Artillery Group Operation Order No. 31.
----------------------------oOo----------------------------

I. On October 18th the Fourth Army will renew the attack in conjunction with the 6th French Army.
    12th Division will attack - 6th Division on right and 30th Division on the left attacking also.

II. Zero, which will be at an early hour before light, will be notified later. 3.40 am 18 Oct

III. Boundary between XVth and XIVth Corps will be a line NORTH and SOUTH through N.21.c.8.0.

IV. Objective of 12th Division will be a line EAST and WEST (approximately) through and including GREASE TRENCH (N.20.b.0.7. to N.21.c.2.9.).

V. 41st D.A.G. will co-operate with barrages etc. as per attached Appendix A.

VI. Heavy Artillery will deal with certain special objectives including villages and distant approaches. There will be no increase of fire from Heavy Hows. before zero.
    From zero onwards counter battery work will be intense.

VII. Watches will be synchronised from this office at 10 pm. October 17th.

VIII. O.P. in SWITCH TRENCH will be manned by 187 Brigade R.F.A. from 5-15 am. October 18th onwards, by which hour telephonic communication will be established.

IX.   ACKNOWLEDGE.

                                                    Major R.A.
17-10-16.   Brigade Major, 41st Divisional Artillery Group.

Copies to :-
        XV Corps R.A.
        XV   "   H.A.
         6th Div.
        12th "   (4 copies).
        30th "
        12th D.A.
        20th D.A.
        30th D.A.   (20 copies).
        41st D.A.   (30 copies).

APPENDIX 'A'.

I. 41st D.A. and 15th Bde. R.H.A. will form a barrage 'A' in depth, as under :-
   (1). From Zero to 3 minutes after zero -
       50% 18-pdrs. on BAYONET Trench from N 20 d 2.6½ to N 13 d 5½.3
       50% 18-pdrs. on line 100 yards SOUTH of above.
   The 189 & 190 Bdes. R.F.A. will take from N 13 d 5½.3 to N 20 a 6.5½.
   The 183 & 187 Bdes. R.F.A. will take from N 20 a 6.5½ to N 20 central.
   15th Bde. R.H.A. will take from N 20 central to N 20 d 2.6½.

   (2). At 3 minutes after zero barrage 100 yards South of BAYONET Trench advance at 50 yards a minute to BAYONET Trench arriving at 5 minutes after zero.

   (3). At 5 minutes after zero barrage EAST of N 20 a 6.5½ swings at 50 yards a minute to the line
           N 20 a 6.5½ to N 20 b 4½.1½.
       183 & 187 Bdes. R.F.A. from N 20 a 6.5½ to N 20 b 2.3
       15th Bde. R.H.A. from N 20 b 2.3 to N 20 b 4½.1½.
       Barrage WEST of N 20 a 6.5½ remains as in (2).
       Whole barrage of 41st D.A. and 15th Bde. R.H.A. remains on this line (viz. N 13 d 5½.3 along BAYONET Trench to N 20 a 6.5½ to N 20 b 4½.1½) until 30 minutes after zero.

II. 30th D.A. (less 1 section see para. III.) and 147 Bde. R.F.A. will form a barrage 'B'. in depth, as under:-
   (1) From zero to 3 minutes after zero on line
       N 20 b 4½.2 to N 20 d 8.8½ along GREASE Trench to N 21 c 1.7½.
       50% of the 18-pdrs. on this line.
       50% of the 18-pdrs. on a line 100 yards SOUTH of this line.
   N.B. The barrage will be especially thick on GREASE Trench.

   (2) 30th D.A. will also form a barrage "not in Depth" at zero from N 21 c 1.7½ to N 21 c 8.7½ advancing at once by 50 yards a minute to line N 21 c 1.7½ to N 21 a 80 and remaining on this line till 5 minutes after zero.

   (3) At 3 minutes after zero all guns SOUTH of line N 20 b 4½.2 to N 21 c 1.7½ advance 50 yards a minute to that line arriving at 5 minutes after zero.

   (4) At 5 minutes after zero whole barrage 'B' (i.e. from N 20 b 4½.2 to N 21 a 80) advances 50 yards a minute to line, N 20 b 4½.2 to N 20 b 8.2 to N 21 a 2.0 to N 21 a 9.6½ 4½ and remains till 30 minutes after zero.

III. One section 30th D.A. will
       from zero to 3 minutes after zero barrage BAYONET Trench from N 20 d 4.5½ to N 20 d 2.6½.
       At 3 minutes after zero this section lifts direct to BAYONET Trench from N 20 a 4.7 to N 13 d 5½.3 and remains till further orders.

IV. At 30 minutes after zero
   (a) 50% of 18-pdrs. on barrage and all guns of 189 and 190 Bdes. and special section 30th D.A. (see para. III.) continue on barrage line searching and sweeping 300 yards North of barrage line until ordered to stop.
       189 and 190 Bdes. will in addition search 50 yards SOUTH of their barrage line (BAYONET TRENCH) returning at irregular intervals to BAYONET TRENCH.

(b).

- 2 -

    (b) 50% 18-pdrs. (less 189 and 190 Bdes. and special Section 301 D.A.) cease barrages and search and sweep all dead ground approaches and sunken roads in their own zones and deal with fleeting opportunities.

   <u>N.B.</u> In addition to their own zones -
     183 Bde. will cover zones of 190 Bde.
     187 Bde. will cover zone of 189 Bde.
     from a line 200 yards NORTH of BAYONET Trench.
   183 Bde. will detail 1 section to continually search LUISENHOF FARM - LIGNY TILLOY road from 30 minutes after zero onwards.

V. Rates of fire for 18-pdrs:-
   Zero to 10 minutes after zero 4 rounds per gun per minute.
   10 minutes after zero to 30 minutes after zero 3 rounds per gun per minute.
   30 minutes after zero to 1 hour after zero 2 rounds per gun per minute.
   1 hour after zero to 'Stop' 1 round per gun per 4 minutes.
  <u>N.B.</u> Above does not apply to fleeting opportunities when there is no limit.

VI. 4.5" Hows. will act as under:-
   (a) From zero to 2 minutes after zero -
     (a) 41st D.A. on BAYONET TRENCH WEST of N 20 d 2.7
     (b) 30th D.A. on GREASE Trench.
       Rate of fire 3 rounds per gun per minute.
   (b) At two minutes after zero all HOWs. will lift direct to following targets in their own zones:-
    BARLEY TRENCH.
    BACON   "
    LUISEN   "
    LUISENHOF Farm
    Sunken roads.
    D/189 will put one 4.5" How. on suspected M.G. emplacement N 13 b 50 - N 13 b 60.
    D/183 will place one section 4.5" Hows. permanently on road, LUISENHOF Farm - LIGNY TILLOY.

    Rates of fire from -
    2 minutes after zero to 1 hour after zero 1 round per gun per minute.
    1 hour after zero to 'Stop' 1 round per gun per 6 minutes.

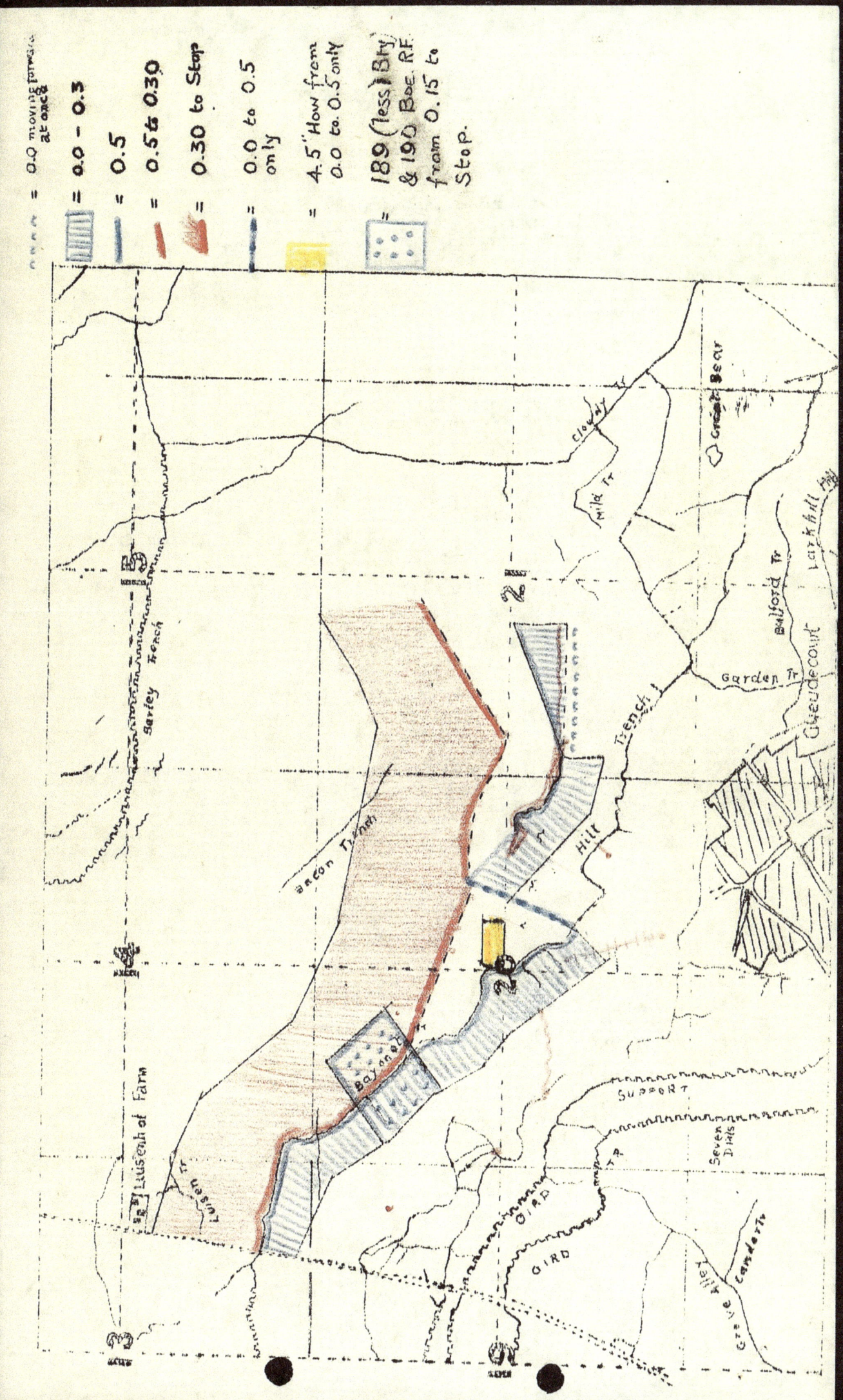

SECRET.

41ST DIVISIONAL ARTILLERY GROUP OPERATION ORDER NO.32

I. On night October 23/24 the 29th Division will "pinch" the portion of BAYONET TRENCH SOUTH EAST of N.20.Central.

II. It is desired to drive the enemy up BAYONET TRENCH to NORTH of N.20.Central.
   The Heavy Artillery will bombard the portion of BAYONET TRENCH from N.20.d.4.5. to N.20.Central from 2.30 pm. on Oct. 23rd onwards.

III. The How. batteries of 189 and 187 Brigades will from 2.30 pm to zero hour maintain a steady rate of fire on BAYONET TRENCH from N.20.d.4.5. to N.20. Central.
   D/189 will fire from 2.30 pm. Oct. 23rd to 4.30 pm.
   D/187 will fire from 4.30 pm. Oct. 23rd to 6.30 pm.
   D/189 will fire from 6.30 pm. October 23rd to 8.30 pm.
   D/187 will fire from 8.30 pm. Oct. 23rd to 10.30 pm.
and so on to zero.
   Fire will be at the rate of 20 rounds per battery per hour up to the time at which the Heavies cease firing.
   From the time the Heavies cease fire, the rate of fire will be increased to 40 rounds per battery per hour.
   Fire will be carefully distributed along the trench from N.20.d.4.5. to N.20.Central.

IV. Necessary registration must be completed before 1 pm. Oct. 23rd.
   N.B. From 1 pm. to 2.30 pm. there will be no firing on BAYONET TRENCH from N.20.d.4.5. to N.20. Central as the H.A. will be registering.

V. 187 Brigade will detail one section 18 pdrs. to stand by to catch any "runners" during the bombardment by the Heavy Artillery from 2.30 pm. onwards.

VI. Officers of L/187 and D/169 conducting the shoot will visit SCAN'S Headquarters as early as possible on Oct. 23rd and arrange any further details.

VII. Zero hour will be notified by Code message "RATS" followed by the hour.

VIII. In addition to above, D/189 will before 1 pm. on Oct.23rd deal with the sap heads (as already arranged) between N.20.c.9½. and N.20.d.1.7½, arranging details direct with LIAISON Officer SCAN.

IX. 30th D.A. will detail one 4.5" How. battery (D/150) to deal with sap heads at N.20.d.3.4. before 1 pm. Oct. 23rd.
   Also two How. batteries (E/150. and D/147) to deal with new trench from N.20.d.4.5. to N.20.d.5.9½ (approximately) from 2.30 pm. Oct. 23rd. to zero hour.

X. ACKNOWLEDGE.

Major R.A.

22-10-16.   Brigade Major, 41st Divisional Artillery Group.

Copies to :-
   189 Bde.   183 Bde.
   187 "   190 "
   30th D.A. (5 copies)   15 "
                       29 Div. G.
                       Scan.
                       Slay.

SECRET   Ref. Map No. X40

41st. DIVISIONAL ARTILLERY GROUP
OPERATION ORDER No. 35

I. In continuation of Warning Order, this Office S.92 of 22nd. October, the bombardment by the Heavy Artillery commences at 8 a.m., October 23rd. and will continue till zero.
  Certain trenches will be cleared for safety.
  There will be no increase of rate of fire before zero.

II. Heavy Artillery will concentrate in particular on the following objectives:-

  (a) Sunken Road N.21.b.6.9. - N.21.b.6.5. (not to commence till result of XIVth. Corps operations of to-day is known)

  (b) STORMY TRENCH N.21.d.5.8½. to N.21.a.7.8. (no fire on this trench SOUTH of N.21.b.2.2. till result of XIVth. Corps operations of to-day is known)

  (c) Road and trenches alongside from N.21.a.3.4. to N.21.a.7.8.

  (d) BAYONET TRENCH from N.20.a.7½.8 & 1½ to LIGNY TILLOY - FACTORY CORNER Road.

  (e) SCABBARD TRENCH.

  (f) BACON TRENCH

  (g) Old gun positions N.14.c.4.4., N.14.c.2.7., N.14.a.1½.1., N.14.a.8.3.

  (h) LUISEN TRENCH

  (i) LUISENHOF FARM

  (j) BARLEY TRENCH from N.15.c.5½.9 to LIGNY TILLOY road

  (k) Road and trenches from N.21.a.7.8. to N.15.b.4.9.

III. The 41st. Divisional Artillery Group will pay special attention to cutting all existing wire on the front and preventing repair by night. This is of the utmost importance and no effort must be spared to ensure that it is successfully carried out.

  N.B. Any available information re wire must be obtained from the Infantry through liaison Officer

IV. 41st. Divisional Artillery Group will also co-operate by concentrating the greater part of all day and night firing by Hows. and 18 pdrs. (the latter using H.E. where safe) on the Trenches and objectives in para II., in their own zones.
  The amount of Ammunition to be expended should be limited only by the amount that can be supplied to the guns and the

physical condition of the men.

At Zero hour on 25th October there should be 600 rounds per 18 pdr. gun and 450 rounds per 4.5" How. at or near the guns.

V. ACKNOWLEDGE.

[signature]

BRIGADE MAJOR,
41st. Divisional Artillery.

23.10.16
HRP

XVth. Corps, R.A.,
30th. Divisional Artillery (20 copies)
183rd. Brigade, R.F.A. (5 copies)
187th. Brigade, R.F.A. (5 copies)
189th. Brigade, R.F.A. (5 copies)
190th. Brigade, R.F.A., (5 copies)
15th. Brigade, R.H.A. (4 copies)
Guards Divisional Artillery
12th. Divisional Artillery Group
29th. Division
SCAN
SLAY
41st. D.A.C.
2 Spare.

SECRET.   Ref. Map X 48.

94

41st Divisional Artillery Group Operation Order No. 36

I. On October 25th at zero hour XV Corps resumes the offensive.
   The 29th Division attacks on the right.
   The 5th Australian Division on the left.
   IIIrd Corps will also attack.

II. For this operation the boundary between 29th and 5th
Australian Divisions will be N.19.b.8.3. - N.14.c.1½.0. - N.14.
a.4.0. Northwards.
   The 189 Brigade will take over the present zone of the 190
Brigade in addition to its own zone, and from zero hour will
come under orders of 12th D.A.G. supporting 1st Australian
Division.
   The 190 Brigade R.F.A. will lend 1-18 pdr. battery each to
187, 183 and 15th Brigades to assist in their zones.

III. 41st D.A.G. will co-operate with barrage as below :-
   (a) Left Barrage.
       (1) From zero to 3 minutes after zero
           on area N.20.a.7½.0 - N.20.d.1½.4 - N.20.d.3½.5 -
           N.14.c.1½.1 (A A. B B. on map)
       (2) At 3 minutes after zero
           Barrage on N.20.a.7½.0 - N.20.d.1½.4 advances at 50
           yards a minute to line N.14.c.1½.1 - N.20.d.3½.5
           arriving at 6 minutes after zero.
       (3) At 6 minutes after zero :-
           Barrage from N.14.c.1½.1 - N.20. Central advances at
           50 yards a minute to line
           N.14.c.2½.3½ to N.20.a.8.8½ to N.20.b.3.2. (C.D.)
           Barrage from N.20.central to N.20.d.3½.5 (15th and
           147th Brigades jumps direct to line
           N.20.b.1.3½ - N.20.b.3.1½ - N.20.b.8.5 in their own
           Brigade zones
       the whole barrage remaining on this line viz :-
           N.14.c.2½.3 - N.20.a.8.8½ - N.20.b.3.1½ - N.20.b.8.5.
           till 13 minutes after zero.
       (4) At 13 minutes after zero whole left barrage advances
           at 50 yards a minute from line
           N.14.c.2½.3 - N.20.a.8.8½ - N.20.b.3.1½ - N.20.b.8.5
           to line N.14.a.4.0 - N.14.d.7½.7½ - N.15.c.2.6½ and
           remains till further orders.

   (b) Right Barrage.
       (1) From zero to 3 minutes after zero on line
           N.20.b.3.1½ - N.20.b.7.2.- N.21.a.0.3. - N.21.a.
           7½.4 - N.21.b.3.½ - N.21.d.5½.8 (D.D' X JJ' K on
           map) and area N.21.a.0.3.- N.21.a.8.8½ - N.21.b.
           3.1½ - N.21.a.7½.4 - N.21.a.0.3.
       N.B. The portion DD' will be carried out by 30th D.A.
           with one section.
       (2) At 3 minutes after zero portion JJ' K swings to
           line N.21.a.7½.4 - N.21.b.   (J.P.) arriving at
           6 minutes after zero.
       (3) At 4 minutes after zero portion J X D' D swings
           to line
           N.21.a.7½.4 - N.20.b.8.5 (JD^2) arriving at 6
           minutes after zero.
       (4) At 7 minutes after zero section on D' D jumps to
           its own zone on line N.20.b.8.5 - N.15.c.8.2.

(5).

2.

III. (b) Contd.
    (5) At 6 minutes after zero barrage on line
        D^2 J P swings to line
        N.20.b.8.5 - N.21.a.8.8 - N.21.b.8½.½ (D^2 L P)
        arriving at 9 minutes after zero.
    (6) At nine minutes after zero barrage on line
        D^2 L P swings at 50 yards a minute to line
        N.20.b.8.5. - N.15.c.8.2 - N.21.b.9.3 (D^2 Z N)
        arriving at 12 minutes after zero and remaining till
        13 minutes after zero.
    (7) At 13 minutes after zero
        whole left [Right] barrage swings from line
        D^2 Z N at 50 yards a minute to line
        N.15.c.2.6½ - N.21.b.9.8½ (F G)
        and remains till further orders.
    (8) At 35 minutes after zero 50% of the 18-pdrs. on the
        barrage lift to BARLEY and BREAD TRENCHES in their
        own zones and remain till further orders.
        The remaining guns open out to cover gaps on final
        barrage line and search back, 41st L.A. 150 yards
        remainder 100 yards at irregular intervals.

IV. At 1 hour after zero
    one 18-pdr. battery of 187 Bde.R.F.A.
    one 18-pdr. battery of 15th Bde.R.H.A.
    one 18-pdr. battery of 30th D.A.
will be detailed to search all communications and dead ground
NORTH of BARLEY TRENCH on 41st D.A.G. front.

V. After 35 minutes after zero any battery not on barrage may
deal with fleeting opportunities as such arise.

VI. Rates of fire for 18-pdrs.:-
From zero to 30 minutes after zero 4 rounds per gun per minute.
From 30 minutes after zero to 45 minutes after zero 2 rounds
per gun per minute.
From 45 minutes after zero to 1 hour after zero 1 round per
gun per minute.
From 1 hour afterzero to 1 hour 30 minutes after zero 1 round
per gun per 2 minutes.
From 1 hour 30 minutes after zero onwards 1 round per gun per
4 minutes.

VII. 4.5" Hows. will deal with tasks as under :-
(a) From zero to 7 minutes after zero
        (Sunken Road N.21.b.6.3 - N.15.b.5½.2.
30th D.A. (
        ("   " N.15.d.2.5. - N.15.b.5½.2.
147 Bde. Trench N.20.b.4.3. - N.20.b.2.4.
41st D.A. BACON TRENCH.
(b) 7 minutes after zero to 13 minutes after zero
30th D.A. Sunken Roads as in VII (a) but NORTH of N.21.b.6½.8.
147 Bde. BACON TRENCH in its own zone.
41st D.A. BACON TRENCH in its own zone.
(c) 13 minutes after zero till further orders
30th D.A. Sunken Roads as in VII (a) but NORTH of N.15.d.7.0
and portion of BARLEY TRENCH in 30th D.A. zone.
147 Bde. (
        (BARLEY TRENCH in their own zones.
41st D.A. (
(d) From 1 hour after zero all 4.5" How. batteries will
detail 1 section per battery to search and sweep all dead
ground and approaches in their own zones NORTH of final
barrage line.
                              VIII.

3.

VIII. Rates of fire for 4.5" Hows. :-
Zero to 30 minutes after zero 2 rounds per gun per minute
30 minutes after zero to 1 hour after zero 1 round per gun per 2 minutes.
1 hour after zero to stop at rate equivalent to 1 round per gun per 4 minutes.

IX. Guards Divisional Artillery on Right is being asked to assist with :-
    (a) One 18-pdr.bty.) On Sunken Roads from N.21.b.6.3.
        One 4.5" How.Bty.) to N.15.b.5.2. from zero to 7 minutes after zero.
    (b) Lifting at 7 minutes after zero to Sunken Road as in (a) but NORTH of N.15.d.7.0. until stop.
    (c) From zero to stop
        1-18 pdr. battery on BREAD TRENCH.
    (d) A continuation of the barrage for 300 yards EAST.

X. The Infantry will vacate trenches N.W. of line shown -∅- -∅- -∅- on map.

XI. Zero will be notified.

XII. Watches will be synchronized at a convenient hour before zero.

XIII. 187 Brigade will man Divisional O.P. from 30 minutes before zero.

XIV. An amendment to extreme Right flank of barrages may be necessary when result of XIVth Corps Operations of to-day is known.

XV. ACKNOWLEDGE.

                                                 Major R.A.

23-10-16.   Brigade Major, 41st Divisional Artillery Group.

Copies to :-
    XV Corps R.A.
    29th Div. (4 copies).
    12th D.A.
    8th Div.
    Guards D.A.
    5th Australian Div.
    30th D.A. (20 copies).
    183 Bde. 5 copies.
    187 "   5 "
    189 "   5 "
    190 "   5 "
    15th Bde. 4 copies.
    41st D.A.C.
    T.M.C. 41st Div.
    5 spare.

SECRET

97

AMENDMENT TO
41ST DIVISIONAL ARTILLERY GROUP OPERATION ORDER NO.36.

A. Para.I - for "October 25th" read "October 28th".

B. Para.II - line 4 to end of para.
    for 189 read 190.
    for 190 read 189.

C. Cancel para.III and substitute the following new paragraph :-

III. 21st D.A.G. will co-operate with barrage as under :-
  (1) Left barrage. (183, 187, 189, and 15th Brigades).
    (a) From zero to 3 minutes after zero
        50% of 18-pdrs. on line
        N.20.a.0.7. - N.20.d.$1\frac{1}{2}$.4 (AA' on map).
        50% of 18-pdrs. on BAYONET TRENCH.
        N.14.c.$1\frac{1}{2}$.0 - N.20.d.2.$6\frac{1}{2}$ (BB' on map).
    (b) At 3 minutes after zero
        barrage on line AA' advances at 50 yards a minute
        to line BB' arriving at 6 minutes after zero.
    (c) At 6 minutes after zero
        Whole left barrage on line BB' advances at 50 yards
        a minute to line
        N.14.c.$2\frac{1}{2}$.4 - N.14.c.8.0 - N.20.b.$3\frac{1}{2}$.3 (CC^{2}C' on map).
        arriving at 9 minutes after zero
        and remains until 13 minutes after zero.
    (d) At 13 minutes after zero
        Whole left barrage advances at 50 yards a minute
        from line CC^{2}C' to line
        N.14.a.4.0 - N.14.d.8.7 (FF' on map).
        and remains till further orders.

  (2) 147th Brigade R.F.A. :-
    (a) From zero to 3 minutes after zero 50% of 18-pdrs.
        on Trench N.20.d.2.7 - N.20.d.$3\frac{1}{2}$.$5\frac{1}{2}$ (B'E on map).
    (b) At zero 50% of 18-pdrs. on line
        N.20.d.$1\frac{1}{2}$.5 - N.20.d.3.4 (VV' on map).
        advancing at zero to line B'E at 50 yards a minute.
    (c) At 3 minutes after zero whole barrage of 147 Brigade
        advances from line B'E at 50 yards a minute to line
        N.20.b.$3\frac{1}{2}$.3 - N.20.b.5.$3\frac{1}{2}$ (C'E')
        arriving at 10 minutes after zero.
    (N.B. Right flank must move via. N.20.b.$4\frac{1}{2}$.0).
    (d) At 10 minutes after zero 147 barrage extends from
        line C'E' to line
        N.20.b.$3\frac{1}{2}$.3 - N.20.b.8.5 (C'Y on map)
        and remains till 13 minutes after zero.
    (e) At 13 minutes after zero 147 barrage advances 50
        yards a minute to line
        N.14.d.7.$7\frac{1}{2}$ - N.15.c.2.6. (F'F^2)
        and remains till further orders.

  (3) Right barrage
    (a) From zero to 3 minutes after zero 50% of 18-pdrs.
        on line
        N.20.b.$7\frac{1}{2}$.3 - N.21.b.3.1 - N.21.d.6.8 (XP'X').
    (b) From zero till overtaken by guns in para.(a) above
        50% 18-pdrs. on trench N.21.a.0.2 - N.21.a.8.$8\frac{1}{2}$ -
        N.21.b.3.1 (PP^{2}P').

                                                          (c).

2.

III. (3) Contd.
(c) At 3 minutes after zero barrage on line XP'
advances 50 yards a minute to line
N.20.d.8.5 - N.15.c.8½.3 - N.21.b.4½.5½ (YY'Y²),
taking guns on line PP²P' with it as it reaches
that line and remains on this line till 13 minutes
after zero.   (YY' Y²)

(d) At 3 minutes after zero barrage on line P'X'
advances at 50 yards a minute to line
N.21.b.4½.5 - N.21.b.9.2½ (Y²Y³)
and remains till 13 minutes after zero.

(e) At 13 minutes after zero whole Right barrage advances
at 50 yards a minute from line
YY' Y² Y³ to line
N.15.c.1½.6½ - N.15.d.4.4 along trench to N.21.b.9.8½
(F²F³F⁴) and remains till further orders.

(4) At 35 minutes after zero 50% of the 18-pdrs. on the
barrage lift to BARLEY and BREAD TRENCHES in their own
zones and remain till further orders.
The remaining guns open out to cover gaps on final
barrage line and search back 41st D.A. 150 yards and
remainder 100 yards at irregular intervals.

D. para.VI line 2 should read
"From zero to 30 minutes after zero not less than 4 rounds per gun
per minute special attention being paid to times of assault".

E. Add to para.VI as follows:-
"From zero to 3 minutes after zero
18-pdrs. on line AA', B' E, XP'X'
will use shrapnel only.
From zero to 3 minutes after zero
18-pdrs. on line BB', PP² P' will use H.E. only.
From 3 minutes after zero till arrival on line FF' F² F³ F⁴
all 18-pdrs will use shrapnel only.
After arrival on line FF' F² F³ F⁴
all 18-pdrs will use 50% H.E. and 50% shrapnel.

F. Add to para IX
(e) If wind is favourable, gas shell on N.15.d. and N.15.c.

G. Delete para. X and substitute
"Infantry will clear GREASE and HILT TRENCHES in N.20.d. as
far EAST as N.20.d.8½.9 and N.20.d.7.4½".

H. ACKNOWLEDGE.

Major R.A.

24-10-16.   Brigade Major, 41st Divisional Artillery Group.

To all recipients of 41st D.A.G. O.O. No.36.

SECRET.

2nd AMENDMENT TO
41ST DIVISIONAL ARTILLERY GROUP OPERATION ORDER NO.36.

I. It is desired to attack BACON TRENCH on a front parallel to the trench - following amendments to amendment to 41st D.A.G. Operation Order No.36 are therefore necessitated.

II. Amend :-
    Amendment to 41st D.A.G. Operation Order No.36.
    para.(2) 147th Brigade R.F.A.
    sub.para.(a) delete "50% of 18-pdrs".
    sub.para.(b) delete whole para.
    sub.para.(e) delete whole para. and substitute
      "At 13 minutes after zero 147 barrage swings
      from line Y C' (N.20.b.8.5.- N.20.b.$3\frac{1}{2}$.3).
      to line N.20.b.8.5. - N.20.b.5.9
      at 50 yards a minute arriving at 18 minutes
      after zero.
      At 18 minutes after zero
      barrage of 147 Brigade advances at 50 yards a
      minute to line
      N.14.d.7.$7\frac{1}{2}$ - N.15.c.2.6. (F'F²)
      and remains till further orders ".

    Para. (3) Right barrage.
    Sub.para.(c) for "13 minutes after zero" read
      "18 minutes after zero".

III. ACKNOWLEDGE.

Maps must be amended accordingly.

                                            Major R.A.

25-10-16.   Brigade Major, 41st Divisional Arty. Group.

TO all recipients of 41st D.A.G. Operation Order No. 36.

SECRET

THIRD AMENDMENT to 41st. DIVISIONAL ARTILLERY GROUP OPERATION ORDER No.36

I. The operations therein referred to have been postponed a further 48 hours and will now take place on November 1st.

II. First amendment para III Night Barrage, sub-paragraph (c) for N.20.d.8.5 - read N.20.b.8.5

Sub-paragraph (c) and (d) for "13 minutes" read "18 minutes".

III. The Divisional O.P. will be manned by 183rd. Brigade, R.F.A., and not by 187th. Brigade, R.F.A.

IV. ACKNOWLEDGE

BRIGADE MAJOR,
41st. Divisional Artillery.

28.10.16
HHP

To all recipients of 41st. Divisional Artillery Group Operation Order No.36.

S E C R E T.

41st. DIVISIONAL ARTILLERY
OPERATION ORDER NO.35.

I.   2nd.Australian Divisional Artillery relieves 41st. Divisional Artillery,if tactical situation permits by Sections on nights October 30th/31st. and October 31st./November 1st.

    On completion of relief G.O.C., R.A., 30th.Division will assume command of the Group.

II.   41st.Divisional Artillery will be relieved as under:-

    (a) 183rd.Brigade by 6th Australian Brigade:-
        A/183 by 16th.Battery
        B/183 by 17th.Battery
        C/183 by 18th.Battery
        D/183 by 106th.Brigade

    (b) 187th.Brigade by 5th.Australian Brigade:-
        A/187th.by 13th.Battery
        B/187th.by 14th.Battery
        C/187th.by 15th.Battery
        D/187th.by 5th.Battery

    (c) 189th.Brigade by 22nd.Australian Brigade:-
        A/189th.by 19th.Battery
        B/189th.by 20th.Battery
        C/189th.by 21st.Battery

    (d) 190th.Brigade by 4th.Australian Brigade:-
        A/190th.by 10th.Battery
        B/190th.by 11th.Battery
        C/190th.by 12th.Battery
        D/190th.by 104th.Battery

III.   All guns and Hows. with sights and sight carriers, but otherwise stripped, will be handed over in position; except the Hows.of D/189, which will accompany the Battery.

    The 2nd.Australian Divisional Artillery will park their guns and Hows. at their present camp at DERNANCOURT D.18.a.(approx) under guard, at which place 41st.Divisional Artillery Batteries will, on relief take them over, except as shown in paragraph V.

IV.   All ammunition at gun positions, and all ammunition in Wagon lines and D.A.C., will be handed over.

    2nd.Australian Divisional Artillery will dump all Ammunition in limbers,Battery wagons and D.A.C., under guard at their camp at DERNANCOURT, D.18.a.(approx) where 41st. Divisional Artillery Batteries and D.A.C. will take it over.

V.   The 11th. and 12th, 17th. and 18th. Australian Batteries are now in Camp at S.25.b.8.3., at which place B/183, C/183, B/190 and C/190 will respectively take over guns.

.1.

B/183, C/183, B/190, and C/190 will not take over Ammunition at S.25.b.8.3., but will fill up limbers and wagons at DE NANCOURT from Ammunition dumped for 41st.D.A.C. by 2nd.Australian D.A.C.

VI. All communications (less instruments) orders registrations air photos maps trench stores, etc., will be handed over to relieving units.

VII? Brigade Commanders -B.Cs - 1 subaltern per Battery - and a proportion of specialists per Battery (with instruments), also "Dump" Officer of 2nd.Australian Divisional Artillery will be at LONGUEVAL X roads, S.17 central, at 10.30 a.m., October 30th.

Guides from Brigades, Batteries, and Dump of 41st.Divisional Artillery will meet them and conduct them to Brigades, batteries, and dump.

These Officers and men will be accommodated by 41st. Divisional Artillery units.

VIII. An Officer of 2nd.Australian D.A.C. ("A" Echelon) will be at 41st.Divisional Artillery Headquarters at 10.30 a.m., on October 30th. where an Officer of "A" Echelon, 41st.D.A.C., will meet him.
Staff Captain and Signal Officer, 2nd.Australian Divisional Artillery will also arrive at 41st.Divisional Artillery Headquarters on October 30th.

IX. Guides from Batteries, 41st.Divisional Artillery will meet relieving sections of Batteries, 2nd.Australian Divisional Artillery at 11 a.m., on road at POMMIERS REDOUBT on October 30th. and October 31st.
Sections 2nd.Australian Divisional Artillery will proceed to Wagon lines 41st.Divisional Artillery, and thence on foot to gun positions.
Detachments will proceed to gun positions singly and at 300 yards interval. Relief will be completed each day, if possible, before dark.
Sections 41st.Divisional Artillery being withdrawn on relief to Wagon lines for the night.

X. On October 31st. Sections 41st.Divisional Artillery relieved on October 30th. and November 1st, Sections 41st.Divisional Artillery relieved on October 31st, will march to area BONNAY - LA NEUVILLE under orders to be issued later.
From this area 41st.Divisional Artillery will march to TALMAS and VILLE S BOCAGE en route for Second Army.

XI. (2) 41st.D.A.C. ("A" Echelon) will be relieved by 2nd. Australian D.A.C. ("A" Echelon) on October 30th. At the same time the Officer and 30 men 41st.Divisional Artillery at Ammunition Dump will be relieved by an Officer and 30 men of 2nd. Australian Divisional Artillery.
41st.D.A.C. ("A" Echelon) proceeding on relief to camp vacated by 2nd.Australian D.A.C. ("A" Echelon) at DE NANCOURT, D.18.a. Details will be arranged direct between O.C., 41st.D.A.C. and representatives of 2nd.Australian D.A.C. - vide para.VII.
Billeting party 41st.D.A.C., "A" Echelon will proceed to DE NANCOURT, D.18.a. (approx) to take over camp of 2nd.Australian D.A.C., on morning October 30th.
(N.B. 41st.D.A.C. ("A" Echelon) will on arrival at DE NANCOURT, send an orderly daily at 9 a.m., 12 noon, and 6 p.m., to BELLEVUE FARM to receive any orders)

(b) "B" Echelon, 41st.D.A.C., will be relieved by "B" Echelon, 2nd.Australian D.A.C., on October 31st., and will proceed on relief to BONNAY via DERNANCOURT area picking up Ammunition at DERNANCOURT en route of 2nd.Australian "B" Echelon (further orders will be issued).

XII. Commands of Batteries, Brigades, etc., and of D.A. will pass on completion of respective reliefs.

XIII. Further orders re march to BONNAY area will be issued.

XIV. Trench Mortars (Medium) will not be handed over.

XV. All wireless installations will be handed over to relieving units.

XVI. Each Battery, 41st.Divisional Artillery will send an Officer with 1 N.C.O., and 4 men on October 30th. to the relieving Battery 2nd.Australian Divisional Artillery to take over guns and Ammunition and take charge of same till removed by Batteries, 41st.Divisional Artillery. Written receipts for guns and Ammunition will be given and obtained.

XVII. Command of 41st.D.A.G. will pass to G.O.C.,30th.Divisional Artillery at 10 a.m., on November 1st., at which hour Headquarters 41st.Divisional Artillery will close at POMMIERS REDOUBT and open at a position in BONNAY area to be notified.

XVIII. All units will report completion of relief by wire to this Office.

XIX. Liaison Officers with Infantry will rejoin their Batteries at 11 a.m., October 31st.

XX. ACKNOWLEDGE.

BRIGADE MAJOR,
41st.Divisional Artillery.

29th.Oct.1916.
HHP
XV Corps,
XVth.Corps,
30th.D.A. (20 copies)
2nd.Australian D.A.
1st.Australian D.A.
41st.Division
183rd.Brigade,
187th.Brigade,
189th.Brigade,
190th.Brigade,
15th.Brigade,H.A., (for information)
41st.D.A.C., "A" & "B" Echelons
T.M.C.,41st.Division
12th.D.A.C.
Left Artillery XIV Corps
41st.D.A.Dump
41st.D.A.Signal Officer

SECRET   Ref.Map ALBERT (combined)
------------   and AMIENS 17.

41st.D.A.G.OPERATION ORDER No.36

I. 41st. D.A. will march on October 31st/& 1st.Nov. to
BONNAY - LA NEUVILLE area in accordance with attached March
Table.

II. Billeting parties of 1 Officer and 1 N.C.O., per Brigade
and two N.C.Os per Battery, mounted will be at POMMIERS REDOUBT
(41st.D.A.Hqrs) at 6.30 a.m., October 31st. to meet Staff
Captain and to proceed to arrange billets.
Rations must be taken.

III. Guides from Billeting party will meet units at N.E.End
of HEILLY(J.2.a.2.2.) at 12.30 pm each day (Oct.31st/Nov.1st)

IV. Rate of March including "short" halts 2½ miles per
hour.
Ten minutes "short" halt at ten minutes before each hour.
"Long" halts of one hour to water and feed at 12 noon.

V. Guns and Ammunition will be picked up as Sections &c.,
pass nearest point on road to D.18.a. Each Brigade will send
forward an Officer a mile in advance to D.18.a., to make necessary
arrangements.

VI. "A" Echelon, 41st.D.A.C., will send billeting party of
two N.C.Os per section under an Officer to meet Staff Captain
at Railway Bridge near DERNANCOURT, E.20.b.2.6. at 7 a.m., on
Oct.31st.
"A" Echelon, D.A.C., will march from D.18.a., to BONNAY
area via BUIRE LIBEMONT and HEILLY starting at 6 a.m., on
Nov.1st. Guide from Billeting party to be at J.2.a.2.2.
at 7 a.m.,to meet "A" Echelon and guide it to Billets.

VII. All units will on arrival in billets send an orderly
to Headquarters 41st.D.A., in BONNAY area - position to be
notified later.

VIII. All T.M. Personnel with equipment, guns, etc., will
be at old dump at F.5.d.1.5. at 11 a.m., on October 31st.,
whence lorries will convey them to billets.

IX. Special orders will be issued to H.Q.,Section 41st.
Divl.Train.

X. ACKNOWLEDGE.

                                        Brigade Major,
30.10.16   41st.Divisional Artillery.

Dst.Anzac Corps   183rd.Bde., F.A.
1st.Australian Divn   187th.   "   "
2nd.Australian D.A.   189th.   "   "
12th D.A.   190th.   "   "
Left ArtilleryXIV Corps   41st.D.A.C. "A" Echelon
30th.D.A.   41st.D.A.C. "B" Echelon
                          T.M.C.,41st.Division
                          FILE.

SECRET

MARCH TABLE

UNIT	Starting Point	Hour of passing Starting point.	ROUTE
		October 31st. All Sections relieved on Oct.30th/31st., and ½ "B" Echelon,D.A.C.	
187th.Bde.R.F.A.	Junction of MONTAUBAN - CAYNOY & MONTAUBAN-FRICOURT rds. S.27.c.7.2.	5.0a.m.	MONTAUBAN - CAYNOY - CROSS ROADS F.18.c.5.2.-F.4.c.5.3.-MIAULTE - DERNANCOURT - CROSS ROADS E.18.b.9.1. E.13.9.1 CROSS ROADS D.12.d.8.8. - CROSS ROADS D.17.b.4.8. - BUIRE - LIBEMONT - HEILLY - to Billets.
189th.Bde.R.F.A.	do.	6.0 a.m.	Do.
190th.Bde.R.F.A.	do.	7.0 a.m.	Do.
183rd.Bde.R.F.A.	do.	8.0 a.m.	Do.
½ "B" Echelon,D.A.C.	do.	9.0 a.m.	Do.

On Nov.1st. all Sections relieved on night Oct.31st/ Nov.1st. and remaining ½ "B" Echelon,D.A.C. as above.

On His Majesty's Service

1st DIV.
R.A., H.Q.
November, 1916

APPENDIX 11.

DIVISION ORDER NO.70.

WAR DIARY or INTELLIGENCE SUMMARY

Army Form C. 2118

Place	Date	Hour	Summary of Events and Information	Remarks and references to Appendices
POMMIERS REDOUBT	1/11/16	10 AM	The 41st D.A. was relieved by 2nd Australian D.A. & marched to the BONNAY - LANEUVILLE area and billeted - a fine day. - 1st Bde were established at the SCHOOL HOUSE BONNAY at 2 PM -	app 1 II + III, app Inny
BONNAY	2/11/16		Rested in Billets - an overcast showery day.	app Inny
VILLERS BOCAGE	3/11/16		Marched from BONNAY to MOLLIENS VILLERS BOCAGE TALMAS area a fine day. 1st Bde were established at THE CHATEAU VILLERS BOCAGE	app 4 app 5 app Inny
DOULLENS	4/11/16		Marched from MOLLIENS VILLERS BOCAGE TALMAS area to AMPLIER ORVILLE area. 1st Bde were established at DOULLENS	app 6
BOUBERS SUR CANCHE	5/11/16		Marched from AMPLIER - ORVILLE area to CONCHY SUR CANCHE BOUBERS SUR CANCHE LIGNY SUR CANCHE - VACQUERIE LE BOURCQ area 1st Bde were established at THE CHATEAU BOUBERS SUR CANCHE	app Inny
MONCHY CAYEUX	6/11/16		Marched from BOUBERS SUR CANCHE - LIGNY SUR CANCHE - VACQUERIE LE BOURCQ area to FONTAINE LES BOULANS - HEUCHIN - BERGENEUSE ANVIN MONCHY CAYEUX area Headquarters were established at MONCHY CAYEUX CHATEAU Rested in Billets - a pouring wet day - horses & men very tired	app 7 app Inny
MONCHY CAYEUX	7/11/16		Rested in Billets	Inny
MONCHY CAYEUX	8/11/16		Rested in Billets	Inny

Army Form C. 2118

WAR DIARY
or
INTELLIGENCE SUMMARY
(Erase heading not required.)

Instructions regarding War Diaries and Intelligence Summaries are contained in F. S. Regs., Part II. and the Staff Manual respectively. Title Pages will be prepared in manuscript.

Place	Date	Hour	Summary of Events and Information	Remarks and references to Appendices
LAMBRES	9/11/16		Marched from FONTAINE les BOULANS - HEUCHIN - BERGENEUSE - ANVIN - MONCHY CAYEUX area to HAM EN ARTOIS - BERGUETTE - NOLINGHEM - LAMBRES - MAZINGHEM area - Head Quarters were established at the CHATEAU LAMBRES	app 8 JCMG
STAPLE	10/11/16		Marched from HAM EN ARTOIS - BERGUETTE NOLINGHEM LAMBRES MAZINGHEM area to WALLON CAPPEL STAPLE HONDEGHEM area Headquarters were established at STAPLE - Battery commanders with subalterns + 3 telephonists went forward in 3 motor buses and 2 lorries to RENINGHELST to prepare to take over positions from the 4th Australian DA.	app 9 JCMG
BOESCHEPE	11/11/16		Marched from WALLON CAPPEL- STAPLE HONDEGHEM area to BOESCHEPE area Headquarters were established at BOESCHEPE	app 10 JCMG
BOESCHEPE	12/11/16		Commenced taking over from 4th Australian DA - A quiet day	app. 10 JCMG
RENINGHELST	13/11/16		Continued taking over from 4th Australian DA. Blips commenced repairing & great deal	app. 11/12
RENINGHELST	14/11/16	10 AM	Assumed responsibility for the ST ELOI and DIEPENDAAL sectors to-day complete. Blips repairing	app 11
RENINGHELST	15/11/16		A fine cold day - Batteries registering - Some hostile shelling of DICKEBUSCH	JCMG
RENINGHELST	16/11/16		A fine cold day - Registration + Calibration carried out - some hostile hostile wire activity. 132 & 58 received 25 rounds from 15 cm at 2.45 pm	app 12

1875 Wt. W593/826 1,000,000 4/15 J.B.C. & A. A.D.S.S./Forms/C. 2118.

Army Form C. 2118

WAR DIARY
or
INTELLIGENCE SUMMARY
(Erase heading not required.)

Instructions regarding War Diaries and Intelligence Summaries are contained in F. S. Regs., Part II. and the Staff Manual respectively. Title Pages will be prepared in manuscript.

Place	Date	Hour	Summary of Events and Information	Remarks and references to Appendices
RENINGHELST	17/11/16		Light rain Good all day. 2/4, TM Battery cut wire from 02c96 to 02c 59½ with apparently good results. 30 rounds were fired. ST ELOI GROUP carried out French Mortar fire DIEPENDAAL GROUP carried out registration - About 80 Hostile Shell were fired on our front. but Some were rather cold day	app 13 Jnry app 14 Jnry
RENINGHELST	18/11/16		a warmer wet day	
RENINGHELST	19/11/16		A fair cold day. cut wire with French mortars	app 15 Jnry
RENINGHELST	20/11/16			app 16 Jnry
RENINGHELST	21/11/16		carried out a dummy Raid - no casualties and no retaliation	app 17 Jnry app 18 Jnry
RENINGHELST	22/11/16		A fine day - Conference held on reorganisation & reallotment of front	app 19 Jnry app a
RENINGHELST	23/11/16		A fair day - tried to retaliation & cut wire with trichure French Mortars	app 20 Jnry
RENINGHELST	24/11/16		A fair day - continued wire cutting with French mortars	app 21 Jnry

1875 Wt. W593/826 1,000,000 4/15 J.B.C. & A. A.D.S.S./Forms/C. 2118.

WAR DIARY or INTELLIGENCE SUMMARY

Army Form C. 2118

(Erase heading not required.)

Instructions regarding War Diaries and Intelligence Summaries are contained in F.S. Regs., Part II. and the Staff Manual respectively. Title Pages will be prepared in manuscript.

Place	Date	Hour	Summary of Events and Information	Remarks and references to Appendices
RENINGHELST	25/11/16		A hot day. TM's out wire - commenced reorganisation	App 23 Army App 23 by
RENINGHELST	26/11/16		A fine day - Completed reorganisation	App 24 Army
RENINGHELST	27/11/16		A fine day - Hostile Aerial activity above normal	App 25 Army
RENINGHELST	28/11/16		A raw day - less hostile activity than usual	App 26 Army
RENINGHELST	29/11/16		A very raw cold misty day - Engaged 2 hostile harch trenches, which produced but slight retaliation under No 42	App 27 App 28 Army
RENINGHELST	30/11/16		A very cold raw misty day but some hostile zone with MTM's	App 29 Army App 29a

J. Wodehughs
G.O.C. R.a
41st Division

SECRET.

41st. DIVISIONAL ARTILLERY
OPERATION ORDER NO.37.

I.   2nd. Australian Divisional Artillery relieves 41st. Divisional Artillery if tactical situation permits by Sections on nights October 30th/31st. and October 31st./November 1st.
   On completion of relief G.O.C., R.A., 30th. Division will assume command of the Group.

II.   41st. Divisional Artillery will be relieved as under:-

   (a) 183rd. Brigade by 6th Australian Brigade:-
       A/183 by 16th. Battery
   LINNET   B/183 by 17th. Battery
       C/183 by 18th. Battery
       D/183 by 106th. Brigade

   (b) 187th. Brigade by 5th. Australian Brigade:-
       A/187th. by 13th. Battery
       B/187th. by 14th. Battery
   STORK   C/187th. by 15th. Battery
       D/187th. by 5th. Battery

   (c) 189th. Brigade by 22nd. Australian Brigade:-
       A/189th. by 19th. Battery
   WREN   B/189th. by 20th. Battery
       C/189th. by 21st. Battery

   (d) 190th. Brigade by 4th. Australian Brigade:-
       A/190th. by 10th. Battery
       B/190th. by 11th. Battery
   ROBIN   C/190th. by 12th. Battery
       D/190th. by 104th. Battery

III.   All guns and Hows. with sights and sight carriers, but otherwise stripped, will be handed over in position; except the Hows. of D/189, which will accompany the Battery.

   The 2nd. Australian Divisional Artillery will park their guns and Hows. at their present camp at DE NANCOURT D.18.a.(approx) under guard, at which place 41st. Divisional Artillery Batteries will, on relief take them over, except as shown in paragraph V.

IV.   All ammunition at gun positions, and all ammunition in Wagon lines and D.A.C., will be handed over.

   2nd. Australian Divisional Artillery will dump all Ammunition in limbers, Battery wagons and D.A.C., under guard at their camp at DE NANCOURT, D.18.a.(approx) where 41st. Divisional Artillery Batteries and D.A.C. will take it over.

V.   The 11th. and 12th, 17th. and 18th. Australian Batteries are now in Camp at S.25.b.8.3., at which place B/183, C/183, B/190 and C/190 will respectively take over guns.

.1.

B/183, C/183, B/190, and C/190 will not take over Ammunition at S.25.b.8.3., but will fill up limbers and wagons at DERNANCOURT from Ammunition dumped for 41st.D.A.C. by 2nd.Australian D.A.C.

VI.   All communications (less instruments) orders registrations air photos maps trench stores, etc., will be handed over to relieving units.

VII.   Brigade Commanders -B.Cs - 1 subaltern per Battery - and a proportion of specialists per Battery (with instruments), also "Dump" Officer of 2nd.Australian Divisional Artillery will be at LONGUEVAL X roads, S.17 central, at 10.30 a.m., October 30th.

Guides from Brigades, Batteries, and Dump of 41st.Divisional Artillery will meet them and conduct them to Brigades, batteries, and dump.

These Officers and men will be accommodated by 41st. Divisional Artillery units.

VIII.   An Officer of 2nd.Australian D.A.C. ("A" Echelon) will be at 41st.Divisional Artillery Headquarters at 10.30 a.m., on October 30th. where an Officer of "A" Echelon, 41st.D.A.C., will meet him.

Staff Captain and Signal Officer, 2nd.Australian Divisional Artillery will also arrive at 41st.Divisional Artillery Headquarters on October 30th.

IX.   Guides from Batteries, 41st.Divisional Artillery will meet relieving sections of Batteries, 2nd.Australian Divisional Artillery at 11 a.m., on road at POMMIERS REDOUBT on October 30th. and October 31st.

Sections 2nd.Australian Divisional Artillery will proceed to Wagon lines 41st.Divisional Artillery, and thence on foot to gun positions.

Detachments will proceed to gun positions singly and at 300 yards interval. Relief will be completed each day, if possible, before dark.

Sections 41st.Divisional Artillery being withdrawn on relief to Wagon lines for the night.

X.   On October 31st. Sections 41st.Divisional Artillery relieved on October 30th. and November 1st, Sections 41st.Divisional Artillery relieved on October 31st, will march to area BONNAY - LA NEUVILLE under orders to be issued later.

From this area 41st.Divisional Artillery will march to TALMAS and VILLE'S BOCAGE en route for Second Army.

XI.   (a) 41st.D.A.C. ("A" Echelon) will be relieved by 2nd. Australian D.A.C. ("A" Echelon) on October 30th. At the same time the Officer and 30 men 41st.Divisional Artillery at Ammunition Dump will be relieved by an Officer and 30 men of 2nd. Australian Divisional Artillery.

41st.D.A.C. ("A" Echelon) proceeding on relief to camp vacated by 2nd.Australian D.A.C. ("A" Echelon) at DERNANCOURT, D.18.a. Details will be arranged direct between O.C., 41st.D.A.C. and representatives of 2nd.Australian D.A.C. - vide para.VII.

Billeting party 41st.D.A.C., "A" Echelon will proceed to DERNANCOURT, D.18.a. (approx) to take over camp of 2nd.Australian D.A.C., on morning October 30th.
(N.B. 41st.D.A.C. ("A" Echelon) will on arrival at DERNANCOURT, send an orderly daily at 9 a.m., 12 noon, and 6 p.m., to BELLEVUE FARM to receive any orders)

(b). "B" Echelon, 41st.D.A.C., will be relieved by "B" Echelon, 2nd.Australian D.A.C., on October 31st., and will proceed on relief to BONNAY via DERNANCOURT area, picking up Ammunition at DERNANCOURT on route of 2nd.Australian "B" Echelon (further orders will be issued).

XII. Commands of Batteries, Brigades, etc., and of D.A. will pass on completion of respective reliefs.

XIII. Further orders re march to BONNAY area will be issued.

XIV. Trench Mortars (Medium) will not be handed over.

XV. All wireless installations will be handed over to relieving units.

XVI. Each Battery, 41st.Divisional Artillery will send an Officer with 1 N.C.O., and 4 men on October 30th. to the relieving Battery 2nd.Australian Divisional Artillery to take over guns and Ammunition and take charge of same till removed by Batteries, 41st.Divisional Artillery. Written receipts for guns and Ammunition will be given and obtained.

XVII. Command of 41st.D.A.G. will pass to G.O.C.,30th.Divisional Artillery at 10 a.m., on November 1st., at which hour Headquarters 41st.Divisional Artillery will close at POMMIERS REDOUBT and open at a position in BONNAY area to be notified.

XVIII. All units will report completion of relief by wire to this Office.

XIX. Liaison Officers with Infantry will rejoin their Batteries at 11 a.m.,October 31st.

XX. ACKNOWLEDGE.

BRIGADE MAJOR,
41st.Divisional Artillery.

29th.Oct.1916.
HHP
XV Corps,
XVth.Corps,
30th.D.A. (20 copies)
2nd.Australian D.A.
1st.Australian D.A.
41st.Division
183rd.Brigade,
187th.Brigade,
189th.Brigade,
190th.Brigade,
15th.Brigade, R.A., (for information)
41st.D.A.C., "A" & "B" Echelons
T.M.C.,41st.Division
12th.D.A.C.
Left Artillery XIV Corps
41st.D.A.Dump
41st.D.A.Signal Officer

SECRET.   240/30. G.

Artillery, 30th Div.   1st Aust. Div.
Artillery, 41st Div.   2nd Aust. Div.
Artillery, 2nd Aust. Div.   5th Aust. Div.   } for information.
                            Artillery, 12th Div.
                            XIV Corps.
                            1st Anzac Corps.

---

1. Para. 2 of XV Corps 240/30.G of 27th Oct. is cancelled (issued only to Artillery, 2nd Aust. Div.; 5th Aust. Div.; Artillery, 12th Div; 2nd Aust. Div.)

2. (a) If the tactical situation admits, Artillery 2nd Australian Div. will relieve Artillery 41st Div. by sections on the nights 30th/31st Oct. and 31st Oct./1st Nov. On completion of relief G.O.C. R.A. 30th Div. will assume command of the 41st Div. Artillery Group, which will thence-forward be known as the 30th Div. Artillery Group.

   (b) Commands of batteries, groups, and D.A's will pass when the respective reliefs are completed.

   (c) All details of relief will be arranged direct between the G.O.C. R.A. 41st Div. and G.O.C R.A. 2nd Aust. Div.

3. Reconnaissance of positions, O.Ps etc. will be carried out as early as possible by Artillery, 2nd Australian Div.

4. (a) Artillery 41st Div. will hand over all communications, orders, registrations, air photos, and maps to Artillery, 2nd Australian Div.

   (b) All dumped ammunition will also be handed over: Amounts taken over will be reported to Corps Headquarters.

5. Divisional Artilleries will retain their own guns and howitzers, except in those forward positions from which, in the mutual opinion of the respective G.O.C , R.A., it is impracticable to withdraw the guns.

6. Detachments of Artillery 2nd Australian Div. marching from Area A (N.W. of DERNANCOURT) will march at 8.30 a.m. on Oct. 30th and 31st respectively.
   Intervals of at least 100 yards will be maintained between sections.
   Route - DERNANCOURT - MEAULTE - FRICOURT. (Horse Track North of road will be used if weather permits).

7. Artillery 41st Div. will on relief be withdrawn to Area BONNAY - LA NEUVILLE under orders which will be issued by 1st Anzac Corps.

H.Q. XV Corps,
29/10/16.

W. H. Anderson
Brigadier-General,
General Staff.

Copy to:- "Q" XV Corps.
B.G.R.A. XV Corps.

SECRET.

Fourth Army. No. QC/806.

I ANZAC Corps.
41st Divisional Artillery.
First Army.)
Second ")
Third   ") (for information).
Fifth   ")
==================================

In continuation of Fourth Army 311/122 G. of 30th.

1.   The 41st Divisional Artillery will be transferred by march route, to rejoin its division in Second Army, and leaves Fourth Army Area on November 3rd.

2.   Supply Railhead will be in Fifth Army Area from November 3rd.

3.   The 41st Divisional Artillery will be accompanied by the supply lorries of No. 17 Divisional Supply Column, and by No. 17 Ammunition Sub Park.

4.   Nature and number of rounds of gun and howitzer ammunition taken by 41st Divisional Artillery will be reported to A.H.Q. by I ANZAC Corps.

R.S. May.

Hd.Qrs.Fourth Army.
30th October, 1916.

Lieut.-Colonel,
A.Q.M.G., Fourth Army.

COPIES to:- D.D.S. & T.
             D.D.O.S.
             D.M.S.
             G.S.

SECRET

S431
2874

Fourth Army No.QC/808.

1 ANZAC Corps.
41st Divl.Arty.
First Army.   )
Second "   ) For information.
Third   "   )
Fifth   "   )

In continuation of my QC/806 of 30th.

All dates therein mentioned are postponed for 24 hours.

R.S.May.

H.Qrs.Fourth Army,
31st Octr.1916.

Lieut.Colonel,
A.Q.M.G.Fourth Army.

Copies to:- D.D.S.&.T.
            D.D.O.S.
            D.M.S.
            G.S.

SECRET.

Copy No. 1

ADMINISTRATIVE ORDER ISSUED UNDER

1st ANZAC ORDER No. 60.

31/10/1916.

1. The 17th Divisional Supply Column Lorries and No. 17 Ammunition Sub Park will accompany 41st Divisional Artillery.

2. No Grenades and no Ammunition normally carried in boxes will be taken out of the 1st ANZAC Area.

3. The last Railhead for the 41st Divisional Artillery in the FOURTH Army Area will be MERICOURT on the 3rd instant when supplies for the 5th instant will be drawn by lorry.

4. Supplies for the 6th instant will be drawn from BELLE EGLISE, FIFTH Army Area on the 4th instant and for the 7th on the 5th instant from same Railhead.

5. Orders for the 6th will be issued by the THIRD Army and for the 7th and 8th by the FIRST Army.

6. Nature and number of rounds of Ammunition taken by the 41st Divisional Artillery will be recorded by wire to 1st ANZAC Corps.

7. Acknowledge by wire.

Brigadier-General.
D. A. & Q. M. G.
1st A. & N. Z. A. C.

Copy No.	To.
1-2	41st Div Art
3	FOURTH Army
4	41st Division
5	X Corps
6	B.G.H.A.
7	G.O.C., R.A.
8	Corps Park
9	A.P.M.
10	A.D.A.S.
11	G.O.C.
12	G.
13	41st Div Train
14	17th Div Supply Col
15	No 17 Ammn Sub Park
16	File
17-21	Retained.

SECRET   Ref.Map ALBERT (combined)
                                    and AMIENS 17.

Appendix II.

41st.D.A.G.OPERATION ORDER No.38

I.   41st. D.A. will march on October 31st/& 1st.Nov. to BONNAY - LA NEUVILLE area in accordance with attached March Table.

II.   Billeting parties of 1 Officer and 1 N.C.O., per Brigade and two N.C.Os per Battery, mounted will be at POMMIERS REDOUBT (41st.D.A.Hqrs) at 6.30 a.m., October 31st. to meet Staff Captain and to proceed to arrange billets.
Rations must be taken.

III.   Guides from Billeting party will meet units at N.E.End of HEILLY(J.2.a.2.2.) at 12.30 pm each day (Oct.31st & Nov.1st)

IV.   Rate of March including "short" halts 2½ miles per hour.
Ten minutes "short" halt at ten minutes before each hour.
"Long" halts of one hour to water and feed at 12 noon.

V.   Guns and Ammunition will be picked up as Sections &c., pass nearest point on road to D.18.a. Each Brigade will send forward an Officer a mile in advance to D.18.a., to make necessary arrangements.

VI.   "A" Echelon, 41st.D.A.C., will send billeting party of two N.C.Os per section under an Officer to meet Staff Captain at Railway Bridge near DERNANCOURT, E.20.b.2.6. at 7 a.m., on Oct.31st.
"A" Echelon,D.A.C., will march from D.18.a., to BONNAY area via BUIRE LIBEMONT and HEILLY starting at 6 a.m., on Nov.1st. Guide from Billeting party to be at J.2.a.2.2. at 7 a.m.,to meet "A" Echelon and guide it to Billets.

VII.   All units will on arrival in billets send an orderly to Headquarters 41st.D.A., in BONNAY area - position to be notified later.

VIII.   All T.M. Personnel with equipment, guns, etc., will be at old dump at F.5.d.1.5. at 11 a.m., on October 31st., whence lorries will convey them to billets.

IX.   Special orders will be issued to H.Q.,Section 41st. Divl.Train.

X.   ACKNOWLEDGE.

30.10.16

Brigade Major,
41st.Divisional Artillery.

Dst.Anzac Corps   183rd.Bde., F.A.
1st.Australian Divn   187th. "   "
2nd.Australian D.A.   189th. "   "
12th D.A.   190th. "   "
Left Artillery XIV Corps   41st.D.A.C. "A" Echelon
30th.D.A.   41st.D.A.C. "B" Echelon
                           T.M.C.,41st.Division
                           FILE.

MARCH TABLE

UNIT	Starting Point	Hour of passing Starting point.	ROUTE

October 31st. All Sections relieved on Oct.30th/31st., and ½ "B" Echelon,D.A.C.

UNIT	Starting Point	Hour	ROUTE
187th.Bde.R.F.A.	Junction of MONTAUBAN - CARNOY & MONTAUBAN-FRICOURT rds. S.27.c.7.2.	5.0 a.m.	MONTAUBAN - CARNOY - CROSS ROADS F.18.c.5.2.- F.4.c.5.3.- MIAULTE - DERNANCOURT - CROSS ROADS F.18.c.9.1. E.13.b.9½.- CROSS ROADS D.12.d.8.8. - CROSS ROADS D.17.b.4.8. - BUIRE - LIBEMONT - HEILLY - to Billets.
189th.Bde.R.F.A.	do.	6.0 a.m.	Do.
190th.Bde.R.F.A.	do.	7.0 a.m.	Do.
183rd.Bde.R.F.A.	do.	8.0 a.m.	Do.
½ "B" Echelon,D.A.C.	do.	9.0 a.m.	Do.

On Nov.1st.all Sections relieved on night Oct.31st/Nov.1st. and remaining ½ "B" Echelon,D.A.C. as above.

appendix 4

291x

SECRET

Ref.Map AMIENS 17 1/10,000
and LENS 11 1/10,000

41st.DIVL: ARTILLERY MARCH ORDER
No.2.

1. The 41st.D.A. will march on Nov.4th. to AMPLIER ORVILLE area in accordance with attached March Table.

2. Billeting parties of 1 Officer and 1 N.C.O., per Brigade, and 2 N.C.Os per Battery; 2 N.C.Os per section under an Officer of "A" Echelon, D.A.C., 1 Officer and 1 N.C.O., "B" Echelon, D.A.C., will be at Junction of roads 200 yds. E.S.E. of R of AMPLIER at 8 a.m., on Nov.4th. to meet Staff Captain and proceed to arrange Billets. Rations must be taken

3. Guides of Billeting parties will meet their unit on the road and guide them to their Billets.

4. All units will report their arrival in Billets in the AMPLIER ORVILLE area and send an orderly to H.Q., 41st.D.A., position will be notified to their units by Billeting party.

BRIGADE MAJOR,
41st.Div; Artillery.

2.11.16
HHP

No.1 183rd.Brigade,R.F.A.
No.2 187th.Brigade,R.F.A.
No.3 189th.Brigade,R.F.A.
No.4 190th.Brigade,R.F.A.
No.5 "A" Echelon, D.A.C.
No.6 "B" Echelon, D.A.C.
No.7 41st.Divl:Train
No.8 FILE

MARCH TABLE

UNIT	Starting Point	Hour of Passing Starting Point	ROUTE
92nd.R.F.A.	Cross Roads 200 yds. N.E. of S. of TALMAS	8.0 a.m.	BEAUVAL HUPPY AUTHEUX AMPLIER
"A" Echelon L.A.C.	Cross Roads 200 yds. N.E. of S. of TALMAS	8.25 a.m.	Do.
127th.Bde.	Cross Roads 200 yds. N.E. of S. of TALMAS	8.50 a.m.	BEAUVAL FIFIT AMPLIER ORVILLE
"B" Echelon L.A.C.	Do.	9.15 a.m.	Do.
9th.Bde.	Do.	9.40 a.m.	BEAUVAL FULTON ORVILLE
103rd.Bde.	Do.	10.0 a.m.	Do.

2424

SECRET.

S.G.20/10/100.

IV Corps.
"Q"
D.D.Signals.
P..
Fourth Army
Third Army
41st Divnl.Artillery) for information.
56th Divnl.Artillery)

___

1.   The 41st Divisional Artillery, on transfer from Fourth Army, will march to "K" area on 3rd November by the AMIENS - DOULLENS road and be administered by the IV Corps, who will allot billets. No restriction is imposed as regards time of movement, but time decided on should be reported to Fifth Army and IV Corps.

2.   Movement will be continued on 4th November to the BOUBERS-sur-CANCHE area under orders of Third Army.

3.   The above orders are identical for the move of the 56th Divisional Artillery 24 hours later.

4.   Acknowledge.

C. H. Macmullen
Major-General,
General Staff.

Headquarters,
Fifth Army,
30th October, 1918.

SECRET

app 5

5119 294

March Table issued with March Order No.2 dated 2/11/16 is cancelled and the attached March Table substituted.

[signature]
Brigade Major,
41st. Divisional Artillery.

3.11.16
HBP

No.1 183rd.Brigade,
No.2 187th.Brigade,
No.3 189th.Brigade,
No.4 190th.Brigade,
No.5 "A" Echelon, D.A.C.
No.6 "B" Echelon, D.A.C.,
No.7 Headquarters,41st.Divl:Train.
No.8 FILE

MARCH TABLE

UNIT	Starting Point.	Hour of passing Starting Point.	ROUTE
"Q"Echelon.			
190th.Brigade	Cross Roads 300 yds N.E. of W of MOLLIENS AU BOIS	7.30 a.m.	PTE. FGOT, PUCHEVILLES, MA IEUX, SAIGON, ORVILLE.
"A" Echelon,D.A.C.	Cross Roads 200 yds N.E. of S. of TALMAS	8.25 a.m.	BEAUVAL, DOULLENS, AMLIN.
187th.Brigade	ditto.	8.50 a.m.	ditto.
"B" Echelon,D.A.C.	ditto.	9.15 a.m.	ditto.
189th.Brigade	ditto.	9.40 a.m.	ditto.
188rd.Brigade	ditto.	10.5 a.m.	ditto.

SECRET   Ref. Map LENS 11 1/100,000

                        41st. DIVL: ARTILLERY
                        MARCH ORDER No.3
                        ━━━━━━━━━━━━━━━━━━━

1.   41 t.D.A., will march on November 5th. to the BOUBERS
area in accordance with the attached March Table.

2.   Billeting parties of 1 Officer and 1 N.C.O., per
Brigade, 2 N.C.Os per Battery, and 2 N.C.Os per Section under
an Officer of "A" Echelon, D.A.C.; 1 Officer and 1 N.C.O., "B"
Echelon, D.A.C., 1 Officer and N.C.O., H.Q., Company, Divl:
Train will be at Junction of roads 300 yds S.E. of the S in
LIGNY SUR CANCHE at 8 a.m., on November 5th. to meet Staff
Captain, and to proceed to arrange Billets.

3.   Guides of Billeting parties will meet their Units on
the road, and guide them to their Billets.

4.   All units will report their arrival in Billets in
the BOUBERS area and sen an orderly to H.Q., 41st.Div. R.A.,
THE CHATEAU BOUBERS SUR CANCHE.

                                      [signature]
                                      Brigade Major,
3.11.18   41st. Divl: Artillery.

No.1 163rd. Brigade, R.F.A.
No.2 187th.   "   "
No.3 189th.   "   "
No.4 190th.   "   "
No.5 "A" Echelon, D.A.C.,
No.6 "B"   "   "
No.7 H.Q., Divl: Train,
No.8 File
No.9 Staff Captain.

MARCH TABLE.

UNIT	Starting Point	Hour of Passing Starting Point.	ROUTE.
183rd.Bde.R.F.A.	Junction of roads 200 yds. S. of AUTHIEULE	7.30 a.m.	DOULLENS - PROVENT - BOUZINS SUR CANCHE.
187th.	"	7.55 a.m.	"
188th.	"	8.20 "	"
190th.	"	8.45 "	"
"A" Echelon,D.A.C.	"	9.10 "	"
"B" " "	"	9.35 "	"

SECRET.

Copy No. 1

THIRD ARMY ORDER No. 85.

31st October, 1916.

Ref. Map LENS 1/100,000

1. The 41st Divisional Artillery will be transferred from the Fourth Army to the Second Army (X Corps) by march route, and will come under the orders of the Third Army from midnight 4th/5th November.

2. The 41st Divisional Artillery will move in accordance with attached March Table.

3. Accommodation Table for billets in the BOUBERS Area on the night of the 5th/6th November is attached.

4. On the 6th November Supply Railhead will be at FREVENT.

5. Acknowledge.

J.F.C. Fuller Maj.
General Staff, Third Army.

Issued at :- 8 pm

Copies to :-

No. 1. 41st Divl. Artillery,
2. Fifth Army,
3. First Army,
4. Second Army,
5-7. Q.
8-9. G.
10. A.
11. P.M.
12. D.D. of Signals,
13. War Diary.
14. Fourth Army.

41st Divisional Artillery March Table.   Issued with Third Army Order No. 85 dated 31st October 16.

Unit.	Date.	From	To.	Route.	Remarks.
41st Divisional Artillery.	5th Nov.	K. area Fifth Army.	BOUBERS area.	DOULLENS - FREVENT - BOUBERS SUR CANCHE.	Head of column to pass Haute Visee by 10 a.m.
—do—	6th Nov.	BOUBERS area.	FONTAINE LEZ BOULANS - HEUCHIN - BERGENEUSE - ANVIN - MONCHY CAYEUX area under orders of the First Army.	Any roads to the WEST and inclusive of the PREVENT - ST POL - HERNICOURT road.	Head of any column using the LIGNY sur Canche - NUNCQ - ST POL road to pass NUNCQ by 9.30 a.m.

Issued with Third Army No. 85 of 31st Oct. 1916

3448
3007

BOUBERS AREA.

AREA.

AUBROMETZ - MONCHEL - BOUBERS sur CANCHE - LIGNY sur CANCHE - VACQUERIE le BOUCQ - CONCHY sur CANCHE.

Divisional Artillery H.Q. - BOUBERS-sur-CANCHE.

ACCOMMODATION.

Name of Village.	Officers.	O.R.	Animals.	Remarks.
AUBROMETZ.	15	500	250	
BOUBERS-sur-CANCHE.	30	450	350	Chateau.
CONCHY-sur-CANCHE.	34	1000	600	
MONCHEL-sur-CANCHE.	7	300	100	
LIGNY-sur-CANCHE.	18	480	300	
VACQUERIE-le-BOUCQ.	12	1100	500	Small Chateau.
Total.	116	3830	2100	

Villages additional to those in above Area.

Villages deducted from those in above Area.

Boubers Area

SECRET   Ref.Map LENS 11 1/100,000

41st. DIVL:ARTILLERY MARCH ORDER NO.4.

BERGUENEUSE

1. The 41st.D.A., will march on November 6th. to FONTAINE LES BOULANS - HEUCHIN - BERGUENEUSE - ANVIN - MONCHY CAYEUX in accordance with attached March table.

2. Billeting parties of 1 Officer and 1 N.C.O., per Brigade, 2 N.C.Os per Battery, and 2 N.C.Os per Section under an Officer of "A" Echelon, D.A.C., 1 Officer and 1 N.C.O., "B" Echelon, and 1 Officer and 1 N.C.O., H.Q., Company Divl:Train will be at junction of roads 100 yds. S.E. of E name of HALTE near MONCHY CAYEUX at 8 a.m., on November 6th. to meet Staff Captain and to proceed to arrange Billets.

3. Guides of Billeting parties will meet their units on the road and guide them to their Billets.

4. All units will report their arrival in the FONTAINE LES BOULANS HEUCHIN BERGUENEUSE ANVIN MONCHY CAYEUX area and send an orderly to H.Q.,41st.Divisional Artillery at MONCHY CAYEUX.

                                               Brigade Major,
                                               41st.Divl:Artillery.

5.11.16
AHP
No.1 183rd Bde., R.F.A.,
No.2 187th.   "   " "
No.3 189th.   "   " "
No.4 190th.   "
No.5 "A" Echelon D.A.C.,
No.6 "B"   "   " "
No.7 H.Q., Train,
No.8 Staff Captain,
No.9 FILE

MARCH TABLE

UNIT.	Starting point	Hour of passing starting point.	ROUTE
190th Bde.	Cross roads 1 mile S.W. of 1st N of NURCQ	7.15 a.m.	NURCQ - ST POL - WAYRANS
189th "	Junction of roads 600 yds S of last R in HAUTE - COTE	7.40 a.m.	NURCQ - ST POL - WAYRANS
"A" Echelon D.A.C.	Cross roads 1 mile S.W. of 1st N of NURCQ	8.5 a.m.	do
"B" "	-- do --	8.30 a.m.	do
163rd Bde.	Junction of xx roads 600 yds N.W. of AUBERMETZ	7.55 a.m.	PILLIMYES - LIETEUX - BEAUVOIS PIEREMONT - WAYRANS.
187th "	-- do --	8.20 a.m.	do

The head of 163rd Brigade R.F.A. will fall in in rear of "B" echelon D.A.C., @ WAYRANS.

SECRET

Ref. map HAZEBROUK 5a
1/100,000.

app 6

41st. DIVL: ARTILLERY MARCH ORDER
No.5

1. The 41st.D.A., will march on Nov.9th. to the HAM EN ARTOIS BERGUETTE MOLINGHEM LAMBRES MAZINGHEM area, in accordance with attached March Table.

2. Billeting parties of 1 Officer and 1 N.C.O., per Brigade, 2 N.C.Os per Battery: 2 N.C.Os per Section under an Officer of "A" Echelon, D.A.C: 1 Officer and 1 N.C.O "B" Echelon, D.A.C., 1 Officer and 1 N.C.O., Headquarters Company Divl: Train, will be at the Cross Roads 400 yds. S. of 2nd. T in COFFRE (St HILAIRE) at 8 a.m., on Nov.7th to meet the Staff Captain and proceed to arrange Billets.

3. Guides of Billeting parties will meet their Units on the road and guide them to their Billets and report position of Hd.Qrs. 41st.D.A.,

4. All units will report their arrival in the HAM-EN-ARTOIS BERGUETTE MOLINGHEM LAMBRES MAZINGHEM area, and send an orderly to Hqrs.41st.D.A.

5. ACKNOWLEDGE.

BRIGADE MAJOR,
41st.Divisional Artillery.

5.11.16

No.1 163rd.Bde.
No.2 187th.Bde.
No.3 189th.Bde.
No.4 190th.Bde.
No.5 "A" Echelon,D.A.C.
No.6 "B" Echelon,D.A.C.
No.7 Hqrs.Train
No.8 Staff Captain
No.9 FILE

MARCH TABLE

UNIT	Starting Point	Hour of Passing Starting Point	ROUTE
187th.Brigade,R.F.A.,	Cross roads 500 yds. S. of F of PALFART.	7.15 a.m.	WESTREHEM ST HILAIRE.
183rd.	"	7.30 "	"
189th.	"	8.0 "	"
190th.	"	8.25 "	"
"B" Echelon, D.A.C.	"	8.50 "	"
"A"	"	9.20 "	"

SECRET Ref; Map HAZEBROUCK 5a.
1/100,000.

41st. DIVISIONAL ARTILLERY MARCH ORDER No.6.

1. The 41st.D.A., will march on Nov.10th. to HAZEBROUCK WALLON CAPPEL STAPLE HONDECHEM, in accordance with attached March Table

2. Guides of Billeting parties will meet their units on the road and guide them to their Billets and report position of Headquarters, 41st.D.A.

3. All units will report their arrival in their Billets and send an orderly to Headquarters, 41st.D.A.

4. ACKNOWLEDGE.

9.11.16
HHP

Brigade Major,
41st. Divisional Artillery

183rd. Brigade
187th.   "
189th.   "
190th.   "
"A" Echelon, D.A.C.
"B"   "   "
Headquarters, Divl: Train
Staff Captain,
FILE

MARCH TABLE

UNIT	Starting Point	Hour of Passing Starting Point	ROUTE	REMARKS
53rd.Bde.R.F.A.	JUNCTION of Roads 20 yds N.of point where Rly.crosses the LAMBRES-AIRE Road	8.10 a.m.	AIRE - HAZEBROUCK.	
187th. " "	Point where Road crosses Rly. ½ mile S. of I of AIRE.	8.40 "	"	
190th. " "	JUNCTION of roads N.of Canal & 1½ M.of H. in GUARBECQUE.	9.20 " 9.25	ST VENANT HAZEBROUCK etc.	190 will fall in behind 187th.Brigade at the Junction of ST.VENANT HAZEBROUCK Road and the AIRE HAZEBROUCK Rd.
18?th. " "	"	9.45 " 9.25 " 9.50 " 9.55 "	"	
"A" Echelon,D.A.C.	Same as "B"Echelon		"	
"B" " "	JUNCTION of roads 20 yds. N. of point where Rly. crosses the LAMBRE-AIRE Road.	10.20 "	AIRE - HAZBROUCK, etc.,etc.	

Officer Commanding,
   183,187,189,190th.Bdes.,D.A.C.,& HQ.Divl:Train

   Billeting arrangements for tomorrow are as under:-

   183rd.Brigade)
   187th.   "   ) will billet at HONDEGHEM

   190th.   "   &   )
   Divl:Hqrs. and   )
   H.Q.Sect.Divl:Train)   "   "   STAPLE

   189th.Bde. and whole)
   of D.A.C.   )   "   "   WALLON CAPPEL

   Billeting Officers will meet Staff Captain in their own
areas at following times:-

   183rd.& 187th.Bdes.   at 9.0 a.m.
   189th.Bde.& D.A.C.   at 8.15 A.M.
   190th.Brigade   at 8.30 a.m.

   Boundaries between Brigades will then be arranged.

                                    Staff Captain,
                              41st.Divisional Artillery
9.11.16

SECRET

App 10

41st. DIVISIONAL ARTILLERY OPERATION ORDER No.1.

RELIEF of 4th. AUSTRALIAN D.A.

11th. Novr. 1916.

RELIEF	1. The relief of the 4th. Australian D.A., will take place by Sections on nights of 12th/13th. and 13th/14th November.
Relief Schedules	2. Schedules showing reliefs by Batteries and Brigades and Groups have already been issued.
Guns.	3. Guns will not be exchanged.
Defence Schemes	4. All Defence Schemes, Trench Maps, 1/10,000 and 1/20,000, registrations, telephone lines, trench stores (Gum boots thigh included) will be taken over by relieving unit, and certificates that this has been done sent to their Group Headquarters.
Command.	5. Command of Batteries will dissolve on 41st. D.A. Bty Comdrs on conclusion of Battery relief. Command of Groups will dissolve on Group Commanders 41st. D.A., on completion of the last Battery relief in the Group. C.R.A., 41st. D.A. will be responsible for the Artillery Defence of the line from 10 a.m., November 14th
Movements.	6. Relieving Sections of 41st. D.A., will arrive at 41st. D.A. Wagon lines at 2 p.m., on November 12th and 13th. Guides from 4th. Australian D.A., will be at the CHURCH, RENINGHELST, at 1 p.m., on November 12th., Batteries will arrange guides for November 13th. No movement of vehicles will take place East of LA CLYTTE - YPRES Road, before 4.30 p.m., on either Relief nights. All Section Reliefs must be completed by 9 p.m.
Ammn. Return.	7. All ammunition at Gun positions will be taken over at noon Novr. 13th., and returns forwarded of the amount taken over. After 12 noon, Novr. 13th. ammunition expenditure will be on account of 41st. D.A.
Relief of DAA.C.	8. 41st. D.A.C., will relieve the 4th. Australian D.A.C., on November 13th. Details to be arranged between D.A.C Commanders, and the relief completed by 4 p.m.
Billets 4th. Australian D.A.	9. The 4th. Australian D.A., will withdraw to the Billets occupied by the 41st. D.A. on relief.
Guides.	10. Guides from each Battery, and Brigade Headquarters will be at the TOWN MAJOR'S OFFICE in the Square at BOESCHEPE at 8.45 a.m., on 12th. November, whence representatives of 4th. Australian D.A., from each Battery and Brigade Headquarters will be met and shown

the Billets and Wagon lines to be taken over.

The 4th.Australian D.A.C. will have a guide from each Section and Headquarters at 41st.D.A.Headquarters at 9 a.m., on November 12th to show representatives of each section and Headquarters, 41st.D.A.C., the positions of their Sections.

An Officer from each Section, 41st.D.A.C., will remain with each Section 4th.Australian D.A.C. from 12 noon November 12th.

Registration byrelieving Sections of 41st. D.A., will be carried out as early as possible on November 12th. and 13th.

12. ACKNOWLEDGE.

A W Dabell L for
BRIGADE MAJOR,
41st.Divisional Artillery.

HNP

183rd.Brigade (10 copies)
187th.   "   (10   "   )
189th.   "   (10   "   )
190th.   "   (10   "   )
41st.D.A.C.   (6   "   )
4th.Australian Division
41st.Division
16th.D.A.,
47th.D.A.,
Xth.Corps.

SECRET.   COPY NO.....8...

AMENDMENT TO
41st DIVISION ORDER NO. 60.

10-11-16.

1.-   The nights 10th/11th and 11th/12th in Para. 1 should read nights 12th/13th and 13th/14th instants.

2.-   Acknowledge.

                                    A C B Kirkpatrick
                                         Capt.
                                for Lt.-Colonel, G.S.

Issued to Signals at 12 noon .

            Copy No   1 - File.
              "   "   2 - War Diary.
              "   "   3)- 10th Corps.
              "   "   4)
              "   "   5 - 10th Corps H.A.
              "   "   6 - 16th Division.
              "   "   7 - 47th Division.
              "   "   8 - 41st Divnl Artillery.
              "   "   9 - 4th Australian Divnl Artillery.
              "   " 10 - 122nd Infantry Bde.
              "   " 11 - 123rd Infantry Bde.
              "   " 12 - 124th Infantry Bde.
              "   " 13 - C. R. E.
              "   " 14 - 19th Bn Middx Regt.
              "   " 15 - 41st Divnl Signal Coy.
              "   " 16 - A.D.M.S.
              "   " 17)- "Q".
              "   " 18)
              "   " 19 - Area Commandant.
              "   Nos 20, 21, 22 Spare.

SECRET. COPY NO......8....

5-10-16.

41st DIVISION ORDER NO. 60.

1.- The 41st Divisional Artillery will relieve the 4th Australian Divisional Artillery on the nights 10th/11th and 11th/12th instants.

2.- Officers and telephonists from batteries of the 41st Divisional Artillery will be attached to those of the 4th Australian Divisional Artillery which they will relieve, on arrival in the 10th Corps Area.

3.- Guns will not be exchanged.

4.- The 41st Divisional Artillery will go into the line as four gun batteries.

5.- All details of the relief will be arranged by the C.R.A's concerned in conjunction with the General Staff, 41st Division.

6.- C.R.A., 41st Division will assume command the morning after completion of relief.

7.- Completion of relief will be wired to Divisional Headquarters.

8.- Acknowledge.

H.C.B. Kirkpatrick
Capt.
for Lt.-Colonel, G.S.

Issued to Signals at ....

Copy No 1 - File.
"   "   2 - War Diary.
"   "   3)- 10th Corps.
"   "   4)
"   "   5 - 10th Corps H.A.
"   "   6 - 16th Division.
"   "   7 - 47th Division.
"   "   8 - 41st Divnl Artillery.
"   "   9 - 4th Australian Divnl Artillery.
"   " 10 - 122nd Infantry Bde.
"   " 11 - 123rd Infantry Bde.
"   " 12 - 124th Infantry Bde.
"   " 13 - C. R. E.
"   " 14 - 19th Bn Middx Regt.
"   " 15 - 41st Div Signal Coy.
"   " 16 - A.D.M.S.
"   " 17)- "Q".
"   " 18)
"   " 19 - Area Commandant.
"   nos 20. 21, 22 Spare.

ENEMY'S ARTILLERY FIRE:-

Time	Locality Shelled	Nos.	Nature	Sound or Flash bearing
10.30 a.m.	YPRES - ST.ELOI ROAD at O.32.a.9.4.	8	7.7 cm	Unknown
10.35 "	H.36.central	8	15.0 "	True bearing from H.35.a.8.2. 105°.
11.5 "	DICKEBUSCHE	15	" "	Not known. Single gun fired at intervals of 3 mins.
11.30 "	H.36 central	4	" "	-
10.30 a.m.) to 12 noon)	DICKEBUSCHE	30	H.V.Gun 10.5 c.m.	Unknown
12.5 p.m.) 12.20 ")	F.IM and SUPPORTS near MOATED GRANGE	2 1	10.5 cm.	-
2.15 p.m.	FRONT LINE TRENCHES O.23	6	7.7 "	-
2 pm.-2115pm	I.33.a.2.5.	6	" "	-
"	I.34.c.3.3.	10	" "	-
"	O.4.b.2.8.		T.M's active	
3.0 p.m.	ROAD at XXX3R H.30.a.3.8.	4	10.5 cm.	Unknown
"	H.35.c.7.9.	3	7.7. "	-

GENERAL SUMMARY

1. **ENEMY'S NEW WORK:-**

    None observed

2. **ENEMY'S MOVEMENTS:-**

    Nil.

3. **OBSERVATION:-**

    Light only good between 12.30 p.m. and 3 p.m.

4. **HOSTILE AIRCRAFT ACTIVITY:)**

    At about 3 p.m. a hostile plane was engaged by one of ours. The enemy plane was forced down, and was observed to land behind its lines in flames. Otherwise, quiet.

5. **CASUALTIES:-**

    PERSONNEL:-
    Capt I.M Brown, R.A.M.C. (killed)
    1 O.R. wounded (Doctor's orderly)

6. **GUNS OUT OF ACTION**
    4.5" Hows. 1
    18 pdrs. 9

BRIGADE MAJOR,
41st. DIVISIONAL ARTILLERY.

16.11.16
HHP

app 11

41st. DIVISIONAL ARTILLERY

DAILY OPERATION REPORT
from 6 p.m. 14.11.16 to 6 p.m., 15.11.16

OUR FIRE:-

Time	Battery	Target	Rounds	Remarks
ST. ELOI GROUP:-				
12.30 p.m.	A/189	HOUSE, O.9.b.9½.6.	28	Registration Zero Lines
3.0 "	B/189	S.O.S. Lines	10	Registration
1 p.m. to 1.15pm	C/189	"	8	Satisfactory
3.30 p.m.	D/189	DOLL HOUSE	2	Calibration.
2 p.m.-4.0 p.m.	"	WHITE CHATEAU and O.4.d.1.4.	28	Registration
12.40 p.m.	A/183	Enemy Front Line Trench.	25	"
3 p.m.- 4 p.m.	B/183	O.8.d.9.7.	24	"
12 noon to 4 p.m.	C/183	WHITE CHATEAU and S.O.S. Lines.	34	"
-	D/183	-	-	-
DIEPENDAAL GROUP -				
11.45 a.m.-12.45 pm.	A/190	THE HOUSE and Night lines	71	-
2 pm.-3 pm.	B/190	Checked Registrations	40	-
11.30 a.m. to 1.0 p.m.	C/190	O.8.d.5½.0. N.10.b.8.2. RD RUIN O.13.c.3.9. SUNKEN RD.N.13.b.7.3.	56	-
12 noon to 1 p.m.	D/190	Checked registration of Night lines.	30	-
-	B/187	Nil	-	-
11.30 a.m. to 12 noon	C/187	O.8.d.7.0.	20	-

.1.

SECRET

app 12

41st DIVISIONAL ARTILLERY

DAILY OPERATION REPORT.
from 6 p.m. 15-11-16
to 6 p.m. 16-11-16.

OUR FIRE

TIME	BTYR	TARGET	RDS.	REMARKS
ST ELOI GROUP				
	A/189			
	B/189	Nil	-	-
	C/189			
2pm to 3 p.m.	D/189	DOME HOUSE	26	Registration & Calibration
11.30 am	A/183	RUINED FARM O.3.c.8½.4½	6	Registration
3.45pm		WIGWAM HOUSE	6	"
4 p.m.	B/183	N.d.4.4.	24	" & Calibration
2.15 p.m.	C/183	S.S. Lines	8	"
2.45 p.m.	D/183	HIELE FARM O.8.a.9.9½	35	"
DIEPENDAAL GROUP				
12 noon	D/19	MARTENS FM. O.8.d.6. N. BRICK BAR N.13.d.2½.8	4	"
12.30 p.m.	B/19	F.N. TR. at N.12.d.3.1	6	"
3.3 p.m. to 4 p.m	B/187	TRENCH at O.7.c.5½.4	27	"
3.15 to 4 pm	C/19	TRENCHES & wire about N.12.d.2. to N.12.d.4.1	16	"

ENEMY'S ARTILLERY FIRE

TIME	LOCALITY SHELLED	RDS	NATURE	SOUND or FLASH bearing
3.45pm to 4pm	FRONT LINE between O.7.b.2.8. & Junction of P. Trench.	6	7.7cm	True sound bearing from H.36.d.8.2. 127°
2.45 pm to 4pm	I.33.d.5.8	25	15cm	"
	I.33.d.5.5	3	"	
	I.33.c.8.2.	3	"	

GENERAL SUMMARY

1. ENEMY'S WORK NEW.   Nothing new observed.

2. ENEMY'S MOVEMENT   At 4pm movement observed at N.8.d.4.4.

3. OBSERVATION   Good.

4. HOSTILE AIRCRAFT ACTIVITY

Above normal. Hostile plane over at 11.30
2.30 pm & 3pm. At about 12.50pm two hostile planes came over our lines

and forced one of our planes to land. They were afterwards driven off by A.A. Gun fire.

5. CASUALTIES   Personnel

                NIL.

6. GUNS OUT OF ACTION.

            18-prs   9
            4.5" Hows. 1

                        Brigade Major

17-11-16.   1st Divisional Artillery

SECRET

app 13

41st. DIVISIONAL ARTILLERY

DAILY OPERATION REPORT
from 6 p.m., 16.11.16 to 6 p.m. 17.11.16

OUR FIRE:-

Time	Battery	Target	Rds.	Remarks
		DICKEBUSCH GROUP:-		
10.45 p.m.	B/190	6 men walking along the road in rear of MARTENS FARM, O.15.a.0.8	5	Men disappeared hurriedly.
11.15 p.m.	"	O.8.d.6.0.	14	-
11.30	"	O.7.c.4.?7 (Night lines)	8	-
12.15 a.m.) to 2 p.m.)	"	Wire at O.7.c.4.4.	64	-
12 noon	C/190	Fire at N.18.b.1½.9	10	
9.30 a.m.	D/190	RED CHATEAU, N.18.b.9.½.	20	Retaliation
12.30 p.m.) to 3 p.m.)	"	CROONAERT CAPEL, O.7.c.4.5. PLATEAU FARM, N.18.b.5.5.	40	Registration
2.55 a.m.	C/187	O.7.c.4.8.	4	S.O.S.test.
12.15 a.m.	"	O.1.d.5.S.	6	
		ST ELOI GROUP:-		
3.0 p.m. to 3.30 p.m.	A/189	Covering fire for Trench Mortars.	24	
"	B/189	"	18	
"	C/189	"	24	
"	A/183	"	30	
"	B/183	"	24	
"	C/183	"	29	
"	D/183	MARTENS FARM,O.8.) d.6.0.)	5	Registration and covering fire.
"	D/189	Nil	-	
"	BELGIAN GROUP	Covering fire for T.Ms.	158	

ENEMY'S ARTILLERY FIRE

Time	Locality shelled.	Rds.	Nature	Sound or Flash bearing.
9.20 a.m.	BRASSERIE at N.6.a.2.2.	8	15.0	From a quarter left.
10.30 a.m. to 11.30 a.m.	Fields 200x N. of DIKKEBUSCHE	10	10.5 HE burst in air.	

.1.

ENEMY'S ARTILLERY FIRE:-

Time	Locality Shelled	Rds.	Nature	Sound or Flash bearing
11.10 a.m.	C/183 Bty.Position	2	10.5 c.m.	-
	H.35.c.7.5.	4	Gas shell	-
5.0 p.m.	"	2	10.5" c.m.	-
		2	Gas Shell	-
10.55 a.m.	TRENCH O 11	2	Heavy T.M.	-
11.20 a.m. to 12 noon	TRENCHES O 11 to O 23.	6	7.7	-
8.45 a.m.	FRONT LINE by TRIANGULAR WOOD	20	T.M.	-
9.15 a.m.	I.32.a.8½.5.	24	7.7	-

GENERAL SUMMARY:-

1. ENEMY'S NEW WORK

    N I L.

2. ENEMY'S MOVEMENTS

    Six men were seen walking from left to right along road in rear of MARTENS FARM (O.15.a.0.8.) at 10.40 a.m.

3. OBSERVATION

    Light good all day.   Observation possible at 8.30 a.m.

4. HOSTILE AIRCRAFT ACTIVITY

    About 12 noon enemy aeroplane passed over DICKEBUSCHE.

5. CASUALTIES:-

    N I L.

6. GUNS OUT OF ACTION

    18 pdrs.   6   -   4.5" How.   1

                                    S. P............
                                    Brigade Major,
                            41st.Divisional Artillery.

18.11.16
HHP

ADDITION

T.M.BATTERIES

    Z/41 Battery was engaged cutting wire between O.2.c.9.6. and O.2.c.5.9½.   30 rounds in all were fired from Zero hour to 0.30, four of which rounds were "duds".   Good results were believed to have been obtained.   Retaliation by the enemy was very slight.   Casualties - Nil.

SECRET

41st. DIVISIONAL ARTILLERY

DAILY OPERATION REPORT
from 6 p.m., 17.11.16 to 6 p.m., 18.11.16

OUR FIRE:-

Time	Battery	Target	Rounds	Remarks
	DIEPENDAAL GROUP:-			
11.40 a.m.	B/190	O.7.c.4.3.	6	
11.50 "	"	O.7.c.3½.7.	3	
3.5 p.m.	"	Night Lines	12	Checking registration.
10.30 a.m.) to 10.45 a.m.)	C/190	Wire at N.18.) b.2.8½.to N.12) a.3½.1.)	15	
3.0 p.m. to 3.15 p.m.)	"	Active T.Ms.	16	
During the morning.)	D/190	SUNKEN ROAD at N.18.b. GRAND BOIS,O.13.a.40		Registration
10.30 p.m.) 1.0 a.m.)	C/187	Test S.O.S.	8	
	ST ELOI GROUP			
8.0 a.m.	A/189	Covering fire for T.Ms.	12	
" "	B/189	"	16	
" "	C/189	"	16	
" "	A/183	"	24	
" "	B/183	"	24	
" "	C/183	"	20	
11.23 "	D/183	Trenches & Supports in front of trenches O.24 & O.25.)	6	Retaliation
11.44 p.m.	BELGES	Test O.11	1	
1.23 a.m.	"	"	1	
8.0 a.m.	"	Covering fire	150	

GENERAL SUMMARY:-

1. **ENEMY'S NEW WORK** NIL
2. **ENEMY'S MOVEMENTS** Nothing observed.
3. **OBSERVATION:-**

Good during the morning, but poor the remainder of the day.

4. HOSTILE AIRCRAFT ACTIVITY:-

        N I L.

5. CASUALTIES:-

        N I L.

6. GUNS OUT OF ACTION:-

    18 pdrs. Q.F.   4
    4.5" Hows.   1

ENEMY'S ARTILLERY FIRE -

Time	Locality shelled	Rds.	Nature	Sound or Flash bearing
6.15 a.m.	O.1.d.8.2.	20	10.5 Sh.	-
8.30 a.m.	O.2.c.2.5.	2	H.T.Ms.	-
9.0 a.m.	VIERSTRAAT & Road	5	7.7	
10.0 "	I.33.b.2.2.	3	"	
11.30 a.m.) to 12.30 p.m.)	N.12.d.central	9	M.T.Ms.	
2.40 p.m.	I.31.c.3½.1.	1	7.7	
5.30 p.m.	H.35.b.7.0.	6	15.c.m.	

Brigade Major,
41st. Divisional Artillery.

19.11.16
HHP

SECRET

41st. DIVISIONAL ARTILLERY

DAILY OPERATION REPORT
from 6 p.m., 18.11.16 to 6 p.m. 19.11.16.

OUR FIRE

Time	Battery	Target	Rds.	Remarks

DIEPENDAAL GROUP:-

Time	Battery	Target	Rds.	Remarks
2.15 p.m.) to) 3.30 p.m.)	A/190	Zero House and points on front line between DIEPENDAAL BECK and BOIS QUARANTE.	80	Registration
12.30 p.m.	B/190	N.18.b.1½.6 to N.18.b.2.8.	38	
2.3 p.m.	"	C.T.N.18.b.3.6½. to N.18.b.7.5. to junction at 0.7.c.4.8½. N.18.b.22.80.	42	
1.0 p.m.		N.12.c.3.1.	6	Working party reported by Infantry.
3.30 p.m.) to) 4.0 p.m.)	C/190	Wire at N.18.b.2.8.	10	
3.40 p.m.	"	N.18.b.7.3.	12	T.M. emplacements
1.0 p.m.) to 4.0 p.m.)	D/190	GRAND BOIS, SUNKEN ROAD at N.18.b.23		Registration
1.30 p.m.	C/187	Front trench in C.7.a.21		"
11.0 a.m.	B/187	Trenches in front of BOIS Quarante.	16	

ST. ELOI GROUP:-

Time	Battery	Target	Rds.	Remarks
11.30 a.m.	A/189	Registration	5	
3.30 p.m.		Covering fire for trench mortars	8	
" "	B/189	"	11	
	C/189	"	6	
	A/183	"	16	
	B/183	"	15	
	C/183		14	
1.0 p.m.	D/189	PICCADILLY FARM	13	
2.0 p.m.	"		13	
	D/183	Not engaged		
3.30 p.m.	BELGIAN GR.	Covering fire for Trench Mortars	220	

ENEMY'S ARTILLERY FIRE:-

Time	Locality shelled	Rds.	Nature	Sound or Flash bearing.
9.0 a.m.) to) 11.0 a.m.)	VIERSTRAAT	20	10.5	
10.0 a.m.	VOORMEZEELE	12	7.7.	
10.30 a.m.	N.36.d.8½.3	10 (7 duds)	7.7.	
10.30 a.m.)) 11.30 a.m.)	Road barrage I.25.b.5.0.to I.25.d.0.½.	25	10.5	
3.30 p.m.	Front line trs.N.18.a.7.7 N.12.c.9½.9½	12	T.M.	N.13.b.

OBSERVATION

Poor.

ENEMY's MOVEMENTS
    Small working party in N.12.c.3.1.

GUNS OUT OF ACTION:-

    18 pdrs.   5
    4.5" How.   1

for Capt Bullock
Staff Capt
BRIGADE MAJOR,
1st.Divisional Artillery.

20.11.16
HHP

SECRET

41st. DIVISIONAL ARTILLERY

DAILY OPERATION REPORT
from 6 p.m., 19.11.16 to 6 p.m. 20.11.16

OUR FIRE:-

Time	Battery	Target	Rds.	Remarks
	DIEPENDAAL GROUP:)			
1 p.m. to 2 p.m.	A/190	Zero House	79	Checked registration of all Guns.
2 p.m. to 3.30 p.m.	B/190	N.18.b.1½.6½. to N.18.b.2.8. N.18.b.2½.7½.to N.18.b.4½.7. O.7.c.4.9. to O.7.c.4.9.6.0.	49	
11.30 p.m. to 12 noon	C/190	Fire at N.18.b.3.8.	12	
3.45 to 4.15p.m.	"	Registered front line about N.12.d.2.0.	10	
12.50 p.m. to 3 p.m.	B/190	Registered O.13.a.4.8. O.13.c.2.6½. N.18.b.5.3½.	30	
3.30 p.m.	"	PLATEAU FARM	15	Work reported here.
2.0 p.m.	B/187	Dug out at O.7.c.3½.3.2½.	19	Several direct hits.
2.45 p.m.	C/187	O.8.d.6.0.	20	Registration
	St ELOI GROUP:-			
8.0 a.m.	A/189	Covering fire for Trench Mortars	11	
3.0 p.m.	"	S.O.S lines	7	Registration
8.0 a.m.	B/189	Covering fire for T.Ms.	7	
2.45 p.m.	"	Registration	9	
3.40 p.m.	C/189	Calibration	4	
8.0 a.m.	"	Covering fire for T.Ms.	11	
" "	A/183	"	10	
2.15 p.m.		Hostile O.P.in tree at O.3.d.6.2½.		A painted shield in tree.
8.0 a.m.	B/183	Covering fire for T.Ms.	16	
" "	C/183	"	12	
" "	D/183	"	10	
12.30 p.m.		O.2.c.9.6.		
11.30 a.m.	D/189	O.3.d.3½.8½.	13	
8.0 a.m.	BELGES	Covering fire for T.Ms.	158	

.P.

T.Ms:-

Two guns fired 51 rounds for wire-cutting between them. Shooting was not good owing to strong wind, and indifferent platforms caused by the state of ground. 2 duds were observed. Many rounds were observed to go into the wire which was fired on for a length of about 60 yards.

Enemy gave no retaliation.

ENEMY'S ARTILLERY FIRE:-

Time	Locality shelled	Rds.	Nature	Flash	Sound or bearing
3.0 p.m.	SCOTTISH WOOD	9	15.0	-	
3.40 p.m. to 3.50 p.m.	N.18.a.7.4.	20	7.7	-	
4.30 p.m.	I.31.c.4.2.	7	7.7.	-	

GENERAL SUMMARY

1. ENEMY'S NEW WORK

No fresh work observed.
Suspected M.G. Emplacement located at O.7.c.3.2½.
An O.P. is visible in a tree at O.3.d.6.2½, a painted shield is to be seen in the tree.

OBSERVATION

Light fair most of the day

GUNS OUT OF ACTION:-

18 pdrs.   5
4.5" Hows.   1

BRIGADE MAJOR,
41st. Divisional Artillery.

21.11.16

SECRET

Ref. Map WYTSCHAETE
28 S.W. 2 1/10000

41st DIVISIONAL ARTILLERY OPERATION ORDER NO. 40.

1. **INTENTION.** The 41st Divisional Artillery will carry out a DUMMY RAID bombardment on the night of Nov. 20th/21st.

2. **BOMBARDMENTS & BARRAGES.** The Officer Commanding St. Eloi Group will detail batteries to carry out bombardments and barrages in accordance with attached schedule.

3. **AMMUNITION.** The expenditure of ammunition will be as in attached schedule and half of the expenditure of 18-pr and 4.5" How. ammunition will be debited to the allotment of the DIEPENDAAL GROUP.

4. **INFANTRY.** The Officer Commanding ST ELOI GROUP will arrange with G.O.C., 123rd Infantry Bde any precautionary measures necessary for the safety of the Infantry.

5. **TIME.** ZERO Hour will be 2.15 a.m. Divisional time will be given to the ST ELOI GROUP by this office at 10 p.m. Nov. 20th, all watches will be synchronised.

6. ACKNOWLEDGE.

[signature]

Brigade Major
41st Divisional Artillery.

18-11-16.

Copy No. 1 File
"   "   2 War Diary
"   "   3 Xth Corps R.A.
"   "   4 41st Divsn.
"   "   5 122nd Inf. Bde
"   "   6 123   "   "
"   "   7 124th "   "
"   "   8 DIEPENDAAL GROUP
"   "   9 ST ELOI   "
"   " 10 19th D.A.
"   " 11 47th D.A.
"   " 12 Xth Corps
"   " 13 Staff Capt.

	Battery	PERIOD	TASK	COORDINATES			Rate of fire in Rds per min.	TM Bty	A	X	BX
(a)	18-pr	10' before Z to Z	Bombard front line trench	O.2.d.1.6½	O.2.d.5½.6		2		20	60	
(b)	"	"	"	O.2.d.1.6½	O.2.d.5½.6		2		20	60	
(c)	1 TM Bty	"	CRATER	O.2.d.1½.6½				20			
(d)	1 18-pr	Zero to 10' after zero	Barrage support trench	C.2.c.9½.5½	O.2.d.3.5.		2		20	60	
(e)	1 Belgian	"	Barrage front line trench	O.2.c.6½.3	O.2.c.9½.5½	O.2.c.9½.3½	3	120			
(f)	1 Belgian	"	"	O.2.d.6½.5½	O.2.d.9.3½		3			48	
(g)	1 18-pr	7' after Z to 10' after Z	"	O.2.d.1.6½	O.2.d.5½.6		4			48	
(h)	"	"	"	O.2.d.1.6½	O.2.d.5½.6		4				
(i)	1 T.M Bty	"	Bombard CRATER	O.2.d.1½.6½				12			
(j)	1 4.5" How	5' before Z to 5' after Z	"	O.3.c.3.2½	O.3.c.6.4½		1				40
(k)	"	3' before Z to 7' after Z	"	O.2.d.4.1.	O.2.d.6½.5		1				40
								32	40	60	276 80

SECRET

41st Divisional Artillery

Daily Operation Report

From 6 p.m. 20-11-16 to 6 p.m. 21-11-16.

OUR FIRE

Time	Battery	Target	Rds.	Remarks

DIEPENDAAL GROUP

Time	Battery	Target	Rds.	Remarks
9.49 a.m.	D/190	LOUWAEGE FARM	19	Registration
10.15 a.m.	C/187	N.12.d.3½.1. to N.12.d.6.0.	19	Registered

ST. ELOI GROUP

Time	Battery	Target	Rds.	Remarks
2.15 a.m.	A/189	Operation Order No.40.	128	
"	C/189	"	84	
"	D/189	"	40	
"	A/183	"	80	
"	B/183	"	113	
"	C/183	"	40	
p.m.	D/189	Covering fire for Trench Mortars	10	
"	C/189	"	6	
"	A/183	"	16	
"	B/183	"	16	
"	C/183	"	6	
2.15 p.m.	BELGIAN GROUP	"	158	
2.15 a.m.	"	Operation Order No.40	120	
4.35	D/183	HEILE FARM MARTENS FARM	6	Retaliation for Enemy T.Ms.

TRENCH MORTARS

2 guns fired on CRATER at 2.15, got off 20 rounds from Centre and 6 rounds from Left Battery. No retaliation.
One gun carried out wire-cutting at 0.8.a.4½.9½, with good result. No retaliation from enemy. No enemy Trench Mortars were observed.

ENEMY'S ARTILLERY FIRE

Time	Locality shelled	Rds.	Nature	Sound or Flash bearing
3.30 p.m.	0.20.a.	12	10.5	
4.30 p.m.	Behind Front line trenches about 0.23.	8	H.T.M.	

GENERAL SUMMARY

1. **OBSERVATION:-**

    Very poor all day

2. **CASUALTIES:-**   PERSONNEL

    1 O.R. accidentally drowned

3. **GUNS OUT OF ACTION**

    18 pdrs.   5
    4.5." How.   1

                                S. Philridge
                                        A.D.C.
                                Brigade Major,
                            41st.Divisional Artillery

22.11.16
HHP

S E C R E T

21st. DIVISIONAL ARTILLERY
DAILY OPERATION REPORT
from 6 p.m., 21.11.16 to 6 p.m., 22.11.16.

OUR FIRE:-

TIME	BATTERY	TARGET	ROUNDS	REMARKS
		DIEPENDAAL GROUP:-		
3 p.m.	B/187.	Trenches about O.7.c.1.1½.	10	Registration
1.15 p.m.	C/187	N.12.d.4.1. to N.12.d.5.1½.	34	"
		ST. ELOI GROUP:-		
3.48	A/189	CRATER No.3	8	New Work
12 noon	B/189	ZERO LINE	2	Calibration
9.53 p.m.	C/189	TEST S.O.S. opposite O.23.	1	Time 9 secs.
1.35 p.m.	D/189	FRONT LINE and SUPPORTS opposite O.25 & O.28	30	Retaliation for enemy shelling
3.0 p.m.	B/183	O.2.c.9.6.	16	Suspected M.M. Emplacement.
3.55 p.m.	BELGIAN GROUP	Over Trench O.22.	10	Retaliation
"	"	O.7.c.4.4., O.7.c.4.5.	15	Registration
4.0 p.m.	"	O.8.a.3.7,) O.8.a.6.5.) O.8.a.7.2½.)	23	Retaliation
3.44½ a.m.	"	TEST S.O.S.O.11.	1	Time 50 secs.

ENEMY'S ARTILLERY FIRE:-

TIME	LOCALITY SHELLED	RDS.	Nature	Sound or Flash bearing
3.0 p.m.	O.2.c.3.4.	10	H.T.M.	
3.45 "	O.7.a.9.8.	10	10.5 c.m.	
3.50 "	TRENCH O.22.	6	15.0 c.m.	
" "	"	10	10.5 c.m.	

GENERAL SUMMARY

(1) <u>ENEMY'S NEW WORK</u>:-
A considerable amount of new work appears to have been done in CRATER No.3.

OBSERVATION:-

    Poor

CASUALTIES:-

    Nil

GUNS OUT OF ACTION:-

    18 pdrs. 5
    4.5 Hows. 1

TRENCH MORTARS:-

    Two guns carried out wire-cutting at O.4.a.0.½. - O.7.a.6.0.
    This was very carefully carried out with the Left Battery at about 12:30. Good observation and steady shooting was obtained with good results, 26 rounds out of 30 were observed to fall into the wire which is effectively cut. 1 "dud" round.
    No retaliation.
    The Right Battery fired 21 rounds at O.7.a.6.0. Supporting observation could not be obtained.
    The enemy retaliated after the first round with Rum Jars, Minenwerfers, and a few 5.9, and although a few rounds dropped within 10" of the gun, most of them fell to the right and left. No casualties occurred.
    The Centre Battery did not fire owing to the Infantry relief being carried out.

                  BRIGADE MAJOR,
               41st, Divisional Artillery.

23.11.16
HHP

appx 19a

WEEKLY SUMMARY OF OPERATIONS

41st. DIVISIONAL ARTILLERY

16th. November to 22nd. November 1916.

16th. Nov. Only registration and calibration was carried out.

17th. " At 9.30 a.m., our Howitzers retaliated on RED CHAPEAU, N.18.b.9.½. Between 3 p.m., and 3.30 p.m., Z/41 T.M.Battery was engaged cutting wire between O.2.c. 9.6 and O.2.c.5.9½. 30 rounds were fired in all with good results. Retaliation very slight. During this period our 18 pdr. & 4.5" How. Batteries, together with the batteries of the Belgian Group, fired 306 (approx) rounds in covering the T.Ms.
At 10.45 p.m., a party of men was dispersed at O.15.a. O.8.
Between 12.15 p.m., and 2 p.m., 74 rounds were fired in cutting wire at O.7.c.4.4. and at N.18.b.1½.9.
Registrations and S.O.S Tests were carried out during the day and night.

18th. " In the morning batteries were engaged in carrying out registrations and cutting wire between N.18.b.2.8½. and N.18.a.3½.1.
At 11.23a.m. our Howitzers retaliated on Hostile Front Line and Supports in front of Trenches O.24. and O.25.
At 8.0 a.m., batteries covered the fire of the Trench Mortars, whilst the latter were engaged wire-cutting.

19th. " During the morning registration was carried out.
At 1 p.m., an enemy working party was dispersed at N.12.c.3.1.
In the afternoon 18 pdr.& 4.5" How. Batteries were engaged covering the fire of our T.Ms, who were wire-cutting. 300 rounds were fired in all.
At 4 p.m., a hostile T.M.Emplacement was shelled at N.18.b.7.3.

20th. " Registration carried out.
Between 11.30 a.m., and 12 noon 12 rounds were fired on enemy wire at N.18.b.3.8. Fifteen rounds were expended on working party at PLATEAU FARM.
At 2 p.m., shelled enemy Dug-out at O.7.c.3.2½; several direct hits were obtained.
Two T.M.Batteries were engaged cutting wire, but shooting was not good owing to strong wind and indifferent platforms caused by the state of the ground. Whilst T.Ms. were cutting wire, our 18 pdr.& 4.5" Hows. were engaged covering T.Ms fire. Enemy did not retaliate.
Fired several rounds at Hostile O.P., in a tree at O.3.d.6.2½., and at an enemy Machine Gun Emplacement, which is suspected at O.7.c.3.2½.

21st. " Batteries carried out operations for the Dummy Raid as detailed in our Operation Order No.40.
Retaliated on enemy Trench Mortars at MARTENS FARM.
Two Trench Mortar guns shelled CRATER, and one T.M. gun cut wire at O.8.a.4½.9½, with good results. 30 rounds were fired in all. No enemy retaliation.

22nd. Nov.   Engaged CRATER No.3 as new work was observed in this locality. Howitzers shelled Machine Gun Emplacement at O.2.c.9.6.
   -Several registrations and retaliations were carried out.

BRIGADE MAJOR,

23rd. Nov. 1916   41st. Divisional Artillery.
HHP

SECRET

41st. DIVISIONAL ARTILLERY

DAILY OPERATION REPORT
from 6p.m., 22.11.16 to 6 p.m., 23.11.16

OUR FIRE:-

Time	Battery	Target	Rds.	Remarks
8.30 a.m.	B/190	M.G.at N.18.b.3.3.	10	M.G. firing at one of our planes
11.0 "	"	N.18.b.7.9. N.12.d.6.0.	20	Registration
3.0 p.m.	"	N.18.b.5.1.3.3	10	T.M.at N.18.b.3.3.
10.0 a.m.	D/190.	O.13.c.2.4.	15	Working party
12.0 noon	"	O.13.b.8.0.	5	Registration
3.15 p.m.	"	N.18.b.5.7.	10	T.M.active
11.45 a.m.	C/187	Support trenches O.7.b.	7	
11.15 a.m.	A/189	CRATERS 3 & 4	12	Retaliation
2.10 p.m.	"	Covering fire for Trench Mortars,	6	
" "	B/189	"	18	
11.35 a.m.	C/189	From O.2.c.5.1½.to O.2.c.9½.6.	9	Retaliation
2.10 p.m.	"	Covering fire for T.Ms.	10	
10.30 a.m.	D/189	No.2 and 4 Craters	22	Retaliation
11.30 a.m.	"	MARTENS FARM	26	"
3.15 p.m.	"	DAM STRASSE	26	"
2.10 p.m.	A/183	Covering fire for T.Ms.	16	
" "	B/183	"	16	
" "	C/183	"	12	
10.5 a.m.	D/183	No.2 Crater	20	Retaliation-
8.0 a.m.	"	DOME HOUSE	6	Working Party
3.0 p.m.	"	O.8.b.2½.2½.	32	Registration by K.B.S.
2.10 p.m.	BELGIAN GROUP	Covering fire	158	

TRENCH MORTARS:-

At 2.10 p.m., three Batteries were engaged cutting wire, as follows:-

"X" Battery O.4.a.0.½. 30 rds.fired
"Y"   "   O.7.a.6.0.   24 "   "
"Z"   "   O.8.a.3½.8¼. 20 "   "

The enemy retaliation was more than usual. He sent about 6 Minenwerfers into ESTAMINET LANE Communication trenches. BOIS CONFLUENT trenches were shelled with 7.7, and also Rum Jars in retaliation against "Z" Battery. 1 man was slightly wounded.
Shooting was good and accurate. Wire was well cut.

.1.

ENEMY'S ARTILLERY FIRE:-

Time	Locality shelled	Rds.	Nature	Sound of Flash bearing
9.30 a.m to 10.0 a.m.	I.31.c.3½.1.	10	7.7.	S.E. of BOIS QUARANTE
10.0 a.m. to 10.50 a.m.	I.31.c.	20	"	"
10.50 a.m. to 11.0 a.m.	Trenches O.24. & O.22.	10	"	
2.55 p.m.	I.31.c.	10	"	
4.30 p.m.	SCOTTISH WOOD	10	10.5	
3.45 p.m.	H.35.b.7.5.	30	"	
2.45 p.m.	O.35 and O.36	20	M.T.M.	12 rounds fired in first minute.
12.30 p.m.	Front Line Trench at N.24.c.	15	7.7.	
1.45 p.m.	N.22.b.	10	"	Rear edge of Wytschaete Wood.
	N.29.b.	6	10.5.	
10.30 p.m.	MOATED GRANGE	20	"	
3.0 p.m.	N.11.c.5.5.	3	7.7.	O.15.b.
3.0 p.m.	Front Line Trench at N.18.a.7.5. to N.12.d.2.4.	20	M.T.M.	N.18.b.3.3.

24th.Nov.1916

12.15 p.m.	H.36.a.	-	H.V.G.	127 degrees

GENERAL SUMMARY:-

ENEMY'S MOVEMENTS:-

    At 8.0 a.m., a working party was observed near DOME HOUSE, and dispersed.
    A working party was also seen at O.13.c.2.4., and likewise dispersed.

OBSERVATION:-
    Fair all day.

CASUALTIES:-
    PERSONNEL:- 1 O.R. slightly wounded (T.M.B.)

GUNS OUT OF ACTION:-

    18 pdrs. - 2
    4.5"Hows. - 1

                                        BRIGADE-MAJOR,
                                41st.Divisional Artillery.

24.11.16
HHP

SECRET

41st. DIVISIONAL ARTILLERY

DAILY OPERATION REPORT from 6 p.m., 23.11.16 to 6 p.m. 24.11.16.

OUR FIRE:-

Time	Battery	Target	Rounds	REMARKS
	DIEPENDAAL GROUP:-			
11.0 a.m.	B/190	O.7.c.4.1.		New work being done here.
"	"	O.7.c.3½.3½	12	
"	"	O.7.c.3½.2½		
10.30 a.m.	C/190	Checked day lines	12	
8.15 a.m.	D/190	O.8.d.8.6.	7	Dispersed a small party of the enemy
1.30 p.m.	"	O.7.d.5.2.	4	Suspected T.M. Emplacement.
3.0 p.m.	"	O.7.b.1½.1½	10	Registration.
	ST ELOI GROUP:-			
12 noon.	A/189	Enemy front line	10	Calibration
2.40 p.m.	B/189	Covering fire for Trench Mortars	12	
4.34 a.m.	C/189	O.2.47.3½.	1	Test S.O.S.Line
2.40 p.m.	"	Covering fire for T.Ms	11	
2.0 p.m.	D/189	O.2.d.3.3. ZILLEBECKE	5 5	Registration "
2.40 p.m.	A/183	Covering fire for T.Ms.	16	
" "	B/183	"	16	
" "	C/183	"	20	
" "	BELGIAN GROUP		162	

TRENCH MORTARS:-

Two Batteries carried out wire-cutting at O.7.a.6.9., and O.2.c.8½.5.

Shooting was fairly good, 46 rounds being fired in all. Two rounds dropped short, probably due to a defective charge. Retaliation normal. The enemy firing a few 5.9 on BOIS CONFLUENT, and a few Rum Jars to the right of CRATER LANE. No damage or casualties occurred.

ENEMY'S ARTILLERY FIRE

Time	Locality shelled	Rds.	Nature	Sound or Flash bearing
9.50 a.m.	I.31.c.	2	7.7.	
10.40 "	"	1	"	
2.20 p.m.	I.32.central	6	10.5 c.m.	
12.50 p.m.	I.31.c.8.2.	10	"	True bearing 121½° I.32.a.3.3½.
12 noon	FRONT LINE) TRENCH at) N.12.d.0.3.)	10	M.T.M.	
"	BRYKERIE FARM	6	7.7.	Direction of WYTSCHAETE.

GENERAL SUMMARY:-

ENEMY'S NEW WORK:-

Fresh planks are visible at O.8.d.6.0. near MARTENS FARM

New work seen at O.7.c.4.1., O.7.c.3½.2½., and O.7.c.3½.3½.

ENEMY'S MOVEMENTS:-

A small party was dispersed at O.8.d.8.6.
An enemy Cookhouse is suspected at O.13.b.7.9.

ENEMY TRENCH MORTARS:-

At 11.30 a.m., a new Trench Mortar was located at O.7.a.8.1.

OBSERVATION:-

Good until 3.30 p.m.

CASUALTIES:-   PERSONNEL:-

NIL.

GUNS OUT OF ACTION:-

18 pdrs. - 3
4.5" Hows. - 1

BRIGADE MAJOR,
41st. Divisional Artillery.

25.11.16
HRP

SECRET

41st. DIVISIONAL ARTILLERY

DAILY OPERATION REPORT
from 6 p.m., 24.11.16 to 6 p.m., 25.11.16.

OUR FIRE:-

Time	Battery	Target	Rds.	REMARKS
		DIEPENDAAL GROUP		
2.15p.m.	C/190	Front Line trench in the HOLLANDSCHESCHURR SALIENT	20	Registration of No.5 Gun
3.0 p.m.	B/190	Trenches from 0.7.c.3½.3. to 0.7.c.3½.6.	25	Retaliation for Hostile T.M.
		ST. ELOI GROUP:-		
7.30 p.m.	A/189	S.O.S. lines	1	Test S.O.S.
8.30 p.m.	"	"	1	"
3.35 p.m.	"	"	6	Retaliation
11.35 a.m.	C/189	0.2.c.5.½ to 0.2.c.9½.6.	4	Indicating zone to incoming Battery.
3.5 p.m.	"	Covering fire for T.Ms.	12	
3.5 p.m.	A/183	"	16	
3.5 p.m.	B/183	"	16	
3.5 p.m.	C/183	"	20	
3.5 p.m.	BELGIAN GROUP		162	

TRENCH MORTARS:-

3 Batteries carried out wire cutting at 0.7.a.6.0.- 0.2.c.8½.5 - 0.8.a.2½.9. 59 rounds were fired in all. Observation bad owing to Fog. Retaliation normal.
1 round from our Right Battery must have hit a dug-out, or possibly a Mortar Emplacement, as a quantity of timber came back near our own trenches. A Hostile Minenwerfer, which had fired three rounds in retaliation, immediately ceased firing and no more came from this direction.

ENEMY'S ARTILLERY FIRE:-

Time	Locality shelled	Rds.	Nature	Sound or Flash bearing.
3 p.m.	FRONT LINE TRENCH N.12.d.4.2. to N.12.d.7.6.	20	M.T.M.	Unknown
3.35 p.m.	TRENCH 0.2.5	12	7.7	-

GENERAL SUMMARY:-

OBSERVATION:-
   Bad, owing to rain and mist.

CASUALTIES:-   PERSONNEL:-

   N I L.

GUNS OUT OF ACTION:-
   18 pdrs.   4
   4.5" How.   1

                              BRIGADE MAJOR,
                           41st. Divisional Artillery.

26.11.16
HHP

Mp 23

**Re-organisation of Artillery Positions
consequent on re-organisation of 41st D.A.**

1. All guns detailed to be handed over, will be handed over with sights complete, but otherwise stripped.

2. Batteries will take over guns and occupy positions as under :-

    A/187 (old style) takes over 4 guns from B/183 (old style) and positions at H.29.c.5.7. also 2 guns A/183 (old style) and half the position at H.29.d.5.5.

    B/187 (O.S.) takes over 4 guns from C/183 (O.S.) and the position at H.35.b.7.5. also 2 guns A/183 (O.S) and half the positions at H.29.d.5.5.

    C/187 (O.S.) takes over 4 guns from C/189 (O.S.) and the positions at H.35.d.0.6, also 2 guns of A/189 (O.S.) and ½ the positions at H.35.d.3½.7.

    D/187 (O.S.) takes over 4 howitzers from D/190 (O.S.) and the position at H.30.c.7.8. also two Howitzers from D/189 (O.S.) and the position at H.36.c.4.7.

    B/189 (O.S.) remains in position at H.30.a.2.7. with its own guns, also takes over 2 guns from A/189 (O.S.) and half the position at H.35.d.3½.7.

    C/189 (O.S.) goes out to rest at N.1.a.4.9 taking with it 2 guns A/187 and 4 guns A/187 and 4 guns B/187.

    D/190 (O.S.) becomes D/189 and goes out to rest at N.6.b.2.2, taking with it 4 howitzers from D/187 (O.S.)

    B/183 (O.S.) becomes A/190 and takes over 2 guns from A/190 (O.S.) and half the position at N.4.d.2.4. also 4 guns from C/187 (O.S.) and the position H.35.c.1.5.
    B/190 (O.S.) remains in position at N.15.b.9.9. with its own guns, also takes over 2 guns from A/190 (O.S.) and half the position at N.4.d.2.4.

    C/190 (O.S.) remains in position at N.16.c.3.8 with its own guns also takes over two guns from A/187 (O.S.) which will be placed in the position N.10.d.6.3.

    D/183 (O.S.) becomes D/190 and remains in position at H.35.a.8.8. with its own 4 Howitzers also takes over 2 Howitzers of D/189 (O.S.) and the position at H.4.c.9.8.

3. RELIEF
    Batteries will take over as follows, four gun positions by Sections at a time at 24 hours interval. Two gun positions by single guns at 24 hours interval.

4. The first sections and single guns will take over at 9 a.m. on the 25th Nov., Second Sections and single guns at 9 a.m. on the 26th Nov.
    Batteries detailed to go to rest will remove their guns to the wagon lines at the same time and in the same detail as in para (3)

5. Re-allotment of wagon lines will be detailed later. In the meanwhile only necessary work should be undertaken on wagon lines.

6. Until this re-allotment all personnel and horses will remain in the lines they are at present occupying.

7. OS.C. Groups will at once submit schemes for re-allotment of wagon lines where necessary.

8. Os.C. St. ELOI & DIEPENDAAL Groups will take command of their respective reconstituted groups at 9 a.m. 26th Nov. Communications will be arranged accordingly.

9. O.C. St. ELOI Group and O.C. DIEPENDAAL Group will submit to this office for approval by 2p.m. 24th Novr. the necessary re-arrangements of S.O.S. lines caused by 2 4.5" Hows. being added to DIEPENDAAL Group and removed from the St-ELOI Group, and two 18-prs being removed from the DIEPENDAAL GROUP to rest.

10. **AMMUNITION.**

    Ammunition will be taken over by respective units at the gun positions which they occupy and at the wagon lines, which they take over on re-organisation. Receipts will be signed by the C.Os. taking over and countersigned by the C.Os. handing over.

    This passing of ammunition will be accounted for by Group.

                                                    [signature]
                                                    Brigade Major
23-11-16.   41st Divisional Artillery.

S 320

With reference to Re-organisation Preliminary Order circulated under our S 304, para 3 should be amended to read as follows:-

3. Batteries will be constituted as follows :-

A/187 from present A/187 and Right half present A/183
B/187   "   "   B/187 " Left   "   "   A/183
C/187   "   "   C/187 " Right "   "   C/183
D/187   "   "   D/187 " Right "   "   A/189
B/189   "   "   B/189 " Right "   "   A/189
C/189   "   "   C/189 " Left   "   "   A/189

D/189 will be constituted by present D/190

A/190 from present B/183 and Right half present A/190
B/190   "   "   B/190 " Left   "   "   A/190
C/190   "   "   C/190 " Left   "   "   C/183
D/190   "   "   D/183 " Left   "   "   D/189.

Guy Bullock
Staff Captain,
41st Divisional Arty.

23-11-16

REORGANISATION

Preliminary Order.

[margin note: keep one copy for Divn HQ ✓   23/11/16]

1. In accordance with G.H.Q. letter No. O.B./1866 dated 16th Nov. 1916, the 41st D.A. will be re-organised as follows :-

    187th Bde. three guns 18-pr Batteries and one 6 gun 4.5 How Bty.

    189th Bde. two 6 gun 18-pr Batteries and one 4 gun 4.5 How Bty.

    190th Bde. Three 6 gun 18-pr Btys and one 6 gun 4.5 How. Bty.

2. The 189th Brigade will then become available for absorption in the Army Field Artillery Brigades, retaining its Brigade number.

3. Batteries will be constituted as follows :-

    A/187 from present A/187 and half present " A/183

    B/187   "   "   B/187 "   "   "   A/183

    C/187   "   "   C/187 "   "   "   C/183

    D/187   "   "   D/187 "   "   "   D/189

    B/189   "   "   B/189 "   "   "   A/189

    C/189   "   "   C/189 "   "   "   A/189

    D/189 will be constituted by present D/190

    A/190 from present B/183 and half present A/190

    B/190   "   "   B/190 "   "   "   A/190

    C/190   "   "   C/190 "   "   "   C/183

    D/190   "   "   D/183 "   "   "   D/189

4. A schedule of officers with their position in Brigades and Batteries will be issued at an early date.

5. No. 2 Section of D.A.C., 41st D.A., will become available for transfer as a section D.A.C., Army Field Artillery Brigades.

                                                                Brigade Major
23-11-16.   fo C.R.A., 41st Divisional Arty.

App 24

S E C R E T

41st. DIVISIONAL ARTILLERY

DAILY OPERATION REPORT
from 6 p.m., 25.11:16 to 6 p.m 26.11.16

O U R   F I R E

Time	Battery	Target	Rds.	REMARKS

DIEPENDAAL GROUP:-

Time	Battery	Target	Rds.	REMARKS
11.30 a.m.	A/190	O.8.d.6½.0.	13	Registration
3.45 p.m.	B/190	N.18.b.8.2. O.8.b.2½.2½.	28	" by K.B.S.
11.0 a.m.	C/190	Front Line) Trench from) N.12.d.4.1.) O.7.c.4.4.)	20	"
Noon to) 1.30 p.m.)	D/190	O.7.d.3.1. Road Junction		" by K.B.S.
11.30 a.m. to 12 Noon	"	N.18.b.6½.8.) N.18.b.5.7.)	19	"

ST. ELOI GROUP:-

Time	Battery	Target	Rds.	REMARKS
6.30 p.m.	A/189	S.O.S. lines	1	Test S.O.S.
10.47 "	"	"	1	
9.55 a.m.	"	Trench O.29	6	Retaliation
1.40 p.m.	A/187	Covering fire for T.Ms.	16	
" "	B/187		16	
1.30 "	C/187	Support Trench in O.2.c.	8)	Reply to enemy sniping at Aeroplane.
1.40 "	B/189	Covering fire for T.Ms..	16)	
7.25 "	BELGIAN GROUP	TRENCH O.11	3	Test S.O.S.
1.40 "	"	Covering fire for T.Ms.	158	

TRENCH MORTARS:-

Two batteries cut wire at O.2.c.9.6½. and O.8.a.3½.9.
50 rounds were fired in all with good results, the wire being well cut. Observation good. Enemy seems to have spotted gun of Left Battery as several rounds fell around it.

Retaliation above normal. Between 2.45 and 3.45 enemy shelled Communication Trench E. of MOATED GRANGE (O.1.a) and also South side of P.& O. Trench, the latter with a large number of Heavy Trench Mortar bombs which reached as far as SNIPER'S BARN (O.1.c.)

ENEMY'S ARTILLERY FIRE:-

Time	Locality shelled	Rds.	Nature	Sound or Flash bearing
3.0 p.m.	I.31.c.	6	7.7.	-
9.45 a.m.	TRENCH O.27	8	"	-
12.0 noon to) 3.30 p.m.)	ECLUSE No.7	1 rd every 10 mins.)	"	From direction of O.9.b.
2.45 p.m.	RIDGE WOOD O.5.a.	6	"	-
3.15 p.m.	Vicinity of B.189.	1	10.5 c.m.	-

GENERAL SUMMARY

ENEMY'S MOVEMENTS:-

At 10.30 a.m., a few men were seen walking along road behind MARTENS FARM.

OBSERVATION:-

Fairly good.

HOSTILE ARTILLERY ACTIVITY

Rather above normal.

HOSTILE TRENCH MORTARS:-

The smoke of a hostile Trench Mortar was seen in the direction of O.2.d.1½.7.

CASUALTIES:-

PERSONNEL:-

NIL.

GUNS OUT OF ACTION

    18 pdrs.   1
    4.5" Hows.   1

BRIGADE-MAJOR,
41st.Divisional Artillery.

27.11.16
HHP

App 25

SECRET

41st. DIVISIONAL ARTILLERY

DAILY OPERATION REPORT
from 6 p.m., 26.11.16 to 6 p.m., 27.11.16.

OUR FIRE:-

Time	Battery	Target	Rds.	Remarks
		ST. ELOI GROUP:-		
2.15 a.m.	B/189	S.O.S. Pt. *Registration*	7	
3.10 p.m.	A/187	S.O.S. Lines	48	Retaliation
11.15 a.m.	B/187	Day and Night lines	4	Testing Registration
10.15 a.m.	C/187	T.M. at O.2.d.9½.3.	15	Retaliation for T.M. fire.
3.30 p.m.	"	S.O.S. Lines	16	Testing registrations
7.8 p.m.	BELGIAN GROUP	Trench O.11.	3	S.O.S. Test.
		DIKKEBUSCH GROUP:-		
3.50 a.m.	A/190 A/A&R	S.O.S. test	2	
1.15 a.m. to 2.30 p.m.	" B/190	O.7.c.4½.8½. O.7.a.9.1. O.7.B.9.5½. O.7.c.2.2. N.12.d.9.1.	48	Registration
10.20 a.m.	B/190	FRONT LINE TRENCH in O.7.c.	20	In reply to hostile rifle fire on our planes.
2.0 p.m.	"	Sunken Road in N.18.b.	16	Registration
3.30 p.m.	"	Trench from N.18.b.9.7. to O.13.a.4.6.	20	In conjunction with F.B.S.
12.30 p.m.	C/190	Checked S.O.S. lines.	10	
10.30 a.m. to 12.0 p.m.	B/190	O.7.b.8.8½. O.13.a.4.7½. O.7.d.1.6. O.7.d.2.7½.	32	Registration

ENEMY'S ARTILLERY FIRE

Time	Locality shelled	Rds.	Nature	Sound or Flash bearing
3.0 p.m. to 3.30 p.m.	DICKEBUSCHE	16	10.5	-
3.0 p.m.	-	10	"	H.E in air -
12.40 p.m.	H.30.d.4.8.	5	"	From direction of O.18
3.0 p.m.	Trench O.29	30	7.7 & 10.5.	-
9.25 a.m.	House at N.11.c.4½.4½	4	10.5	H.E.in air -

GENERAL SUMMARY:-

ENEMY'S MOVEMENTS

Smoke seen coming from a dug-out at O.8.d.6½.2.

OBSERVATION

Light good between 8 a.m., and 4 p.m.

HOSTILE AIRCRAFT ACTIVITY

Two hostile planes overhead about 12.45 p.m., and disappeared in N.W.direction.
General activity throughout the day.

CASUALTIES:

PERSONNEL:-
N I L.

GUNS OUT OF ACTION

18 pdr.   1.

S. Philip. A.D.C.
BRIGADE MAJOR,
41st.Divisional Artillery.

28.11.16
HWP

SECRET

41st. DIVISIONAL ARTILLERY

DAILY OPERATION REPORT
from 6 p.m., 27.11.16 to 6 p.m., 28.11.16.

OUR FIRE:-

Time	Battery	Target	Rds.	REMARKS
DIEPENDAAL GROUP				
9.45 a.m.	B/190	FRONT LINE TR. in O.7.c.	6	
3 p.m.,- 4 p.m.	"	Sunken Road in N.18.b.	60	Group Shoot
"	C/190	"	60	" "
"	D/190	PLATEAU FM) SUNKEN ROAD)	30	" "
ST. ELOI GROUP				
6.58 p.m.	C/187	S.O.S. lines	1	Test S.O.S.
10.25 "	"	"	1	" "
5.35 a.m.	"	"	1	" "
5.5 "	"	"	1	" "
8.44 p.m.	BELGIAN GROUP	TRENCH O.11	3	" "

TRENCH MORTARS:-

Our Trench Mortars did not fire in consequence of a relief taking place.

ENEMY'S ARTILLERY FIRE

Time	Locality shelled	Rds.	Nature	Sound or Flash bearing
9.45 - 10.0 a.m.	Trench IV 12.1 IV. 12.2	3	Light T.M.	Unknown

GENERAL SUMMARY

OBSERVATION:-

    Bad, owing to thick mist.

CASUALTIES:-

        PERSONNEL:-

        N I L.

GUNS OUT OF ACTION:-

    18 pdrs.   1

[signed]
BRIGADE MAJOR,
41st. Divisional Artillery

29.11.16
HHP

SECRET

41st. DIVISIONAL ARTILLERY

DAILY OPERATION REPORT
from 6 p.m., 28.11.16 to 6 p.m., 29.11.16

OUR FIRE:-

TIME	BATTERY	TARGET	Rds.	REMARKS
DIEPENDAAL GROUP:-				
11.30 ,-) 11.45 a.m.)	B/190	Hostile T.M. O.18.b.9½.3.	40	In accordance with Operation Order No.42
"	C/190	"	40	" "
"	D/190	"	60	" "
ST. ELOI GROUP:-				
1.30 p.m.	B/189	Covering fire for T.Ms.	9	
11.30 a.m.	A/187	Hostile T.M. O.2.a.6½.5.	36	
1.30 p.m.	"	Covering fire for T.Ms	15	
" "	B/187	"	24	
11.30 a.m.	C/187	Hostile T.M. O.2.a.6½.5.	36	
1.30 p.m.	"	Covering fire for T.Ms.	14	
11.30 a.m.	D/187	Hostile T.M. O.2.a.6½.5.	60	
1.30 p.m.	"	Covering fire for T.Ms.	12	
2.15 a.m.	BELGIAN GROUP	Test O.11.	3	
1.30 p.m.	"	Covering fire for T.Ms.	158	
5.22 p.m.	"	Test O.11.	4	

TRENCH MORTARS

The daily shoot was carried out on the enemy's wire yesterday from 1.30 p.m. to 2 p.m., with good results. One round which dropped in front line near O.2.c.8.5. threw up entrenching materials, duckboards, and timber, into the air. Casualties - Nil.

ENEMY'S ARTILLERY FIRE:-

Time	Locality shelled	Rds.	Nature	Sound or Flash bearing
2.30 p.m.	FRONT LINE TR. N.18.a.7.6.	2	Light T.M.	Unnamed Wood
11.40 a.m.	Trench O.25	6	7.7.	

GENERAL SUMMARY

OBSERVATION:-

Impossible. Wire-cutting impossible owing to bad light, Heavy mists shrouded front line all day.

CASUALTIES:-

PERSONNEL:-

N I L.

GUNS OUT OF ACTION:-

18 pdr.   1

S. Rudlip
A.D.C.

BRIGADE MAJOR,
41st. Divisional Artillery.

30.11.16
HEP

SECRET

War Diary

Ref. Map WY-SCHEME
28 S.W. 2 1/10,000

41st DIVISIONAL ARTILLERY OPERATION ORDER No. 42.

INTENTION.
1. The 41st Divisional Artillery will destroy hostile trenches Mortars at C.8.a.7.4 and N.18.b.9½.3½ on November 29th 1916.

TACTICS.
2. A square barrage will be placed all round these mortars which will take in trenches near them, thus blocking all exits, meanwhile the mortars will be bombarded by 4.5" Howitzers assisted by the Heavy Artillery.
The operation will be in 3 phases.

Phase 1. Howitzers bombard mortars for 5', after the Howitzers have been shooting 2' the 18-prs form the barrage and shoot for 3'.

Phase 2. All guns and Howitzers cease firing.

Phase 3. Phase 1. repeated.

DETAIL.
3. O.C. St Eloi Group will detail batteries to destroy CUPID in accordance with attached schedule A.
O.C. DIEPENDAAL Group will detail batteries to destroy FREDERICK in accordance with attached schedule B.
FREDERICK's pin point verified by the latest air photographs is N.18.b.9½.3½.

HEAVY ARTILLERY. The Heavy Artillery will be asked to co-operate.

RATES OF FIRE. AMMUNITION. Rates of fire and allotment of ammunition will be as laid down in schedule A & B.

PREPARATION. O.C Groups will make all arrangements at once for carrying out this operation.

ZERO HOUR Watches will be synchronised with this office at 9 a.m. on November 29th Zero Hour will be 11.30 a.m.

8. ACKNOWLEDGE.

J.H.Hilton

Brigade Major
41st Divisional Ary.

Copy No. 1 War Diary.
"   "   2 FILE.
"   "   3 St Eloi Group
         6
"   "   7 DIEPENDAAL group
         10   "
"   "   11 187th Bde.
"   "   12 41st Divsn G
"   "   13   "   Q
"   "   14 10th Corps H.A.
"   "   15 10th   "
"   "   16 Belgians 7th !G..

SCHEDULE "A"

Guns	Period	TASK	Co-ordinates	rds per gun per min	AX	BX	Total
(a) 3 18-prs	2' after Z to 5' after Z	Barrage	0.8.a.6.7..48-0.8.a.78.48	1	9		9
(b) 3 "	"	"	0.8.a.78.48 - 0.8.a.78.35	1	9		9
(c) 3 "	"	"	0.8.a.78.35 - 0.8.a.67.38	1	9		9
(d) 3 "	"	"	0.8.a.67.38 - 0.8.a.67.48	1	9		9
(e) 6 4.5" Hows	Z to 5' after Z	Bombard	0.8.a.7.4.	1		30	30
(f) 3 18-prs	12' after Z to 15' after Z	Barrage	(as in (a))	1	9		9
(g) 3 18-prs	"	"	" (b)	1	9		9
(h) 3 "	"	"	" (c)	1	9		9
(i) 3 "	"	"	" (d)	1	9		9
(j) 6 4.5" Hows	10' after Z to 15' after Z	Bombard	" (e)	1		30	30
					72	60	132
			From Schedule B		72	60	132
			GRAND TOTAL		144	120	264

SCHEDULE B

Guns	Period	TASK	Co-ordinates	rds per gun per min	AX	DX	Total
(k) 3 18-prs	2' after Z to 5' after Z	Barrage	N.18.b.97.45 - O.13.a.02.56	1	9		9
(l) 3 18-prs	"	"	O.13.a.02.56 N.18.b.55.50	1	9		9
(m) 3 18-prs	"	"	N.18.b.95.30 - N.18.b.89.57	1	9		9
(n) 3 18-prs	"	"	N.18.b.99.57 N.18.b.97.45	1	9		9
(o) 6 4.5" How.	Z to 5' after Z	Bombard	N.18.b.92.58	1		30	30
(p) 3 18-prs	2' after Z to 15' after Z	Barrage	as in (k)	1	9		9
(q) 3 18-prs	"	"	as in (l)	1	9		9
(r) 3 18-prs	"	"	as in (m)	1	9		9
(s) 3 18-prs	"	"	as in (n)	1	9		9
(t) 6 4.5" How	10' after Z to 15' after Z	Bombard	as in (o)	1		30	30
					72	60	132

SECRET

41st. Divisional Artillery

DAILY OPERATION REPORT
from 6 p.m., 29.11.16 to 6 p.m., 30/11/16

OUR FIRE:-

Time	Battery	Target	Rds.	Remarks
11.45 a.m.	A/190	Registrations	46	
2.0 p.m.	"	O.7.d.4½.4.-) O.8.c.½.2½.)	75	Operation Order 39.
2.0. -) 2.30 p.m.)	C/190	LOUWAEGE FARM		" "
"	D/190	" "	50	" "
12 noon.	B/189	Covering fire for T.Ms.	11	
"	A/187	"	16	
"	B/187	"	16	
"	C/187	"	20	
"	D/187	"	12	
2.59 a.m.) 8.44 p.m.)	C/187	Test Trench O.25	2	
12 noon	BELGIAN) GROUP))	) Covering fire) for T.Ms.)	158	

OUR TRENCH MORTARS:-

The daily shoot was carried out on the enemy's wire from 12 noon to 12.30 p.m., 71 rounds being fired in all. The result again appeared to be very good, duckboards, entrenching materials, etc., being blown in the air, especially at O.2.d.1½.6½.

ENEMY'S ARTILLERY FIRE

Time	Locality shelled	Rds.	Nature	Sound or Flash bearing
10.30 a.m.	VIERSTRAAT	20	10.5	O.29.b.
11.50 a.m.	O.7.a.Central	50 (about)	M.T.M.	No retaliation was fired as our T.Ms.opened at 12 noon
12.10 p.m.	Feeble retaliation on Front Line Tr. in reply to our T.M. at N.12.d.1.3.-O.7.c. O.½.	5	Light T.M.	Direction unknown.

-1-

GENERAL SUMMARY

OBSERVATION:-

    Poor.   Possible from 10 a.m., to 2.0 p.m.

CASUALTIES:-

        PERSONNEL:-

        N I L.

GUNS OUT OF ACTION:-

    18 Pdrs.   1.

                      BRIGADE MAJOR,
                  41st. Divisional Artillery.

1.12.16
HHP

app=9a

41st. Divisional Artillery

WEEKLY SUMMARY OF OPERATIONS from 24th. November to 30th. November 1916

24th. November

At 8.30 a.m., shelled Machine Gun at N.18.b.3.3., which had been firing at one of our Aeroplanes.

At 3.0 p.m., and 3.15 p.m., fired on active Trench Mortars at N.18.b.3.3, and N.18.b.5.7.,respectively

Working parties at DOME HOUSE and O.13.c.2.4. were fired on and dispersed.

Retaliated on CRATERS Nos.2,3,and 4, MARTENS FARM, DAM STRASSE, and Trenches from O.2.c.5.1½ to O.2.c.9½.6.

At 2.10 p.m., whilst our Trench Mortars were wire-cutting, our 18 pdrs. and 4.5" Hows., together with the Belgian Group, were engaged covering their fire, expending in all about 236 rounds.

Our Trench Mortars fired about 74 rounds during their wire-cutting operations on wire at O.4.a.O.½, O.7.a.6.O., and O.8.a. 3½. 8¼.   Their shooting was good and accurate and wire was well cut.   The enemy's retaliation was rather heavier than usual.

A few registrations were also carried out.

25th. November

At 11 a.m., fired a few rounds at O.7.c.4.1., O.7.c.3½.3½. and O.7.c.3½.2½., as new work was being carried out at these points.

At 8.15 a.m., a working party was observed at O.8.d.8.6., and was dispersed by our fire.

At 1.30 p.m., fired a few rounds at a suspected Trench Mortar Emplacement at O.7.d.5.2.

At 2.40 p.m., our Trench Mortar Batteries were engaged cutting wire at O.7.a.6.O. and O.2.c.8½.5., 46 rounds being fired in all.   During this operation our 18 pdrs and 4.5" Howitzers, together with the Belgian Group, fired 247 rounds as a covering fire.

Enemy retaliation - Normal.

Several registrations were also carried out.

At 11.30 a.m., a new Trench Mortar was located at O.7.a.8.1.

26th. November

At 2.15 p.m., fired several rounds on Front Line Trench in the HOLLANDSCHESCHUUR SALIENT.

At 3.0 p.m., fired 25 rounds on Trenches from O.7.c.3½.3 to O.7.c.3½.6, in retaliation for Hostile Trench Mortar.

At 3.5 p.m., our Trench Mortars cut wire at O.7.a.6.O.- O.2.c.8½.5 - O.8.a.2½.9., during which operation our 18 pdrs and 4.5" Hows., assisted by the Belgian Artillery, expended 216 rounds in covering their fire. One round from our Right Trench Mortar Battery apparently hit a dug-out, or possibly a Trench Mortar Emplacement, as a quantity of timber was hurled back near our own trenches, and a hostile minenwerfer, which had fired three rounds in retaliation, immediately ceased firing - no more rounds coming from this direction. Observation was bad owing to heavy fog.   Enemy retaliation - normal.

A few registrations and S.O.S.tests were carried out.

27th. November

Several registrations by K.B.S., and otherwise, were carried out.

At 1.30 p.m., a few rounds were fired at Support Trench

in O.2.c., in retaliation for enemy sniping at one of our Aeroplanes.

At 1.30 p.m., our Trench Mortars were again engaged cutting wire at O.2.c.9.6½., and O.8.a.3½.9., our 18 pdrs and 4.5" Hows.,assisted by the Belgian Group, covering their fire - expending in all about 206 rounds. Our Trench Mortars fired 50 rounds in all with good results, the wire being well cut.

Retaliation by the enemy was rather above normal.

28th.November

Carried out several registrations and S.O.S. tests.
At 10.15 a.m., retaliated on hostile Trench Mortar at O.2.c.9½.5.
At 10.20 a.m., fired several rounds at Front Line Trench in O.7.c., in reply to hostile rifle fire at our Aeroplanes.
At 3.30 p.m.,in conjunction with K.B.S., fired several rounds at Trench from N.18.b.9.7. to O.13.a.4.6.
Our Trench Mortars did not fire owing to an Infantry relief taking place.

29th.November

From 3 p.m., to 4 p.m., carried out operations on SUNKEN ROAD in N.18.b., and FLATEAU FARM, firing 150 rounds in all. Observation bad in consequence of heavy mist.
Carried out several S.O.S. tests.
Our Trench Mortars did not fire on account of Infantry relief being carried out.

30th.November

Carried out operations on Hostile Trench Mortars, in accordance with our Operation Order No.42, expending about 430 rounds in all.
Our Trench Mortars were again engaged in cutting wire, good results being obtained. One round dropped in front line near O.2.c.8.5., causing entrench materials, duckboards, and timber, to be hurled into the air.
Some S.O.S.tests were carried out.

BRIGADE MAJOR,
41st.Divisional Artillery.

30.11.16
HHP

On His Majesty's Service.

Secret

D A G
3rd Echelon

HQ RA HR's
U 8

Army Form C. 2118

WAR DIARY
41st Div. Arty.
INTELLIGENCE SUMMARY
for month December 1916
(Erase heading not required.)

Instructions regarding War Diaries and Intelligence Summaries are contained in F. S. Regs., Part II. and the Staff Manual respectively. Title Pages will be prepared in manuscript.

Place	Date	Hour	Summary of Events and Information	Remarks and references to Appendices
RENINGHELST	1/12/16		A fine cold day	App 30. Intry
RENINGHELST	2/12/16		A fine day	App 31. Intry
RENINGHELST	3/12/16		Issued out operation order 39 & Sketches	App 32. App 33 App 34 App 1. Intry
RENINGHELST	4/12/16		Retaliated successfully on a hostile trench mortar at 0.13.a.1½.4½.	App 35. Intry
RENINGHELST	5/12/16		A fine day. Retaliated on hostile trench mortar at 0.13.a.1½.4½.	App 36. Intry
RENINGHELST	6/12/16		A fine day. Conditions normal. Old Etonian Founders day at Dinner at CASSEL 8PM	App 37. Intry

Army Form C. 2118

WAR DIARY
or
INTELLIGENCE SUMMARY
(Erase heading not required.)

Instructions regarding War Diaries and Intelligence Summaries are contained in F.S. Regs., Part II. and the Staff Manual respectively. Title Pages will be prepared in manuscript.

Place	Date	Hour	Summary of Events and Information	Remarks and references to Appendices
RENINGHELST	7/17/16		A damp cold day	app 58 smy
RENINGHELST	8/17/16		A normal day.	app 39 smy
RENINGHELST	9/17/16		Retaliated on trench mortar 0747.7	app 40 smy
RENINGHELST	10/17/16		Wired rd. Shoot BLISTER and 14TH Bde 00-43 not burst hostile retaliation - Blister was most successful	app 41 app 42 app 43 smy
RENINGHELST	11/17/16		A normal day.	app 44 smy

1875   Wt. W 593/826   1,000,000   4/15   J.B.C. & A.   A.D.S.S./Forms/C. 2118.

Army Form C. 2118

WAR DIARY
or
INTELLIGENCE SUMMARY

(Erase heading not required.)

Instructions regarding War Diaries and Intelligence Summaries are contained in F.S. Regs., Part II. and the Staff Manual respectively. Title Pages will be prepared in manuscript.

Place	Date	Hour	Summary of Events and Information	Remarks and references to Appendices
RENINGHELST	14/10/16		Enemy more active than usual - both with trench mortars & guns	app 45 my.
RENINGHELST	15/10/16		nothing to report.	my
RENINGHELST	16/10/16		much more activity than usual - no trenches were raided by the foe opposite Bois QUARANTE - The enemy probably lost heavily	app 46 app 47 my
RENINGHELST	15/10/16		Enemy more active with retaliation fire - warned by tops to over expend our ammunition allotment if the situation was thought to demand it	app 48 my
RENINGHELST	16/10/16		Issued ont 4139 A A order no 44. Some retaliation otherwise nothing of importance - Duds to Whizbits or hostile T.M.s with strangers instead of nuts, T.M.S	app 49 app 50 my
RENINGHELST	17/10/16		Fired in retaliation - hits of hostile Batteries & active hostile trench mortars were identified	app 51 app 52 app 53 my

1875 Wt. W593/826 1,000,000 4/15 J.B.C. & A. A.D.S.S./Forms/C. 2118.

Army Form C. 2118

WAR DIARY
or
INTELLIGENCE SUMMARY
(Erase heading not required.)

Instructions regarding War Diaries and Intelligence Summaries are contained in F.S. Regs., Part II. and the Staff Manual respectively. Title Pages will be prepared in manuscript.

Place	Date	Hour	Summary of Events and Information	Remarks and references to Appendices
RENINGHELST	18/10/16		A variety of hostile shelling occurred today giving the appearance of speaker activity	app 54 Int'y
RENINGHELST	19/10/16		There was nothing abnormal today	app 55 Int'y
RENINGHELST	20/10/16		Hostile shelling further lack than usual	app 56 Int'y
RENINGHELST	21/10/16		A normal day	app 57 Int'y
RENINGHELST	22/10/16		A wet day	app 58 Int'y app sig 4y
RENINGHELST	23/10/16		A grey day with clouds activity normal	app 60 Int'y
RENINGHELST	24/10/16		The enemy shelled road Sr Eloi group batteries heavily but did no damage	app 61 Int'y

1875 Wt. W593/826 1,000,000 4/15 J.B.C. & A. A.D.S.S./Forms/C. 2118.

WAR DIARY
or
INTELLIGENCE SUMMARY
(Erase heading not required.)

Army Form C. 2118

Place	Date	Hour	Summary of Events and Information	Remarks and references to Appendices
REDOUBT EAST	26/12/15		Carried out operation order no 45	Appx 63 / Appx 64
REDOUBT WEST	26/12/15		A quiet day.	
"	Dec 27th		A quiet day - Shelled enemy M.G. party at British aeroplane at 11.35am	Apx
"	28th		A normal day. Registration carried out on various points - No one with R.R.A. Broutin	Cont
"	29th		A quiet day - weather very bad & no strafing.	Cont
"	30th		A fine day - enemy arty active on St Eloi later. Shots in assistance into Afangier to trenched out successfully.	Cont.
"	31st		A fine day - observation good - were nothing but but but our rear pretty. Carried out no fire 20 mins H.B. "strafes". Hostile retaliation slight. Hostile arty activity normal.	Good.

31/12/16

[signature]
Brig. Gen. Commanding 2nd Battn.

SECRET

41st. DIVISIONAL ARTILLERY

DAILY OPERATION REPORT
from 6 p.m., 2/12/16 to 6 p.m., 3/12/16.

OUR FIRE:-

Time	Battery	Target	Rds	REMARKS
	DIEPENDAAL GROUP:-			
12.20 a.m.	B/190	-	285 BX	41st.D.A.Opera-
			127 BX	tion Order No.39.
12.30 a.m.	A/190	-	251	"
3.30 p.m.	B/190	N.18.c.6.9.	30	Retaliation (T.M.)
12.5 a.m.	"	-	580	41st.D.A.Opera-
				tion Order No.39
" "	C/190	-	900	"
	ST.ELOI GROUP:-			
12.30 a.m.	A/187	-	336	"
11.10 p.m.	"	Working Party O.8.d.2.7	4	Result unobserved
12.30 a.m.	B/187	-	307	41st.D.A.Operation Order No.39.
12.53 &) 12.56 p.m.)	"	Test Rounds	2	
12.0 midn't	C/187	-	529	41st.D.A.Operation Order No.39
5.55 a.m.	"	Test S.O.S.	1	
3.35 p.m.	D/187	RUINED FARM, O.3.c.8.4.	30	
			20	Confirming Registration.
12.30 a.m.	B/189	-	146	41st.D.A.Operation Order No.39.
4.15 p.m.	"	Active T.M., ANDREW.	36	

OUR TRENCH MORTARS:-

Fourteen rounds were fired in retaliation by our X/41 Battery. The enemy opened fire on CABARET LANE with heavy Minenwerfers about 3.15 p.m. We replied two minutes later on his Front Line. The enemy ceased firing about 3.35 p.m., we, about ten minutes later. The Stokes Mortars co-operated.

Casualties - Nil.

ENEMY'S ARTILLERY FIRE

Time	Locality Shelled	Rds.	Nature	Sound or Flash bearing
2.0 p.m.) to 4 p.m.)	Unknown	20	15 c.m. & T.M.	About O.4.a. 4.5.
3.0 p.m.,-) 3.30 p.m.)	N.12.d.	6 - 10 (Hvy.T.M.) Trench) 20 - 30) (Light.TM) Mortars)		-

GENERAL SUMMARY:-

OBSERVATION:-

Visibility poor but better than previous few days.

CASUALTIES:-

        PERSONNEL:-

        N I L.

GUNS OUT OF ACTION:-

    18 pdr.   1   (Spring trouble)

S. Pinney
A.D.C.
BRIGADE MAJOR,
41st. Divisional Artillery.

4.12.16
HHP

SECRET

41st. DIVISIONAL ARTILLERY

DAILY OPERATION REPORT
from 6 p.m., 3.12.16. to 6 p.m., 4.12.16.

OUR FIRE:-

Time	Battery	Target	Rds.	REMARKS
		DIEPENDAAL GROUP:-		
11.30 a.m.	A/190	Active T.M. EDWARD.	100)	
"	C/190	" " "	70)	Very effective
"	D/189	" " "	40)	
2.30 p.m.	A/190	CROONAERT CHAPEL,	60)	
"	C/190	O.7.c.3½.4.	60)	Group shoot
"	D/190	" "	54)	
"	B/190	FRONT LINE TRENCH O.7.c.3½.5½.	20	Registration
		ST. ELOI GROUP:-		
10.15 p.m.	A/187	Enemy's Trench at O.2.d.3.4½.	1	S.O.S. Test
7.10 a.m.	"	Working Party on the WYTSCHAETE - ST.ELOI Road at O.8.a.7½.5.	6	
12.12 p.m.	"	Enemy's Trench at O.2.d.3.4½.	1	S.O.S. Test
9.15 p.m.	B/189	S.O.S. lines covering O.38.	2	" "
12.30 p.m.	"	Strong Point at O.4.a.2½.3½.	12	Checking Registration
3.50 p.m.	"	ROAD from O.4.a. 4.4. to O.3.d.3.1.	12	Group Orders
9.57 p.m.	C/187	S.O.S. lines covering O.26.	1	Test S.O.S.
11.30 a.m.	D/187	Trench Mortars at O.8.a.8.7.	12	Observed by F.O.O.
2.30 to 3.45 p.m.)	"	PICCADILLY FARM, O.8.a.2½.7., and Trenches from O.2. c.4.0.-O.8.a.0.7½.)	61	Registration

OUR TRENCH MORTARS:-

                                          were fired

Thirteen rounds in retaliation by X/41 T.M. Battery. The enemy opened fire on our front line close to the Canal Bank. We immediately replied, and after the tenth. round from our Mortars the enemy ceased firing. This was between 2.45 p.m., and 3.10 p.m.

    The Stokes Mortars co-operated.
    Our Casualties - Nil.

ENEMY'S ARTILLERY FIRE:-

Time	Locality shelled	Rds.	Nature	Sound or Flash bearing
10.a.m.	ROADS, DICKEBUSCH - YPRES, and Trenches from O.7.b.1.8. - O.7.b.5.9.	10	10.5 c.m.	LOUTARGE FARM
10.30 a.m.	H.29.c.5.8.	6		
10.45 "	FRONT LINE TRENCH in O.1.d.	6	T.M.	O.8.a.8.7.
10.50 "	N.12.c.8.0.	12	T.M. EDWARD	EDWARD
2.45 p.m.	O.1.b.5.5.	15	10.5 cm	134° True bearing
3.15 p.m.	TRENCHES in O.3.c. & O.3.d.	10	T.M.	-
3.30 p.m.	Shelling FARM, O.2.b.8.1.	20	7.7 cm	-
3.45 p.m.	SCOTTISH WOOD	40	10.5 cm.	LOUBALGE FARM

GENERAL SUMMARY:-

ENEMY'S NEW WORK:-

A working party was dispersed by our fire at 7.10 a.m., at O.8.a.7½.5.

OBSERVATION:-

Fair.

At 10.50 a.m., EDWARD showed considerable activity, and was observed firing from O.4.c.7½.7½., by one of our F.O.Os. At 11.30 a.m., EDWARD was suppressed by a combined shoot with the Heavy Artillery and our 18 pdrs. and 4.5" Hows. The F.O.O. reported that all the shells fell on or very near EDWARD. Since this shoot EDWARD has shown no activity.

A Hostile T.M. is suspected at O.8.a.8.7.

CASUALTIES:-

PERSONNEL:-

NIL

GUNS OUT OF ACTION:-

18 pdrs.   2

5.12.16.
BHP

BRIGADE MAJOR,
41st. Divisional Artillery.

SECRET

41st. DIVISIONAL ARTILLERY

DAILY OPERATION REPORT
From 6 p.m. 4.12.16 to 6 p.m. 5.12.16

OUR FIRE:-

Time	Battery	Target	Rds.	REMARKS
DIMPENDAAL GROUP:-				
2.15 p.m.	D/190	CROONAERT CHAPEL O.7.c.3½.4.	7 H.E.	Verifying Registration
2.45 p.m.	A/190	T.M.EDWARD	40	X5xxz T.M. Retaliation
"	C/190	"	40	"
"	D/190	"	22 H.E.	"
ST. ELOI GROUP:-				
9.45 p.m.	A/187	Enemy's Trench at O.29	1	S.O.S. Test
10.49 p.m.	B/187		3	"
10.52 "	"			"
10.57 "	"			"
3.0 p.m.	C/187	Enemy Front Line	1	"
4.30 "	"	"	1	"
10.32 "	"	"	1	"
10.46 "	"	"	1	"
12.6.15 a.m.	"	"	2	"
12 noon to)		Hostile Trench		
5.0 p.m.)	"	O.2.c.6.3. to O.2.d.4.6.	21 20	Registration
11 a.m.	D/187	O.8.a.3.8½	20	Confirmation of registration
12.30 p.m.	"	O.3.c.8½.4	24	"
10.30 p.m.	B/189	S.O.S. Lines	3	Test S.O.S.
11.15 p.m.	"	S.O.S. Test	3	"
12 Noon	"	O.4.a.25.35	6	Checking Registration
5.0 p.m.	"	O.10.b.6.5.	4	Group Orders
5.20 "		"	4	"
5.30 "		"	4	"

ENEMY'S ARTILLERY FIRE:-

Time	Locality shelled	Rds.	Nature	Sound or flash bearing
Time Intermittent shelling	H.29.c.5.	10 10.5 cm		
4.0 p.m.	H.35.a.6.0.	5	10.5	
9.30 a.m.	H.35.d.8.8.	10	"	
12 Noon to 1.0 p.m.	-	20	"	

11.0 a.m.	In the vicinity of SCOTTISH WOOD	20	10.5	
2 p.m.to 4 p.m.	Vicinity of H.35.c.1.5.	5	"	T.B.Unknown
9.30 a.m. to 11 a.m.	Vicinity of H.35.b.central	10	Time H.E.	"
	CHICORY LANE	10	7.7 a.m.	

GENERAL SUMMARY:-

CASUALTIES

PERSONNEL:-
N I L

GUNS OUT OF ACTION

18 pdrs. Q.F.   2

Guy Bullock
Staff Capt.

BRIGADE MAJOR,
41st DIVISIONAL ARTILLERY.

6.12.16

SECRET

41st. DIVISIONAL ARTILLERY

DAILY OPERATION REPORT
from 6 p.m., 5.12.16 to 6 p.m., 6.12.16.

OUR FIRE:-

Time	Battery	Target	Rds.	Remarks
DIEPENDAAL Group:-				
10.30 p.m.	A/190	O.7.b.3.3.	8	Enemy working party
1.30 a.m.	B/190	HOSTILE T.M. ZAMBUK	20	T.M. retaliation
" "	C/190	"	20	"
" "	A/189	"	20	"
2.30 p.m.	B/190	N.19.b.3.9.	8	H.E. New work in Enemy Communication Tr.
ST ELOI GROUP:-				
	A/187	Working party at O.8.b.9.3.	6	
5.46 p.m.) 10.41 p.m.) 10.45 p.m.)	B/187	S.O.S.Test - Trench O.36.	3	
10.50 p.m. 10.53 p.m. 1.5 a.m. 3.24 a.m. 1.56 a.m. 1.55 p.m.	C/187	S.O.S.Test	6	
8.40 a.m.	"		6	Retaliation.
11.30 a.m.	D/187	Working Party at O.8.d.8.3.	12	
12.30 p.m.	"	HIELE FARM, O.8.b.9.0.	15	Confirmation of Registration.
9.30 p.m.) 10.0 p.m.) 10.15 p.m.) 12.30 p.m.)	B/189	S.O.S.Lines	4	Test S.O.S.
5.0 p.m.	C/187	Hostile Trenches opposite (O.23 - O.25 Trenches O.25 - O.27.	21) 16)	Registration of new zones.

OUR TRENCH MORTARS:-
X/41 T.M.Battery fired 10 rounds on the top of Enemy's Communication Trench at O.4.a.O.½., with good results, rounds being observed to drop into Trench.
    Casualties - Nil.

ENEMY'S ARTILLERY FIRE:-

Time	Locality shelled	Rds.	Nature	Sound or Flash bearing
10.30 a.m.	VIERSTRAAT	10	10.5 cm	From direction of O.22 central, taken from N.16.b.8½.9.

8:1&xxxxx	I.33.d.0.0.	10	—	—
12 noon.	I.32.c.7.1.	4	10.5	—
12.30 p.m.	Front Trench O.24 (approx)	13	10.5 & 7.7cm	165° Magnetic Sound from N.36 d.6.2.
1.30 a.m.	Fr. Line S.12.d.	—	—	—

GENERAL SUMMARY:-

ENEMY'S NEW WORK

    Communication Trench N.18.b.3.9.

ENEMY'S MOVEMENTS

    Hostile working party at O.7.b.3.3.
    "   "   "   " O.8.b.9.3.
    "   "   "   " O.8.d.8.3.

OBSERVATION:-

    Fairly good from 8.10 a.m.   Wind very strong from N.E.

CASUALTIES:-

PERSONNEL:-

    N I L.

GUNS OUT OF ACTION:-

    18 pdrs Q.F.Gun   2

                                BRIGADE MAJOR,
                         41st. Divisional Artillery.

7.12.16.
HMP

app 38

SECRET

41st. DIVISIONAL ARTILLERY

DAILY OPERATION REPORT
from 6 p.m., 6.12.16 to 6 p.m. 7.12.16.

OUR FIRE:-

Time	Battery	Target	Rds.	REMARKS
DIEPENDAAL GROUP:-				
12 to 12.25 p.m.	A/190	O.13.c.9.7½ to O.14.c.3½.1½. & ONREET FARM, O.14.a.1½.0.	70	Group Shoot
"	B/190	O.13.a.3.6. to O.14.c.7.8. and ONREET FARM, O.14.a.1½.0.	70	" "
12.20" "	C/190	ONREET FARM, O.14.a.1½.0.	20	" "
" "	D/190	"	20	" "
ST. ELOI GROUP:-				
12.30 p.m.	A/187	Enemy Front Line Trench at O.2.d.3½.6.	8	Suspected O.P.
11.55 a.m.	B/187	S.O.S.Lines	1	Test S.O.S.
3.45 p.m.	C/187	"	1	" "
4.45 p.m.	"	"	3	" "
3.15 p.m.	C/187	O.3.c.7.1.	20	Retaliation
3.45 p.m.	D/187	O.8.a.7½.2, CUSTARD.T.M.	20	
12.15 a.m.	B/189	S.O.S.Lines	1	Test S.O.S.
11.0 a.m.	"	"	1	" "
3.30 p.m.	"	"	1	" "

OUR TRENCH MORTARS:-

No shooting was was done by our duty Mortar yesterday.

ENEMY'S ARTILLERY ACTIVITY:-

Time	Locality shelled	Rds.	Nature	Sound or Flash bearing
1.45 p.m.	Front line of Left Battalion	-	T.M.	-
3.30 p.m.	VOORMAOUME, I.31.c.	4	10.5	-

GENERAL SUMMARY:-

ENEMY'S MOVEMENTS

Movements were seen at a suspected O.P., being built in the enemy front line trench at C.2.d.3).6. A periscope is also visible.

OBSERVATION:-

Front line not visible until about 11 a.m. The fog then lifted somewhat and visibility improved, but remained poor all day.

CASUALTIES:-   PERSONNEL:-

NIL.

GUNS OUT OF ACTION:-

18 pdrs.   2

GENERAL:-

Hostile machine guns were more active than usual in consequence of our working parties being out.

BRIGADE MAJOR,
61st.Divisional Artillery.

8.12.16.
HHP

SECRET

41st. DIVISIONAL ARTILLERY

DAILY OPERATION REPORT
from 6 p.m., 7.12.16 to 6 p.m., 8.12.16.

OUR FIRE:-

	Time	Battery	Target	Rounds	Remarks
DIEPENDAAL GROUP	10.30 a.m.	A/189	EVANS FARM	3	)
	12.0 mid-day	"	OSTAVERNE FARM	3	)
	1.0 p.m.	"	ONRERT FARM	3	) Suspected working
	2.0 p.m.	"	RENTY FARM	3	) parties.
	3.0 p.m.	"	LOUVAEGE	3	)
	3.45 p.m.	"	OSTAVERNE	4	)
	3.50 p.m.	"	EVANS FARM	2	)
	4.0 p.m.	A/190	O.7.c.4.5., DANIEL	55	Hostile T.M. (Retaliation)
	4.0 p.m.	B/190	"	60	"
	2.0 p.m.	"	"	20	"
ST.ELOI GROUP	1.36 a.m.	A/187	Enemy's front) line at O.2.d.) 3½.6.)	1	S.O.S.Test
	2.36 a.m.	"	"	1	"
	11.55 a.m.	B/187	S.O.S.Lines	1	"
	6.5 p.m.	"	"	1	"
	9.40 p.m.	C/187	"	1	"
	11.8 p.m.	"	"	1	"
	9.40 p.m.	"	"	1	"
	11.0 a.m.	B/189	"	1	"
	5.0 p.m.	"	"	1	"

OUR TRENCH MORTARS:-

Our "duty" Trench Mortar did not fire, there being no hostile Trench Mortar activity, on their front.

ENEMY'S ARTILLERY FIRE:-

Time	Locality shelled	Rounds	Nature	Sound or Flash bearing
12 noon to 3 p.m.	O.12.	12	10.5 cm	154° Mag. from H.36.a.8.2.
1.30 p.m. to 3.45 p.m.	FRONT LINE TR. (BYRON FARM, N.18.a, N.18.c, & N.24.a.)	-	T.Ms.	-

GENERAL SUMMARY:-

OBSERVATION:-

Very bad. Thick mist prevailed throughout the day.

CASUALTIES:-

    PERSONNEL:-
    NIL.

GUNS OUT OF ACTION:-
    18 pdrs.   2
    4.5" How.(Overhauled) 1

9.12.16.

BRIGADE MAJOR,
41st.Divisional Artillery

S E C R E T

41st. DIVISIONAL ARTILLERY
DAILY OPERATION REPORT
from 6 p.m., 8.12.16 to 6 p.m., 9.12.16.

OUR FIRE:-

Time	Battery	Target	Rounds	Remarks
DIEPENDAAL GROUP:-				
2.0 p.m.	A/190	T.M., DISMAL	70	Retaliation on T.M.
12.0 a.m.	C/190	Smoke rising from Trench at O.13.a.3.7.	4	Effect good. Smoke ceased.
2.0 p.m.	B/190	Hostile T.M.DISMAL	70	Retaliation on T.M.
"	D/190	SNIPER'sp late at O.7.b.4.3.	30	Group Shoot
2.30 p.m.	A/189	T.M.DISMAL	55	Retaliation on T.M.
ST:ELOI GROUP:-				
10.15 a.m.	A/187	O.8.d.9½,7.(DOME HOUSE)	12	Working Party dispersed, two of the enemy believed to have been hit.
12.30 p.m.	"	Registration of front line trench, O.8.a.2.7½.	19	-
8.15 a.m.	B/187	On RUINED FARM, 2x8½x4.	2	-
10.30 a.m.	"	O.3.c.8½.4.	2	-
11.15 a.m.	"	On Support Trenches O.3.d.8.0.	2	-
12.15 p.m.	"	On Trenches- O.4.d.½.3.	2	-
2.40 p.m.	"	On communication trenches - O.4.central.	2	-
3.15 p.m.	"	On Trenches -O.4.c.0.4.	2	-
4.10 p.m.	"	On communication trenches,O.4.c.0.4½.	2	-
11.3 p.m.	C/187	S.O.S.lines	1	Test S.O.S.
8.21½ am	"	do.	2	"
		Front line trench in O.2.c. & O.2.d.	10	Retaliation called for by Group
	"	Front line Trenches, O.2.d.2.7.- O.2.d.3.8½.	15	Testing registration of new zone.
11.0 a.m.	B/189	S. O. S. Lines	1	Test, S.O.S.

OUR TRENCH MORTARS:-

About 2.30 p.m., Y/41 Trench Mortar Battery, opened fire on the enemy's trenches in the BOIS QUARANTE, in retaliation for Fish tail bombs. After firing six rounds, the Infantry requested us to cease firing as the enemy counter retaliation was too strong. Several large Minenwerfers fell within 30 yds of the Mortar.

ENEMY's ARTILLERY FIRE

Time	Locality shelled	Rds.	Nature	Sound or flash bearing
2.0 p.m. 2.30 p.m.	N.11.c.4½.8.	12 rds.	7.7	~~DISMAL~~ ~~90°~~ true ~~North from G.7.~~

1.30 p.m.	O.7.a.3½.1.	14	T.M.L.	Unknown
3.40 p.m.	South of Sunken Road	20	"	"
1.30 p.m.) 3.0 p.m.)	Front line at O.7.a.9.5.	-	"	"
3.30 p.m.	VIERSTRAAT	8	10.5 H.E.	WYTSCHAETE

GENERAL SUMMARY:-

ENEMY's MOVEMENTS

Smoke was observed coming from O.18.a.3.7.

OBSERVATION:-

Possible on front line at 8 a.m., but poor during the morning and improving towards afternoon.

CASUALTIES:-

PERSONNEL:-
NIL

GUNS OUT OF ACTION:-

18 pdr.   1.

BRIGADE MAJOR,
41st. Divisional Artillery.

10:12:16
HHP.

SECRET   Copy No. 2.

DIVISIONAL SHOOT BLISTER

GENERAL ORDER   (1) The following Divisional Shoot will take place on 10th December 1916 - Zero 1.45 p.m.

INTENTION.   (2) Intention is to destroy enemy front line trenches in the given area, as it is suspected he intends to make a raid from that point.

DETAIL OF BATTERIES & TARGET.   (3) Batteries will take part as under:-

       D/190 from 0.7.b.0.0½ - 0.7.b.3.2½.
       A/189   "   0.7.b.3.2½ - 0.7.b.5½.4½.
       D/187   "   0.7.b.5½.4½ - 0.7.b.7.5.

1 18 pdr. Battery to be detailed by Officer Commanding, Diependaal, from 0.7.b.0.0½ - 0.7.c.3½.7½.

1 Belgian Battery to be detailed by Officer Commanding, St. Eloi, from 0.7.b.7.5½ - 0.8.a.3.9.

1 Trench Mortar Battery from 0.7.b.3.3. - 0.7.b.4.3½, detailed by Diependaal Group.

TIME and AMMUNITION   (4) All Howitzers from Zero to 30 after Zero

       40 rounds per Howitzer

6 18 pdrs. from Zero to 30 after Zero

       10 rounds AX per gun

1 Belgian Battery from Zero to 30 after Zero

       100 rounds

1 Trench Mortar Battery 2" from Zero to 30 after Zero

       12 Bombs per Trench Mortar

SPECIAL INSTRUCTIONS FOR 18pdrs & BELGIAN BATTERY   (5) Their fire is intended to cover the Trench Mortars hence it must be fairly evenly distributed at moderately even rate, to keep down F.L.T. observers.

       ACKNOWLEDGE

                                           BRIGADE MAJOR,
                                           41st. Divisional Artillery

9.12.16
HHP

Copy No.1 FILE   Copies   6 - 10 ST. ELOI GROUP
Copy No.2 War Diary   "   11- 15 DIEPENDAAL GROUP
Copy No.3 41st. Division (G)   "   16. D.T.M.O.
Copy No.4 7th. Belgian Regt.
Copy No.5 124th Infantry Brigade

SECRET. 41st. DIVISIONAL ARTILLERY COPY No. 2

OPERATION ORDER No.43 - AMENDMENT (3).

AMENDMENT (2), dated 9-12-16 is cancelled - substitute :-

DATE.   This operation will be carried out on December 10th. 1916.

ZERO HOUR. Zero hour will be 6.p.m.

ACKNOWLEDGE.

Brigade Major,
41st. Divisional Artillery.

Copy No. 1 War Diary.
     2 FILE.
     3. Staff Captain.
     4. 41st. Division 'G'
     5. 41st.   "   'Q'
     6. 122 Inf: B'de.
     7. 123 Inf: B'de.
     8. 124 Inf: B'de.
     9. Xth. Corps H.A.
    10. Xth.   "   R.A.
    11. 47th. D. A.
    12. 16th. D. A.

    13 to) ST.ELOI
    24.)

    25 to) DIEPENDAAL.
    30.)

    31. 7th. Belgian Regt.

SECRET   Copy No. 2

41st. DIVISIONAL ARTILLERY
OPERATION ORDER No. 43 - AMENDMENT (2)

Amendment dated 7.12.16 is cancelled - substitute

DATE. This operation will be carried out on December 11th. 1916.

ZERO HOUR ZERO hour will be 6 p.m.

ACKNOWLEDGE.

BRIGADE MAJOR,
41st. Divisional Artillery.

9.12.16.
HHP

Copy No. 1 War Diary
     2 FILE
     3 Staff Captain
     4 41st. Division (G)
     5 "   "   (Q)
     6 122nd. Infantry Brigade
     7 123rd. Infantry Brigade
     8 124th. Infantry Brigade
     9 Xth. Corps, H.A.
    10 Xth. Corps, R.A.,
    11 47th. D.A.
    12 16th. D.A.,
    13
    24 ST. ELOI GROUP
    25
    30 DIEPENDAAL GROUP
    31 7th. Belgian Regt.
     5 SPARE

SECRET.   41st. DIVISIONAL ARTILLERY OPERATION   Copy No. 2
           ORDER No.43 - AMENDMENT.

DATE.   This operation will be carried out on Decr. 10th. 1916.

ZERO HOUR.   Zero hour will be 6.p.m.

             ACKNOWLEDGE

                                        H Hinton
             7-12-16.   Brigade Major,
                                             41st. Divisional Artillery.

             Copy No. 1   War Diary.
                      2   FILE.
                      3   Staff Captain.
                      4   41st. Divn. 'G'
                      5   41st. "   'Q'
                      6   122 Inf: B'de.
                      7   123 "   "
                      8   124 "   "
                      9   X Corps H.A.
                     10   X Corps R.A.
                     11   47th. D. A.
                     12   16th. D. A.
                     13.
                     24   ST.ELOI GROUP
                     25
                     30   DIEPENDAAL GROUP.
                     31   7th. Belgian Regt.
                      5 spare.

War Diary

SECRET   COPY No. *I*

Ref. Map YTSCHAETE 28 S" 2
1/10,000.

41st DIVISIONAL ARTILLERY OPERATION ORDER NO. 43.

1. **INTENTION**   The 41st D.A. will carry out an M.M.P. shoot on Dec. 8th
   DATE   1916.
   ZERO HOUR.   Zero hour will be notified later.

2. **GENERAL IDEA.**   Howitzers bombard suitable localities on the roads and chief lines of communications of the enemy and thus act as policemen stopping the traffic, with the result that a block and congestion takes place in a fixed area. When this area is full, it is subjected to a rapid Heavy Bombardment.

3. **BOMBARDMENTS.**   Bombardments will be arranged and carried out as follows.

   Those in Appendix A by O.C., St ELOI GROUP.
   Those in Appendix B by O.C., DIEPENDAAL GROUP.

4. **RATES OF FIRE AMMUNITION EXPENDITURE.**   The rates of fire and expenditure of ammunition will be as laid down in Appendices A, B & C.

5. **TIME.**   Watches will be synchronised under 41st D.A. arrangements.

6.   **ACKNOWLEDGE.**

                             Brigade Major
5-12-16.   41st Divisional Artillery.

Copy No. 1   War Diary
" " 2   FILE
" " 3   Staff Captain
" " 4   41st Divsn G
" " 5   " " Q
" " 6   122nd Inf Bde.
" " 7   123rd "
" " 8   124th "
" " 9   10th Corps R.A.
" " 10   " " H.A.
" " 11   47th D.A.
" " 12   19th D.A.
" " 13
" " 14   ST ELOI GROUP
" " 15   DIEPENDAAL GROUP
" "   " " B " Regt.
5 spare

APPENDIX A.

ST ELOI GROUP

GUNS	TASK	PERIOD	Co-ordinates	rds per gun per min	A	AX	BsLG.	EX	TOTAL
(a) 1 4.5"How	Bombard road	1 hr before Z to Z	O.9.c.9.0½	⅓				20	20 *
(b) 1 4.5"How	Bombard road junction.	- do -	O.10.b.6.5.	⅓				20	20 *
(c) 1 4.5"	Bombard tramline	- do -	O.10.b.5.5.	⅓				20	20 *
(d) 18 18-prs	Bombard tramline	Z to 1'30" after Z	O.11.a.8½.5½ - O.9.d.3.4	6	32	130			162
(e) 8 75 mm	Bombard road	- do -	O.15.a.3½.1 - O.15.b.6.8	6			72		72
(f) 4 75 mm	Bombard road	- do -	O.15.a.3½.1 - O.9.d.3.4.	6			36		36
(g) 6 4.5 Hows	Bombard OOSTAVERNE	Z to 10' after Z	O.21.b.6.7	1½				90	90
(h) 6 4.5 Hows	Bombard GOUDZAUWE FARM.	2 hrs after Z to 2 hrs 5' after Z	O.15.b.0.3½	2				60	60
(i) 18 18-prs	Bombard tramline	2 hrs after Z to 2 hrs 1'30" after Z.	O.11.a.8½.5' - O.9.d.3.4	6	32	130			162
(j) 8 75 mm	Bombard road	- do -	O.15.a.3½.1 - O.15.b.6.8.	6			72		72
(k) 4 75 mm	Bombard road	- do -	O.15.a.3½.1 - O.9.d.3.4	6			36		36

* Irregular intervals between rounds but never more than 4'30" between rounds.

NOTE. 18-pr and 75 mm batteries will divide their portions of their road or tramline as evenly as possible between the guns so that each gun can quickly cover the whole of its target and thus a long and continuous line of road or tramline can all be engaged at the same time.

APPENDIX B

Guns	Task	PERIOD	Co-ordinates	rds per gun per min	A.	AX.	EX.	TOTAL
(a) 1 4.5"How	Bombard road	1 hour before Z to Z	0.14.c.4.2½	⅓			20	20 *
(b) 1 4.5"How	Bombard road & tramline	- do -	0.15.a.0.5.	⅓			20	20 *
(c) 14 18-prs	Bombard Road	Z to 1'30" after Z	0.19.b.8½.4 - 0.15.a.3½.1	6	25	101		126
(d) 4 18-prs	- do -	- do -	0.20.a.3.9 - 0.20.c.2.8	6	8	28		36
(e) 6 4.5 Hows	Bombard OOSTAVAERNE	Z to 10' after Z	0.21.b.6.7.	1½			90	90
(f) 6 4.5 Hows	Bombard EVANS FM.	2 hrs after Z to 2 hrs 5' after Z	0.14.b.3.2.	2			60	60
(g) 14 18-prs	Bombard road	2 hrs after Z to 2 hrs 1'30" after Z.	0.19.b.8½.4 to 0.15.a.3½.1	6	25	101		126
(h) 4 18-prs	- do -	- do -	0.20.a.3.9 - 0.20.c.2.8.	6	8	28		36
					66	258	190	514

* Irregular intervals between rounds, but never more than 4' 30" between rounds.

NOTE. 18-pr Batteries will divide their portions of their road or tramline as equally as possible between the guns so that each gun can cover the whole of its target and thus a long and continuous line of road or tramline can all be engaged at the same time.

APPENDIX C

TOTAL AMMUNITION EXPENDITURE.

	A	AX	BX	BELG	TOTAL
From Appendix A	64	260	210	216	750
From Appendix B	66	258		190	514
GRAND TOTAL	130	518	210	406	1264

SECRET

41st. DIVISIONAL ARTILLERY

DAILY OPERATION REPORT
from 6 p.m., 9.12.16 to 6 p.m. 10.12.16.

OUR FIRE:-

Time	Battery	Target	Rds.	REMARKS
DIEPENDAAL GROUP:-				
1.45 p.m.	A/190	$0.7.b.0.0\frac{1}{2}$. $0.7.c.3\frac{1}{2}.7\frac{1}{2}$.	60	Div: Shoot "BLISTER"
"	D/190	$0.7.b.0.0\frac{1}{2}$. $0.7.b.3.2\frac{1}{2}$.	40	"
3.15 p.m.	"	HOSTILE T.M. DRAKE, $0.7.d.7.3$.	20	Retaliation
11.30 a.m.	A/189	Hostile T.M. DISMAL, $0.7.c.7.7$.	20	)
12.5 p.m.	"	Hostile T.M. DONKEY, $0.7.c.4\frac{1}{2}.8\frac{1}{2}$.	20	) "
11.45 p.m	"	$0.7.c.3\frac{1}{2}.5$.	20	Registration
3.50 p.m.	"	$0.7.b.9\frac{3}{4}.8\frac{3}{4}$, Hostile T.M. DAPHNE	30	Retaliation.
1.45 p.m.	"	$0.7.b.3.2\frac{1}{2}. -5\frac{1}{2}.4\frac{1}{2}$	133	Div. Shoot "BLISTER"
ST ELOI GROUP:-				
	B/187	-	9	Registration
12 noon	C/187	$0.2.c.9\frac{1}{2}.6$	14	"
3.20 p.m.	"	Front Line Trenches over 023 & 024	20	Retaliation called for by Inf.
4.15 p.m.	"	Do.	14	Retaliation called for by Group
1.45 p.m.	D/187	$0.7.b.5\frac{1}{2}.4\frac{1}{2}.- 0.7.b.7.5$.	163	Div; Shoot "BLISTER"
12 Noon	"	-	22	Registration
2.30 p.m.	"	-	16	"
4.0 p.m.	"	PICCADILLY FARM	12	
8.15 p.m.	"	-do-	30	
	D/190	$0.7.c.4.5$.	20	Retaliation for T.Ms on our front line

OUR TRENCH MORTARS:-

At 1.45 p.m., Y/41, opened in accordance with Shoot "BLISTER" from $0.7,a.7.8$. on enemy's front line between $0.7.b.3.3$. and $0.7.b.4.3\frac{1}{2}$. The result appeared to be very good the enemy's front line being breached in several places.

The enemy's retaliation was heavy for first five minutes, but after our Artillery got going it died away to practically nothing. Casualties Nil.

At 3.30 p.m., the enemy started to bombard our front line in O.1.d. Our "duty" Trench Mortar Battery, Z/41, immediately retaliated and after the tenth round the enemy Trench Mortars ceased firing.

ENEMY'S ARTILLERY FIRE:-

Time	Locality Shelled	Rds.	Nature	Sound or Flash bearing
9.30 a.m.	F.L.T. N.12.d.1.3.	5	L.T.M.	Unknown
11.30 a.m.	VIERSTRAAT	10	10.5	WYTSCHAETE
1.20 p.m.	"	6	"	(S.B.True 119° from N.16.b.9.8.
1.50 p.m.	F.L.T. N.12.d.	10	L.T.M. & 7.7.	) Flash seen) in Wood about) O.10.d.
2.0 p.m.	VOORMEZEELE	10	10.5	154½° True Bearing from H.36.d.6.2.
3.0 p.m. to 4.0 p.m.	Front Line -O2C & D.	Bombardment intense	"	154½° & 148° true bearing from H.36.d.6.2.
3.15 p.m. to 4.15 p.m.	Front Line & support	75	15.0cm.	
3.4.30 p.m.	F.L.T.,N.12.2 - N.12- 5	20	LTM	-
3.25 p.m.	VIERSTRAAT	13	10.5 cm	-
3 to 5 p.m.	BUS HOUSE & vicinity	40	-	-

GENERAL SUMMARY

OBSERVATION:-

A screen has been put up along DAMSTRASSE ROAD from DOME HOUSE.

Fair all day.

CASUALTIES:-

PERSONNEL:-

N I L.

GUNS OUT OF ACTION

18 pdrs.   3

J. A. Fordham
/o BRIGADE MAJOR,
41st. Divisional Artillery.

11.12.16.
HHP

SECRET

app 44

41st. DIVISIONAL ARTILLERY

DAILY OPERATION REPORT
from 6 p.m., 11.12.16 to 6 p.m. 12.12.16.

OUR FIRE:-

Time	Battery	Target	Rds	Remarks
	DIKKEBUSCH GROUP:-			
3 p.m.	B/190	N.(8.b.9.2.)		Suspected working
		O.14.d.3.1.)	9	parties.
		O.8.d.6.0.)		
4 p.m.	D/190	MARTENS FARM		
		O.8.d.7.0.	5	"
	"	ZERO HOUSE		
		O.14.a.6.6½.	5	"
12.30 p.m.	A/189	LOUBARGE FM.		
		O.7.c.8.3½.	3	"
1.45 p.m.	"	EVANS FARM,		
		O.14.b.3.2.	3	"
3.0 p.m.	"	OOSTAVERNE xx.		
		CROSS ROADS,		
		O.21.b.5⅜.7⅛.	3	"
4.30 p.m.	"	T.M.DAPHNE.	30	Retaliation.
	ST.ELOI GROUP:-			
2.30 p.m.	B/187	Checking regis-		
		tration.	12	
9.47 a.m.	B/187	S.O.S.Lines	1	Test S.O.S.
12.30 p.m.	"	Suspected M.G.	10	
		emplacement,		
		O.2.c.8½.3.		
6.15 p.m.	D/187	T.M.("BERTIE")	25	
		at O.3.c.8.4.		
7.45 p.m.	D/190	"	40	

OUR TRENCH MORTARS:-

Our duty trench mortar battery did not fire.

ENEMY'S ARTILLERY FIRE:-

Time	Locality shelled	Rds.	Nature	Sound or flash bearing
6.25pm.	O.3.c.6.8.	10	7.7cm	
7.30p.m	(F.L.T.)			

GENERAL SUMMARY:-

OBSERVATION:-
　　Very poor.

CASUALTIES:-
　　　　　　　　　　　PERSONNEL:-
　　　　　　　　　　　　NIL.

GUNS OUT OF ACTION:-

　　18 pdrs.　　　　　　3 guns.

　　　　　　　　　　　　　　　S. Plumer
　　　　　　　　　　　　　　　　B.M.
　　　　　　　　　　　　BRIGADE MAJOR,
13.12.16.　　　　　41st. Divisional Artillery.
BMP.

SECRET

41st. DIVISIONAL ARTILLERY

DAILY OPERATION REPORT
from 6 p.m., 12.12.16 to 13/12/16 6 p.m.

OUR FIRE:-

	Time	Battery	Target	Rds.	Remarks
EPENDAAL OUP	5 p.m.	A/190	Communication Trs: from C.7.Central to LOUWAEGE FARM	34	Retaliation to 7.7 c.m.
	11.30 a.m.	C/190	O.13.a.2½.6.	6	Smoke rising Affect good.
	3.0 p.m.	D/190	N.18.b.7.5., T.M. FUNK	20	Retaliation
	11.45 a.m.	A/189	T.M.DOUGLAS,O.7.b. 6¼.4¾.	20	"
			T.M.DEVIL,O.7.b.5½. 4½.	20	"
	12.30 p.m.		O.13.a.4.8.	7	Registration
T.ELOI ROUP	3.1 a.m.	A/187	Front Line Trench.	1.	S.O.S.Test
	8.35 p.m.	B/187	S.O.S.Lines	2	"
	5.0 p.m.	"	CROSS ROADS, O.10. b.5¼.5¼.	18	
	1.20 p.m.	C/187	O.2.d.4½.0.	2	2 Rounds fired on dead ground
	1.30 p.m.	"	O.2.c.9.6½.	5	
	3.20 to 4.0 p.m.	D/187	T.M.ALBERT,O.4.c. 0½.7.	20	
	2.30 p.m.	D/189	WIGWAM FARM,O.9.b. 9.6.	9	Registration

OUR TRENCH MORTARS:-

At 11.15 a.m., the enemy fired two Rum Jars on to our front line trench. The duty gun of "Y" Battery immediately retaliated by firing 5 rounds, after which the gun had to be abandoned as the enemy got two direct hits with Fish tail bombs on the emplacement, and five others within a few yards of it. No other gun in this battery could be got into action to carry on the retaliation, as the enemy were by this time firing all along our front line in N.12.d., and N.7.a., and c., with fish tail bombs, rum jars and H.T.Ms.

Our 4.5" Hows. and the Heavy Artillery also retaliated, and the enemy stopped firing at 12 mid-day

ENEMY'S ARTILLERY FIRE

Time	Locality shelled	Rds.	Nature	Sound or flash bearing
10.0 a.m.	VIERSTRAAT	6	7.7.	97° T. from N.16.b.9½.8½.
10.5 to 10.20 a.m.	WOOD, H.29.d.5.1.	12	"	-
7.30 a.m.	O.41 TRENCH	1	"	Fuze picked up from one of these shells set at 42½.
7.35 a.m.	ESTAMINET LANE, O.3.b.7.5½.	6	"	
3.30 p.m.	-do-	2	"	
7.30 a.m.	-do-	3	Minenwerfers.	-
1.10 p.m. to 3.15 p.m.	SPOIL BANK & behind ,I.33.c.6.6.	6	7.7.	84° T.Bearing from I.33.c.7½.8½
3.30 p.m.	I.33.d.0.7.	1	"	
9.45	VIERSTRAAT	10	4.5. How. H.E.	-
12 noon	"	4	"	-
11-12 a.m.	N.125 to N.122	Very active T.Ms.		-

GENERAL SUMMARY:-

OBSERVATION:-

Fair

ENEMY'S MOVEMENTS:-

Smoke was observed at O.13.a.2½.6 (approx)

ENEMY AIRCRAFT ACTIVITY:-

Enemy A.A.Guns were busy firing at our Aeroplanes. One Hostile A.A.Guns was observed firing T.B.122° from H.35.b.5.6½.

CASUALTIES:-

PERSONNEL:- NIL.

GENERAL:-

A large white smoke cloud, possibly an ammunition dump ablaze, was seen near HEILE FARM, O.8.d.9.9., at 11.30 a.m. None of our guns were active at the time.

GUNS OUT OF ACTION:-

| 18 pdrs. | 2 |
| 4.5" Hows. | 1 |

BRIGADE MAJOR,
41st.Divisional Artillery.

14.12.16.
HHP

SECRET

App 46

41st. DIVISIONAL ARTILLERY

DAILY OPERATION
REPORT from 6 p.m., 13.12.16. to 6 p.m.,
14.12.16.

OUR FIRE:-

Time	Battery	Target	Rds.	Remarks
DIEPENDAAL GROUP:-				
11.30 am.	A/190	T.M.DESMOND	20	Retaliation
12 - 12.30	"	Checking registrations	17	"
3.40 pm.	"	T.M.DAVID	20	"
Noon	B/190	Hostile T.M. at 0.7.c.6½.9½.		"
12.30	"	0.13.a.35.75) 0.7.d.32.10.)	32	Registration
1 - 1.30	C/190	Sunken Road at 0.13.a.4.2	130	
	"	T.M.DAVID	30	Retaliation
	"	" DESMOND	30	"
1 p.m.	D/190	0.13.a.6.2½.- 0.15.c.7.9½.	20	" (Good effect)
2.45 p.m.	"	GRAND BOIS,0.13. a.4.8.	5	Registration
3.50 p.m.	"	CROSS ROADS, 0. 15.a.3.1.	20	Retaliation
4.15 p.m.	A/189	T.M.DOUGLAS	30	"
10.a.m.	"	T.M.FOOL	30	"
10.30 a.m.	"	T.M.DAPHNE	20	"
11.45 a.m.	"	T.M.DESMOND	15	"
1 p.m.	"	T.M.FOOL	40	"
2.55 p.m.	"	0.13.a.4.4. 0.13.c.3.9.	20	Retaliation
3.40 p.m.	"	T.M.DAVID	15	"
ST.ELOI GROUP:-				
11.5 p.m.	A/187	F.L.T.	1	S.O.S.Test
1.2 a.m.	"	"	1	"
9.45 p.m.	"	0.8.d.8½.5.	20	Working Party
9.10 a.m.	B/187	S.O.S.Lines	1	S.O.S.Test
9.59 a.m.	"	"	1	"
11.25 p.m.	"	"	1	"
12.50 to 1.30pm.	C/187	0.8.a.9½.9½.& Vicinity	20	Working parties suspected.
	D/187	T.M.COOT	6	
4.30 p.m.	B/189	0.3.c.8.4.T.M. BERTIE	12	Group Order
11.12 a.m.	"	WIGWAM HOUSE,0. 9.b.9.6.	49	Registration
10.30 a.m.	D/190	S.O.S.Lines	1	S.O.S.Test
11.0 a.m.	"	MARTENS FM.0.8. a.5½.0.	20	Group Order
2.30 p.m.	"	HEILE FARM,0.8. d.9.9½.	10	"
1.30 p.m.	"	T.M.COOT	6	"

OUR TRENCH MORTARS:-

At 4.15 p.m., the enemy fired 1 Minenwerfer on to ESTAMINET LANE at about O.3.b.5.5. Our "duty" gun of "X" Battery immediately fired 10 rounds on top of Enemy Communication Trench at O.4.a.0.0½. No further rounds were fired by the enemy.

ENEMY'S ARTILLERY FIRE:-

Time	Locality shelled	Rds.	Nature	Sound or Flash bearing
9.30-9.45	VIERSTRAAT	10	10.5	Unknown
11.15 a.m.	"	2	"	"
12.15 p.m.	"	6	7.7	"
3.15 p.m.	"	6	10.5	"
9.45 a.m.	N.12.b.)	5	L.T.M.	"
10.45 a.m.	")			
9.40 a.m.	CARRE FARM	10	H.T.M.	"
3.15 p.m.	VIERSTRAAT	1 per min for 40 mins	10.5 10.5	Behind GRAND BOIS (O.14) WYTSCHAETE
1.20 p.m.	CONVENT LANE & BUS HOUSE, O.2.a.4.7.	16	7.7mm	
10.5 to 10.25 a.m.	I. 31. c.	12	10.5	About 162° T.B. at I.31.c.3½.1.
1.10 p.m. to 1.30 p.m.	"	12	"	"
1.15 p.m.	TRENCHES	25	T.Ms	?
3.15 p.m.	Right Sector	20	10.5	?
3.45 p.m.	H-18.a.	2	7.7	?
9.0 a.m. till 10.45 a.m.	Ridge of North Canal Bank I.33.d.	1 H.E. every 5 mins.	7.7.	110° from I.33.c.7.9.
4.0 till 4.40 pm	I.33.d.0.3.	20	"	125° SB " "

GENERAL SUMMARY:-

OBSERVATION:-

Light good for observation at moderate ranges.

Smoke was seen coming from Hostile Trench in the vicinity of O.9b.3.7.

ENEMY AIRCRAFT ACTIVITY:-

NORMAL

CASUALTIES:-

PERSONNEL:- NIL

GUNS OUT OF ACTION

18 pdrs. 3
4.5" Hows. 1

S. Phillips
BRIGADE MAJOR,
41st. Divisional Artillery.

15.12.16.
HHP

App 47.

9.18 p.m.	ST. ELOI informed me heavy firing on their front. Signal Officer called in had just received message from Infantry Brigade Major that it was on DIEPENDAAL Sector. All guns were firing slowly on their S.O.S. lines.
9.19 p.m.	Warned 10th.Corps R.A., that a raid was likely on our front and asked them to stand by.
9.20 p.m.	DIEPENDAAL reported that they had three Batteries firing on their S.O.S.lines and had received an S.O.S.call from the Right Battalion.
9.21 p.m.	10th.Corps, R.A., asked to fire slowly on S.O.S.lines.
9.22 p.m.	Informed DIEPENDAAL, who reported that they were firing slowly on their S.O.S.Lines.
9.25 p.m.	Informed 41st.Division "G" of situation as we knew it, and what we were doing.
9.26 p.m.	Informed ST.ELOI of situation
9.27 p.m.	DIEPENDAAL reported chief fire was on N.12.4 and N.12.5.
9.28 p.m.	Turned one Belgian Battery on to CROONAERT CHAPEL, O.7.c.1.0. Rate of fire 1 round per gun per minute.
9.32 p.m.	Informed 47th.D.A. of situation.
9.33 p.m.	No.2 Belgian Battery ordered on to Double Area - 1 round per gun per minute.
9.34½ p.m.	Informed 16th. D.A. of situation.
9.37 p.m.	Informed 41st.Division "G" of situation
9.40 p.m.	Informed by DIEPENDAAL GROUP S.O.S. received from Left Battalion
9.42 p.m.	Belgian Battery double rate of fire from CROONAERT CHAPEL at O.7.c. O.1.
9.45 p.m.	Informed 10th. Corps R.A., of situation.
9.47 p.m.	Informed 10th.Corps R.A., of situation
9.48 p.m.	Stopped ST.ELOI GROUP
9.49 p.m.	Informed of raid opposite Right Company of Left Battalion DIEPENDAAL (vide other sheet)
9.51 p.m.	ST.ELOI. co-operate II .
9.52 p.m.	2nd.Belgian Battery 4 rounds per per minute.

9.49 p.m.	DIEPENDAAL informed me that trenches from C..7.1. - 0.7.8. had been raided, and that they had speeded up their fire throughout front though 4 minutes before they had been asked by Infantry to slacken fire.
9.55 p.m.	Co-operate II was firing.
9.56 p.m.	Speed up your S.O.S. DIEPENDAAL (10th.Corps R.A.)
10.1 p.m.	Talked to X Corps Brigade Major, said it was not time for hard and fast rules, although co-operate II was firing.
10.4 p.m.	Rang up 18th.D.A.
10.4½ p.m.	Engaged ring when they get them
10.6½ p.m.	Again rang up 18th.D.A.
10.8½ p.m.	Ammunition Park rang up. Told to get off line
10.9 p.m.	Rang up 18th.D.A. "Priority"
10.12½ p.m.	Got 18th.D.A. HELP RABBIT - 18th. D.A. did not answer until 10.14⅜ p.m.
10.15½ p.m.	Rang up DIEPENDAAL.
10.16 p.m.	Anything further to report - Left Battalion know nothing - Company raidedwires gone - Left Company of Left Battalion say things are quiet, asked to slacken fire. Right reported O.K. Right Battalion asked to slacken fire
10.18 p.m.	Rang up "O".
10.18½ p.m.	Talked to "G.S.O.1." till 10.21 p.m.
10.22 p.m.	10th.Corps, R.A., rang up.
10.23 p.m.	10th.Corps R.A., asked to slacken fire to about half - and stop 12"
10.24 p.m.	10th.Corps R.A., rang up. Situation explained. Rang off 10.26 p.m.
10.27 p.m.	Rang up ST.ELOI.
10.28 p.m.	Rang ST.ELOI again.
10.28½ p.m.	Talked to Colonel of ST.ELOI. Slacken off Belgian Batteries to 1 round per gun per two minutes. Situation explained to Colonel. Rang off 10.30 p.m.
10.28½ p.m.	DIEPENDAAL rang up. Reports Left of Right Battalion O.K. Infantry Brigade Major said things were quietening. Left Battalion rang up and asked them to slacken rate of fire, but still keep up a slow rate. Left Battalion 1 round per gun per two minutes. Right Battalion stopped. Infantry Brigade Major reports T.Ms. on left are still active.
10.34½ p.m.	Rang up 10th.Corps R.A.
10.35½ p.m.	Told 10th.Corps R.A., to drop fire to 1 round per gun per 4 minutes.

10.36 p.m.	Rang up ST. ELOI.
10.37 p.m.	Told ST. ELOI to slacken fire to one rd. per gun per 4 minutes.
10.38 p.m.	Rang up Xth. Corps H.A.
10.38½ p.m.	Told Xth. Corps H.A. to slacken ½. Told situation. Asked if they might stop as soon as possible.
10.40 p.m.	Rang up "G".
10.41 p.m.	Talked to "G.S.O.I". Asked if Heavies might stop - Told to stop liaison Barrage, on N.L.S. DIEPENDAAL to fire on T.M's with Hows: Heavies to stop. - Everybody to stand by.
10.45½ p.m.	DIEPENDAAL rang up and said Lt. Bn. report enemy ejected (unofficial). Told to stand by.
10.47 p.m.	Told Xth. Corps H.A. to stop firing but to stand by.
10.47½ p.m.	Rang up ST. ELOI.
10.48 p.m.	ST. ELOI - stop firing, stand by.
10.48¼ p.m.	16th. D.A. Rang up.
10.48½ p.m.	60 pr. reported 'Stand by'.
10.49 p.m.	Rang up 16th. D.A. again.
10.50 p.m.	16th. D.A. 'Stop firing' - 'Stand by'.
10.54 p.m.	Lt. Btn. 'O.K', asked 'Stop firing'. Everything quiet.
10.54¾ p.m.	Rang up 'G'.
10.55 p.m.	Talked to G.S.O.1 situation explained - everyone stand by.
10.45 p.m.	Germans reported out of our trenches - confirmed.
10.50 p.m. 10.56 p.m.	Rang up DIEPENDAAL.
10.57 p.m.	DIEPENDAAL 'stop firing' - 'stand by'.
11.36 p.m.	DIEPENDAAL reported trenches knocked about. Not many casualties.
11.37 p.m.	Spoke to G.S.O.1. can batteries get out ordinary S.O.S. Lines.
11.38 p.m.	Xth Corps H.A.
11.40 p.m.	Resumed normal conditions. Xth Corps H.A.
11.42 p.m.	Resume normal conditions 16th D.A.
11.43½ p.m.	Resume normal conditions ST. ELOI, DIEPENDAAL.
12.15 a.m. (about)	Informed by DIEPENDAAL that our casualties on right of Left Battalion were small - 4 killed, 6 wounded.

SECRET

41st. DIVISIONAL ARTILLERY

DAILY OPERATION REPORT
from 6 p.m., 14.12.16 to 6 p.m., 15.12.16.

OUR FIRE:-

	Time	Battery	Target	Rds.	REMARKS
DIEPENDAAL GROUP:-	9.10 p.m. to midnight	A/190	SCHEME H - S.O.S. (Right Company of Left Battalion)	852	Retaliation Scheme "H" fired twice. S.O.S all guns 9.26 p.m.
		B/190	S.O.S.(Left Company of Right Battalion.	380	9.15 p.m
		C/190	S.O.S.(Right Company of Right Battalion)	298	9.13 p.m
		A/189	S.O.S.Lines	80	
	9.10 a.m.	A/190	O.12.d.9.1.	8	T.M.Retaliation
	9.55 a.m.	"	O.13.a.3.5."EAGLE"	20	"
		C/190	" "	20	"
		A/189	" "	15	"
	8.30 a.m.	B/190		4	To keep down M.G. fire
	12.30 p.m.	"	N.18.b.7.8.	13	New work
	4.30 p.m.	"		4	Retaliation
	5. 0 p.m.	"	PLATEAU FARM, N.18.b.3½.6.	30	"
ST.ELOI GROUP:-	8.45 p.m.	A/187	Front Line Trenches O.7.Central - O.7.b.6.5.	222	Group Order
	6.30 a.m.	"	Front Line Trench	1	S.O.S.Test
	2.36 a.m.	B/187	S.O.S.Lines	1	"
	9.5 p.m.	C/187	"	28	Slow rate of fire.Group Order
	10.15 p.m.	D/187	"CO-OPERATE 2"	60	Group Order
	8.45 a.m.	"	T.M."ANDREW" & Registration.	86	" "
	11.0 a.m.	D/190	ESTAMINET, O.9.c.3½.3, DOME HOUSE, O.8.d.9½.7, PICCADILLY FARM, O.8.a.2½.8, and suspected Battalion Headquarters at O.9.a.O.5½.	36	

OUR TRENCH MORTARS:-

At 9 p.m., 14.12.16, the enemy vigorously bombarded on the right of Z/41 Sector, and, as the Battery Commander was uncertain whether any of the fire was directed against his front, he opened fire with his "Duty" Gun, expending 4 rounds.

On being assured by an Officer of the Durham Light Infantry that nothing was falling in his sector, he ordered the

"Duty" gun to cease firing.

Up to 6 p.m., 15.12.16, no hostile Trench Mortars lamded on our front, and the "Duty" guns did not fire.

ENEMY'S ARTILLERY ACTIVITY:-

Time	Locality Shelled	Rds.	Nature	Sound or Flash bearing
9.30 a.m. " ")	O.13.a.3.5.	Few	T.M.	
12.30 to 1.15pm 3.30 to 4 p.m.)	VIERSTRAAT	15	10.5	From direction of WYTSCHAETE taken from N.16.b.8.9.
10.15 a.m.	Right of our Front (very heavy)	-	-	
11.0 a.m.	H.29.d.8.7.	6	10.5	
9 p.m. - 11p.m.	I.33.c.O.3 near ARUNDEL HOUSE	-	7.7.	125°T.B.from I.33.c.7.9.
7.20 a.m. - 10.0 a.m.	I.33.d.1.9. to I.34.c.4.2.	-	7.7 & 10.5	133°T.B. from I.33. c.7.9.
3.15 p.m. - 4.30 p.m.	) Trench Mortar Activity) about BOIS QUERENTI &) GRAND BOIS.	-	T.M.	
9.0 p.m.- 11.0 p.m.	O.2.Central		All calibres of TM.	-
6.30 a.m.- 10.0 a.m.	) Our Trenches on either) side of Canal I.34.c. and O.4.a. Heavy Bombardment.	-	T.M.	-

GENERAL SUMMARY:-

ENEMYSNEW WORK:-

New work was observed at N.18.b.7.8.

OBSERVATION:-

Poor.

A Battalion Headquarters is suspected at. O.9.a.0.5½., and was registered by one of our batteries.

CASUALTIES:-

PERSONNEL:-

N I L

GUNS OUT OF ACTION

  18 pdrs.   3
  4.5" Hows   2

              BRIGADE MAJOR,
16.12.16.   41st.Divisional Artillery.

SECRET   R.A. X Corps No.17/2.

R A War Diary.
———————————

1. Reference O.O.12, appendix A. In the objective for
two 4.5" How. Batteries 47th Division for "I.35.a.60.85. to
I.29.c.93.26." read "I.29.d.10.45. to 37. to 45.55."

2. Watches will be synchronized from this office at
11 a.m.

3. Zero hour for Appendix A will be at 3.30 p.m.
           ,,   B   ,,   1 p.m.

4. ACKNOWLEDGE.

                            [signature] Lt Col
                               Major, R.A.
15-12-16.   Staff Officer, R.A. X Corps.

SECRET.   41st. DIVISIONAL ARTILLERY.   Copy No. 2

                OPERATION ORDER No. 44.   Reference Map 1/10,000.

INTENTION.   1.   A bombardment of the enemy's front line system will take place to-morrow December 16th. by Heavy Artillery, 4.5" Howitzers and Trench Mortars.

2.   The neighbourhood of HILL 60 will be bombarded.

3.   The trenches East of the BLUFF will be bombarded.

4.   Tasks are allotted and will be arranged and carried out as follows:-

By O.C. ST.ELOI Group.

    (a) 2   4.5" Hows. from 0.4.a.20.35 to 0.4.a.27.38.

    (b) 2   4.5" Hows. from 0.4.a.27.38 to 0.4.a.40.44.

    (c) 1   Medium Trench Mortar Bty from 0.4.a.0.1 to 0.4.a.1.2.

By O.C. DIEPENDAAL Group.

    (d) 4   4.5" Hows. from 0.4.a.40.44 to 0.4.a.55.50.

AMMUNITION.   5.   Special ammunition allotment is as follows:-

    For (a) 50 rds. BX   For (b) 50 rds. BX
    For (d) 100 rds. BX   (c) will fire 40 rds.

ZERO HOUR.   6.   Zero hour will be notified later. Watches will be synchronised with this office at 9.a.m. 16-12-16.

7.   ACKNO:LEDGE.

Issued at   Brigade Major,
12 15-12-16.   41st. Divisional Artillery.

Copy No. 1 War Diary.
       2   File.
       3. 41st. Division 'G'
       4. Staff Capt.47th.D.A.
       5. 16th. D.A.
       6. Staff Capt.41st.D.A.
       7. Xth.Corps H.A.
       8. Xth. Corps R.A.
       9. Commdt. Belgian Group.
      10. 7th. Belgian Regt.
    11 - 15. Diependaal Group.
    16 - 20. St. Eloi Group.
      21. D.T.M.O.

Copy No. 2

S E C R E T

41st DIVISIONAL ARTILLERY OPERATION ORDER NO.44.

AMENDMENT.

Reference to Operation Order No.44.

The duration of Bombardment will be 15 minutes.

The rate of fire as rapid as ammunition will allow.

ACKNOWLEDGE.

Brigade Major,
41st Divisional Artillery.

15.12.16.

Copy No. 1 War Diary.
         2 File.
         3 41st Division G.
         4 Staff Captain 47th D.A.
         5 56th D.A.
         6 Staff Captain 41st D.A.
         7 X Corps H.A.
         8 Xth Corps R.A.
         9 Commandant Belgian Group.
        10 7th Belgian Regt.
    11 -15 DIEPENDAAL Group.
    16 -20 ST ELOI Group.
        21 D.T.M.O.

S E C R E T.   Copy No. 2

Reference O.O.No. 44 of 15.12.16.

1. Zero hour will be at 1 p.m.
2. Watches will be synchronized from this office at 11.15 a.m.
3. ACKNOWLEDGE.

Sd Porahawk
Brigade Major,
41st Divisional Artillery.

16.12.16.

Copy No. 1 War Diary.
      2. File.
      3 41st Division G.
      4 Staff Captain 47th D.A.
      5 16th D.A.
      6 Staff Captain 41st D.A.
      7 Xth Corps H.A.
      8 Xth Corps H.A.
      9 Commandant Belgian Group.
    10 7th Belgian Regt.
11 -15 Diependaal Group.
16 -20 St.Eloi Group.
    21 D.T.M.O.

SECRET   Copy No. 1

XTH CORPS ARTILLERY OPERATION ORDER No. 12.

15th December, 1916.

Reference Sheets 1/10,000 WYTSCHAETE and ZILLEBEKE.

1. A bombardment of the enemy's front system will take place tomorrow December 16th.

2. The neighbourhood of HILL 60 will be bombarded in accordance with Appendix A.

3. The trenches East of the BLUFF will be bombarded in accordance with Appendix B.

4. Zero hours will be notified later.

5. Trench Mortars will assist under Divisional arrangements.

6. Acknowledge.

Major, R.A.

Issued at   Staff Officer, R.A. X Corps.

1. R.A. 41st Division.
2. R.A. 47th Division.
3. Lowe's Group R.A.
4. Heavy Arty. X Corps.
5. 23rd Division.
6. 41st Division.
7. 47th Division.
8. X Corps "G".
9. X Corps "Q".
10. 6th Squadron R.F.C.
11. No.7 Balloon Coy. R.F.C.
12. M.G.R.A. Second Army.
13. War Diary.
14. Office.

15 to 18. Spare.

Appendix A.

Bombardment of HILL 60 area by Heavy and Field Howitzers and Trench Mortars on 16th instant.

Battery.	Objective.	Ammunition.
One 12" How.	Trench Junction at I.35.b.62.42 and communication trench N. of Railway for 50 yards. North West.	10 rounds per gun.
One 12" How.	Support line from I.36.a.00.92 to I.30.c.13.08.	10 ,,
One 9.2" How.	Support line crossing railway I.35.b.00.90 and trench junction.	15 ,,
One 9.2" How.	Support line and trench junction at I.35.a.80.70.	15 ,,
One 9.2" How.	Communication trench from I.35.b.00.90 to I.35.b.35.60.	15 ,,
One 9.2" How.	Minenwerfer at I.35.b.65.95.	15 ,,
(Note. M.W. is just South of the South West corner of the house shewn in the 1/10000 map.)		
Four 6" Hows.	Rectangle of trenches I.29.c.90.05 - I.29.d.0.0.; I.29.d.1.1, I.29.d.0.12.	60 rounds per battery.
Four 6" Hows.	Support line from I.29.d.5.3. to I.29.d.8.5.	60 rds per bty.
Two 4.5" How Batteries. 47th Divn.	Front line from I.35.a.60.85 to I.29.c.93.26. (Our front trenches in places should be cleared.)	100 ,,
Two 4.5" How Batteries Lowes Grp.	Front line from I.29.d.60.55 to I.29.d.90.45.	100 ,,

Note. Bombardment to last for 15 minutes.

As rapid a rate of fire as ammunition will allow.

Appendix B.

Bombardment of BLUFF area by Heavy and Field Howitzers and Trench Mortars on 16th instant.

Battery.	Objective.	Ammunition.
One 12" How.	O.4.b.90.35 (Minenwerfer just West of this point).	10 rounds per gun.
One 12" How.	Rectangle of trenches O.4.a. 90.40., O.4.b.10.40., O.4.b.10.30., O.4.a.90.30.	10 ,,
One 9.2" How.	Communication trench from O.4.a.74.46 to O.4.a.90.36.	15 ,,
One 9.2" How.	Communication trench from I.34.d.25.22 to I.34.d.50.20.	15 ,,
One 9.2" How.	Bend in communication trench at O.4.b.44.74. (M.W. on or close to road at this point)	15 ,,
One 9.2" How.	I.34.d.78.88 (M.W. and dugouts here).	15 ,,
Four 6" Hows.	Support trench from O.4.b.10.75 to O.4.b.25.95.	60 rounds per battery.
Four 6" Hows.	Support line from I.34.d.45.60 to I.34.d.55.30.	60 rounds per battery.
Two 4.5" How Batteries 41st Divn.	Front line from O.4.a.20.35 to O.4.a.55.50.	100 ,,
One 4.5" Battery 47th Divn.	Support line from O.4.b.25.95 to I.34.d.22.22.	100 ,,
One 4.5" Battery 47th Divn.	Support line I.34.d.45.60 to I.34.d.60.80.	100 ,,

SECRET

41st. DIVISIONAL ARTILLERY

DAILY OPERATION REPORT
from 6 p.m., 15.12.16. to 6 p.m., 16.12.16.

O U R   F I R E :-

	Time	Battery	Target	Rds.	Remarks
DIEPENDAAL GROUPS	3.5. p.m.	A/190	S.1.	21	
	9.0 a.m.	"	"NASTY"	8	Machine Gun active
	11.30 "	"	"	6	on plane
	2.45 p.m.	"	"	4	"
	3.15 p.m.	"	"	4	"
	3.35 p.m.	"	"	8	
	2.30 p.m.	B/190	New work at N.18.b.7½.8½.	8	New Work
	3.15 p.m.	"	M.G.at CROONAERT CHAPEL.	7	M.G.firing at plane
	11.0 a.m.	C/190	N.18.b.3.9½.	12	Three direct hits on new work.
	1.35 p.m.	D/190	T.M.FERRIER	8	T.M. silenced. Bombs or ammunition blown up
	1.0 p.m.	A/189	O.4.a.40.44 - O.4.a.55.50	100	Group Shoot
	1.40 p.m.	"	T.M.FROSTY	20	Retaliation
ST.ELOI GROUP	7.30 p.m.	A/187	F.L.T.	1	S.O.S.Test
	9.15 a.m.	"	Enemy Working Party at O.8.d.7½.7.	12	Working party dispersed.
	11.15 a.m.	"	Hostile M.Gs active against our aircraft pp posite Trenches O.33 to O.37.	8	Hostile machine guns silenced.
	3.30 p.m.	B/187	S.O.S.Lines	1	S.O.S.Test
	10.30 a.m.	C/187	O.4.c.4.4.	6	Registration by aeroplane which failed owing to bad weather.
	1.0 p.m.	D/187	Hostile Trench - O.4.a.20.35 - O.4.a.40.44.	100	41st. D.A. O.O. No.44.
	11.15 a.m.	D/190	T.M. ALBERT	6	Group Order.

OUR TRENCH MORTARS:-

In accordance with our Operation Order No.44, X/41, assisted in the bombardment of the enemy trenches between 0.4.a.0.1 and 0.4.a.1.2.

Nos. 5 and 6 Mortars were in action, and fire was opened at 1 p.m. No.5 gun detachment fired 20 rounds in 15 minutes, and No.6 fired 20 rounds in 8 mins. The latter

Most of the rounds fired were observed to fall in the trenches, and duckboards, timber, etc., hurled into the air.

Y/41 battery was engaged in an aeroplane shoot, but in consequence of some misunderstanding about the pin-point it was not successful. This Battery ceased firing after the ninth round as the bed gave way.

ENEMY'S ARTILLERY ACTIVITY:-

Time	Locality Shelled	Rds	Nature	Sound or Flash bearing.
8.0 a.m.- 12 Noon.	O.8.d. and O.9.c.	-	A.A. guns	-
2.45 p.m.	Neighbourhood of I.33.c.7.8. near ARUNDEL HOUSE, I.33. c.8.9. SPOILBANK	16 -	10.5 cm 7.7 mm	- -
1.0 p.m.	O.23	12	" "	-
2.30 p.m.	O.23	6	10.5 cm	-
3.50 p.m.	VOORMEZEELE	6	7.7 mm	158° from H.32.d.8.2.
1.0 p.m.	O.23	17	7.7 "	
3.0 p.m.	AEROPLANE	12	A.A.C.	Approx. O.13 Central
8.0 a.m.-) 2.0 p.m.)	Three British Planes.	40	"	Sound bearing of A.A. firing at 11.5 a.m. was 102°.30' from TEA HOUSE, N.16.b.85.90.

GENERAL SUMMARY

ENEMY'S NEW WORK:-

Enemy working party were observed at O.8.d.7½.

New work appears to be done at N.18.b.3.9½., and also at Machine Gun Emplacement at N.18.b.5.6½.

OBSERVATION:-

Very difficult.

CASUALTIES:-

PERSONNEL:-
N I L.

GUNS OUT OF ACTION:-
18 pdrs.   2
4.5" Hows. 1

GENERAL:-

During the retaliation on some Trench Mortars at about 4.15 p.m., the enemy were observed to send up a rocket breaking into 7 orange coloured stars from each end of the shelled area. Three minutes after a Battery of 4.2 fired 16 rounds rapid into VIERSTRAAT. On a single green light being sent up the shelling ceased.

BRIGADE MAJOR,
41st. Divisional Artillery

17.12.16
HHP

app 51

SECRET

41st. DIVISIONAL ARTILLERY

DAILY OPERATION REPORT
from 6 p.m., 16.12.16 to 6 p.m., 17.12.16

OUR FIRE:-

	Time	Battery	Target	Rds.	REMARKS
DIEPENDAAL GROUP	3.33 - 3.40	A/190	O.7.b.8.6½. to O.7.Central.	100	Scheme K (Retaliation to Heavy Tr. Mortaring)
	3.0 p.m.	B/190	O.13.a.2.7.T.M. EMU - O.7.c.4.5. T.M. DANIEL	12	Retaliation.
	1.0 p.m.-3.0pm	"	O.13.a.4.8. O.7.d.3.1.	6 6	T.M.Retaliation " "
	3.0p.m.-4.0 "	"	O.7.c.4.4.-N.18.b.9.7.	50	Scheme "J"
	2.55 p.m.	D/190	T.M.DOUGLAS	20	Retaliation
	3.0 p.m.	C/190	N.12.d.8.0. to O.7.c.2.1.	20	T.M.Retaliation.
	10.15 a.m.	A/189	EVANS FARM, O.14.b.3.2.	3	Registration check
	3.0 p.m.	"	T.M.EVIL	20	Retaliation.
ST.ELOI GROUP	1.18 a.m.	A/187	Front Line Trench	1	Test S.O.S.
	3.20 a.m.	B/187	" " "	1	" " "
	1.12 a.m.	C/187	" " "	1	" " "
	12.45 p.m.	"	O.9.a.5.½.	6	

OUR TRENCH MORTARS:-

41st.D.A., Trench Mortar Batteries did not fire.

ENEMY'S ARTILLERY FIRE:-

Time	Locality shelled	Rds.	Nature	Sound or Flash bearing
2.45 p.m.) to 3.30 p.m.)	Front Line -O.2.3.- O.1.5.	85	T.M's.(M.) & (Hvy.)	
2.30 p.m.	do.	-	T.Ms.	156½° T.B.from R.36.d.8.2.
2.45 p.m.) to 4.0 p.m.)	Front Line Trench	100	H.& L. T.Ms.	Unnamed Wood

.1.

GENERAL SUMMARY

OBSERVATION :-

    Very difficult owing to heavy mist.

CASUALTIES :-   PERSONNEL :-

                       N I L.

GUNS OUT OF ACTION :-

    18 pdrs.   2
    4.5" Hows.   1

S. Phillip.
A.D.C.

for BRIGADE MAJOR,

18.12.16   41st. Divisional Artillery.
HHP

app 52

SHEET 28

HOSTILE BATTERIES
located in action between 1st. and
15th. December 1916.

Map Position	Nature	Aeroplane Photograph	Zone of Fire
Q.5.b.5.5.	F.H.	6 B. 1024	H.33 - O.31
Q.6.b.75.20	"	" 556	I.28. - I.34.
Q.6.c.35.85	"	" 1093	I.23 - I.27
Q.6.d.7.9.	15 cm.H. (4)	" 914	H.30. - I.32
Q.11.b.75. 40	" (1)	" 796	I.27 - O.2.
Q.11.c.1.9.	F.H.	" 1083	H.30. - I.28.
Q.12.c.3.8.	" (4)	" 922	I.2. - I.26.
Q.12.d.3.7.	"	" 38	I.26 - O.27
Q.14.d.05.7.	F. or F.H.	" 1114	
Q.15.a.9.1.	F.	" 1006	H.12. - O.7.
Q.15.b.4.4.	F. (2)	I.B. 598	H.35 - O.2.
Q.15.d.8.6.	F.	6 B.1070	H.35 - O.7.
Q.16.a.85.65	F.H.	B.B. 131	O.7.
Q.16.a.55.15		6 B.1071	I.29
Q.16.c.75.55	F. (2)	" 614	H.15 - O.7.
Q.16.c.15.90	F. (2)	" 1071	I.15 - O.7.
Q.17.b.05.05	F.H.	" 1098	H.13 - O.3.
Q.18.a. 05.30	15 c.m. H.(1)	" 925	H.18 - I.31.
Q.20.b.8.1.	F.	1 B. 590	N.11 - N.21.
Q.21.a.9.1.	F.H. (1)	" 465	N.12. - O.2.
Q.21.a.6.5.	F.	" 587	N.11 - N.17
Q.21.b.05.40	F.H.		N.6. - N.17.
Q.21.c.15.10.	F. (2)	" 599	N.12. - N.36
Q.21.d.7.6.	F.H. (3)	" 836	N.4. - N.29.
Q.21.d.45.50.	F.H. (1)	6 B 832	N.11. - O.1.
Q.22.a.3.8.	F.H. (2)	" 831	I.26. - N.11.
Q.26.a.45.75	F.H. (1)	" 531	I.26. - N.11.
Q.27.a.6.5. 85.	F. (4)	1 B 684	N.30. - O.4.
Q.27.b.2.3.	F. (4)	" 684	N.10. - N.29.
Q.27.b.05.55.	F. (4)	20 K 372	N.23. - O.4.
Q.27.c.55.55.	F.H. (2)	1 B 684	N.24. - U.1.
Q.27.d.7.3.	F. (4)	" 684	N.18. - I.6.
Q.28.a.70.25.	F.H.	" 793	N.23. - N.29.
Q.28.a.40.05.	15 cm.H.	BC. 531	
Q.28.c.9.2.			
Q.34.a.35.90.	F.H.		N.29. - U.8.
Q.35.c.5.9.	F.	1 B 374	U.1. - U.21

Officer Commanding,

Forwarded for your information.

A.E.C., R.A.,
41st. Divisional Artillery.

18.12.16.
HHP

app 53

(5635)

SECRET   Copy No....1....

HOSTILE T.M. CODE

O.4.c.05.75	ANGUS	O.7.d.30.60	DANIEL
O.1.c.75.75	ARTHUR	O.7.d.10.55	DENT
O.1.c.50.50.	ALFRED	O.7.d.50.15.	DONAVAN
O.3.c.80.40.	BENJAMIN	O.7.d.55.20.	DORA
O.2.c.95.50.	CUTHBERT	O.13.a.15.45.	EVELYN
O.2.d.16.60.	CHARLES	O.13.a.30.65.	EUSTACE
O.8.a.45.87	CECIL	O.13.a.50.20.	EGBERT
O.8.a.65.50	CLARENCE	O.13.a.30.30.	ETHELRED
O.7.b.50.30.	DAVID	O.13.a.90.55.	EDGAR
O.7.b.62.47	DESMOND	O.13.a.95.60.	EDRED
O.7.c.40.50	DONALD	O.13.b.00.70.	EDMUND
O.7.c.6½.9½.	DANDY	O.13.b.10.75.	ESTHER
O.7.c.97.87.	DEODAR	N.18.b.60.90.	FANNY
		N.18.b.70.50.	FIRSTLY
		N.18.b.95.30.	FRIGHTENS
		N.18.b.80.30.	FATHER.

Herewith coded list of Trench Mortars on 41st.
Divisional Front.   Previous lists should be destroyed.

[signature]

BRIGADE MAJOR,
41st.Divisional Artillery.

18.12.16
HHP
Copy 1 War Diary
      2 File
   3 -13 St.Eloi Group
  14 -19 Diependaal Group
  20 -22 189th.Brigade
      23 Xth Corps H.A.
  24 -25 41st.Division

SECRET

41st. DIVISIONAL ARTILLERY

DAILY OPERATION REPORT
from 6 p.m., 17.12.16 to 6 p.m., 18.12.16.

OUR FIRE:-

Group	Time	Battery	Target	Rds.	REMARKS
DIEPENDAAL GROUP.	2.15 a.m.	A/190	S.O.S. Lines	1	S.O.S. Test
	3.40 a.m.	"	F.L.T. 0.7.c.4½.8½ - 0.7.b.8½.5½.	8	Retaliation
	4.30 a.m.	"	F.L.T. 0.7.c.4½.8½ - 0.7.b.1.1.	60	Scheme H. Appeared to be very effective
	3.25 a.m.	"	CROONAERT CHAPEL 0.7.c.4½.4½.	10	Retaliation.
	11.30 a.m.	B/190	Trench Junction 0.7.d.5.4.	6	"
	12.1 p.m.	"	Trench Junction 0.7.b.8.3.	3	"
	3.0 p.m.	D/190	T.M. "ELI"	3	Registration. Last two rounds good effect
ST. ELOI GROUP	10.35 a.m.	A/187	F.L.T. 0.3.d.0.3.- 0.3.d.6.6.	20	Retaliation for Hostile T.M.s firing on our F.L.T.
	3.0 "	B/187	Test S.O.S.	1	
	11.16 "	B/187	Trench 0.4.c.7½.7½.	12	Retaliation
	12.15 p.m.	C/187	F.L.T.0.2.c.9.6.- 0.2.d.1.7.-0.2.d.3½. 6.-0.2.d.5.6½.	25	Registration
		D/190	0.9.c.4.9.	4	Smoke seen to be coming from this point.

OUR TRENCH MORTARS:-

The 41st.D.A., Trench Mortar Batteries did not fire.

ENEMY'S ARTILLERY FIRE

Time	Locality shelled	Rds.	Nature	Sound or Flash bearing
11.25 a.m.	F.L.T. 0.3.8. to 0.3.1.	30	T.Ms.	-
4.5 p.m.	I.33.c.5.3. S. of ARUNDEL HOUSE	-	7.7 mm	160° from G.2.- I.33.c.7.9.
11.28 a.m. to 12.30 pm	CARRE FARM	-6	4.2"	119° from H.3.
11.30 a.m. to 12.12 p.m. & 3 to 3.30	VIERSTRAAT	39	"	105° " Q.7.
1.30 p.m.	VOORMEZEELE	-	5.9" G.	143° " K.9.
"	P.& O. TRENCH	-	" How.	143° " K.9.
1.39 "	VOORMEZEELE	-	" G.	1400° " H.35.b.
1.42 "	-	-	4.2"	152° " K.9.
2.6 p.m to 2.37 p.m	VOORMEZEELE	21	7.7 mm	136° " K.9.
12 Noon	Front Line Trs.	10	" "	
1.15 p.m.	EZENVALLE CHATEAU	6	5.9" c.m.	145° " K.9.

GENERAL SUMMARY

ENEMY'S NEW WORK

Coils of wire were seen on enemy's parapet at O.3.d.2.6. and O.3.b.6.9.½.

OBSERVATION:-

Dull and misty.

CASUALTIES:-   PERSONNEL:-
                  N I L.

GUNS OUT OF ACTION:-

3.

GENERAL:-

One of our Battery Commanders reports that he is troubled with Snipers and Machine gun fire from the direction of Sap O.31.b.6½.2, suspected strong point and Machine Gun emplacement.

S. Philip

BRIGADE MAJOR,
41st. Divisional Artillery.

19.12.16
HHP

SECRET

DAILY OPERATION REPORT
from 6 p.m., 18.12.16 to 6 p.m. 19.12.16

OUR FIRE:-

	Time	Battery	Target	Rds.	REMARKS
DIEPENDAAL GROUP	9.40 a.m.	A/190	O.7.d.4.9½.	1	Working party
	11.30 a.m.	"	ZERO Line	1	Corrector test
	11.30 a.m.	B/190	O.13.a.1.8.	19	Motor truck reported by Infantry. Believed to be very effective.
	1.45 p.m.	D/190	O.13.a.5.2. O.7.c.3½.4. N.18.b.4½.6. O.13.a.4.8.	8	Registrations.
ST.ELOI GROUP	12.35 p.m.	A/187	F.L.T.(O3.6)	1	S.O.S (25 secs) Test
	2.25 p.m.	B/187	F. L. T.	1	" Test.
	9.43 p.m.	C/187	S.O.S.Lines (O2.7)	1	" " (20 secs.)
	11.20 p.m.	"	S.O.S.Lines	1	" " (26 secs.)
	12.15 p.m.	"	O.8.a.3.8.- O.8.d.6.0.	35	Suspected Working Parties.
	9.15 a.m.	D/187	T.M."CHARLIE"	4	Group Order.

OUR TRENCH MORTARS:-

41st.D.A.Trench Mortar Batteries did not fire.

ENEMY'S ARTILLERY FIRE:-

Time	Locality shelled	Rds.	Nature	Sound or Flash bearing
8.0 a.m. 10.51 "to)	TRACK - I.25.d.5.3½.	8	7.7	O.8.d.9½.1½.
11.7 a.m.)	BOIS CARRE	4	4.2"	105° from Q.2.
11.0 "	-	-	"	115° " H.3.
11 a.m. to) 11.7 a.m)	-	2	7.7	104° " H.3.
12.10 p.m.) to.12.34p.m)	VOORMEZEELE Trenches	16	HOG	HOG
1.35 p.m.to) 1.50 p.m.))	O.11 to O.38.	2	M.T.M	141½°T.B. from K.9.
2 p.m.-2.8pm	O2.3 O2.4.	-	HOG	HOG.
2.45 p.m.	N.11.d.	6	7.7	141½°T.B. from K.9.
9.0 p.m	O2.4	2	M.T.M.	102° from Q.2.

GENERAL SUMMARY

ENEMY'S NEW WORK
New work observed in remains of HOLLANDSCHECHOUR FARM N.18.b.4.9½.

OBSERVATION:-
Visible Possible from 10.45 a.m. to 3 p.m.

CASUALTIES:-

PERSONNEL:-
NIL.

P.T.O.

GUNS OUT OF ACTION:-

        18 pdrs.   3
        4.5" Hows.   1.

GENERAL:-

        At 12.40 a.m., a white pigeon was seen flying low at N.10.c.0.2½, from the direction of N.8.b.3.4. to Front line.

CORRECTION:-

        The sap mentioned in our Daily Operation report of yesterday should read "O.3.b.6½.2" and not "O.31.b.6½.2."

20.12.16.
HHP

                                    for Brigade Major,
                                  41st. Divisional Artillery.

App 56

S E C R E T

41st. DIVISIONAL ARTILLERY

DAILY OPERATION REPORT
from 6 p.m., 19.12.16 to 6 p.m., 20.12.16

OUR FIRE:-

	Time	Battery	Target	Rds.	REMARKS
DIEPENDAAL GROUP:-	10.16 a.m.	B/190	N.12.b.2.9½.	10	M.G. active. Effect good
	12.30 p.m.	C/190	N.18.b.9.7.	10	Scheme K.(Retaliation)
	12.55 p.m.	A/189	O.5.a.3.1½ CROSS ROADS O.20.a.3.9.	20	Aeroplane registration
ST. ELOI GROUP:-	2.46 p.m.	A/187	F.L.T.	1	S.O.S. Test (17 secs)
	11.0 a.m.	"	"	4	Verification of S.O.S. Lines.
	1.49 p.m.	"	F.L.T.(036)	1	S.O.S. Test (14 secs.)
	12.30 p.m.	"	DOME HOUSE, O.8.d.9½.6	18	Verification of Zone Line.
		B/187	S.O.S. Lines	1	Test S.O.S.
	12.1 p.m.	"	"	1	" "
	2.7 p.m.	C/187	O.2.d.6½.6	1	Test S.O.S. (15 secs)
	11.15 a.m.	"	O.2.c.9.6.	12	Working party
	9.15 a.m.	D/187	T.M.CECIL	5	
	12.45 p.m.	D/190	O.9.c.3½.9½	4	Suspected Dug-outs
	2.0 p.m.	"	O.4.d.1.7.	10	Registration
	2.30 p.m.	"	O.9.c.3½.9½.	4	Registered Dug-outs

OUT TRENCH MORTARS. The 41st. D.A. T.M. Batteries did not fire.

ENEMY'S ARTILLERY FIRE.

Time.	Locality Shelled	Rounds	Nature	Sound or Flash bearing.
10.15 a.m. to 10.22 a.m.		-	4.2"	125° from Q 2.
10.40 a.m.	West of RIDGEWOOD	-	4.2"	119° from H3
10.40 a.m.	RIDGEWOOD	25	5.9"	132½° from K 7
10.40 a.m.	O.1.a.8.4.	6	10 cm.	120° from K1
10.40 to 11.30 a.m.	RIDGE WOOD	25	5.9"	132½° from K 7
10.45 a.m. to 3.45 p.m.	H.35.d.1.7	40	5.9"	131½° from H.35.b 2.5.
10.53 a.m.	CHOCORY LANE	-	7.7cm	118° from H3
11.8 a.m.	-	-	5.9"	120° from DEAD DOG'S FM.N.6.b.2.0.

Time	Location		Rounds	Calibre	Bearing
11.20 a.m.	–	–	–		131°30' from H.35.d.9.6 Time of flight 18 secs.
11.22 a.m. to 12 noon.	–		–	–	119° from H.3. 120° from Q 8.
11.26 a.m.	–		–	–	146° from X9
11.46 a.m.	–		–	4.2"	103° from Q2 119° from H3
11.20 a.m.	H.35.c.Central		20.	5.9"	165° from Q 4.
12.31 p.m.	N.17.b.		–	7.7cm.	116° from Q 7.
12.15 p.m.	N.17.b. – N.18.a.		10	7.7.	Grand Bois.
1.30 p.m.	Front Line Trench.		5	L.T.M.	N.18.b.9.3.
3. p.m.	H.35.c.Central		3	5.9"	165° from Q4.
3.23 p.m.	H.35.c.5.5.		–	5.9"	103° from Q2.
9.45 a.m.	Crater-O.2.c.5.6.		10	7.7.	–

GENERAL SUMMARY.

Enemy's New Works.

A working party was observed repairing Crater No. 2 at O.2.c.9.6. New work appears to be done at N.18.b.1.5. to loophole in mound of earth — *apparently a* ~~suggested~~ M.G. or O.P.

Observation very good.

Enemy Aircraft Activity.

2 hostile planes were active during the morning *and* ~~which~~ were heavily engaged by our aircraft guns, and driven back.

Casualties.   Personnel
               Nil.

Guns out of Action.

                18-pdrs.   3.

S. Philip
A.D.C.
Brigade Major,
41st. Divisional Artillery.

21/12/16.

SECRET.

41st. DIVISIONAL ARTILLERY

DAILY OPERATION REPORT.
from 6 p.m. 20.12.16 to 6 p.m. 21.12.16.

OUR FIRE.

	Time	Battery	Target	Rds.	Remarks.
DIEPENDAAL GROUP.	12.40 a.m.	A/190	Front line trench. 0.7.b.3.3	10	Retaliation Scheme.
	3.10 p.m.	A/190	0.7.c.9.7	12	-do-
	3.45	B/190	Front line Trench 0.7.a.5.0	12	-do-
	12.30 p.m.	A/189	Hostile active Battery 0.14.b.2.5½.	30	Retaliation on Hostile Battery.
ST. ELOI GROUP.	1.10 a.m.	A/187	Front line trench	1	S.O.S Test
	3.30 p.m.	"	0.9.d.9.8 (POND HOUSE)	20	
	4.0 p.m.	"	Front line trench opposite 0.3.7	15	
	1.30 a.m.	E/187	S.O.S. lines	1	Test S.O.S.
	10.20 a.m.	C/187	0.8.d.9½.7	20	Group Order
	10.30 a.m.	"	0.8.a.5.0	15	Registration of dug-outs, where smoke has been seen.
	2.0 p.m.	"	0.2.c.9.6	8	Registration
	2.15 p.m.	"	0.2.c.7.6	18	Sniper post hit. Infantry asked for this to be fired on.
	4.20 p.m.	"	0.3.c.5.4 to 0.3.c.1.3	20	Group Order
	2.0 p.m.	D/190	0.8.d.9.7.	4	Registration.

OUR TRENCH MORTARS. The 41st. D.A. T.M. Batteries did not fire.

ENEMY'S ARTILLERY FIRE.

Time.	Locality Shelled.	Rds.	Nature.	Sound or flash bearing.
7.52 - 8.30 a.m.	-	-	HOG	
7.30 a.m.	0.31.c 0.1.d (CONVENT LANE)		7.7cmm.& 10 cm .7.7cm	140° T.B. from 1.31.c.3½.½
9.30 a.m.	Front line about 0.2.4	7	7.7cm	
9.57-10.15 a.m.	-		HOG	
10.30 a.m.	VOORMEZEELE	3	4.2"	145°R. of Mag.
10.15 a.m.	"	16	7.7cm	140°T.B. from K 9
10.30 a.m.	0.2.4	4	7.7cm	h.36.d.8.2
10.52.a.m.	N 17.a Central	6	4.2"	S.B.
1033 a.m.	-	-	Hoy Gun	150° from L.31.c.5.2
10.52 -11.9) a.m.) 11./o-11.48) a.m.)	F.L & 0.2.4		7.7cm	144° from K 9
11.20 - 12 noon.	near BUS HOUSE	10	4.2"	H.36.d.8.22
11.30 a.m.	N.2	6	4.2"	140°R. of Mag.

2.40 p.m.	n.18.b.2.6.	4	T.Ms.	96° from Q3
	M.12.d.6.6	7	"	
3.15 p.m.	POPPY LANE	20	7.7cm	s.b. 98° from Q7
3.15 p.m.	-		4.2" or 5.9	140° from K9
3.0 p.m to 3.45 p.m.	Near Bus Ho.	10	4.2"	H.36.d.8.2
3.30 p.m.	D/190-H.30.a.7½.8.	20	4.2"	-do-

INTELLIGENCE SUMMARY.

2. <u>Enemy's Movements.</u>
    Whilst C/187 were firing at 0.8.d.9½.7 at 10.20 a.m. two green lights were sent up behind enemy trenches near target.
3. <u>Observation.</u>
    Light fair up to 8 a.m. but bad during the day. Misty.

5. <u>Casualties.</u>

            Guns.   3.

6. <u>Guns out of action.</u>
        2 18-prs. One with spring trouble, and one at I.O.M.
        2 4.5" Hows.

22/12/16.

Brigade Major,
41st. Divisional Artillery.

1.35 p.m.	VOORMEZEELE	2	4.2"	HOG 0.20.b.8.1
1.15 p.m.	KRUISSTRAATHOEK		4.2"	123° from H4
7.0 p.m.	Neighbourhood of DICKEBUSCH	2	15cm How.	87° from N.6.c.2½.9½
	-do-	3	10.5cm	83° -do-

GENERAL SUMMARY.

2. **Enemy's Movements.**
   Smoke was seen at. O.9.a.4.0 at 3.15 p.m. Suspected Infantry dugouts.

3. **Observation.**
   Fair to good.

5. **Casualties.**   Guns.... 3

6. **Guns out of Action.**   2-18 prs.   2-4.5" Hows.

S. Riley
Brigade Major,
41st. Divisional Artillery

23/12/16.

41st. DIVISIONAL ARTILLERY.

DAILY OPERATION REPORT.

From 6 p.m. 21st. to 6 p.m. 22nd. Dec.

OUR FIRE.

	Time.	Bty.	Target.	Rds.	Remarks.
DIEPENDAAL GROUP.	8.15 p.m.)			1	S.O.S. Test.
	8.45 a.m.)	A/190	LOUSAKGE Farm.	12	Retaliation at request of Infantry.
	3.30 p.m.)		O.7.c.4.3.	10	
	12 noon)	B/190	Plateau Farm	20	M.G. firing at our 'plane N.18.b.4.6.
	3.45 p.m.)		Martens Farm O.8.d.60.	20	
			Suspected M.G. Emplacements	16	M.Gs. firing at our 'planes.
	2.15 p.m.	A/189	Hostile battery at O.15.c.½.6	20	Battery ceased firing.
ST. ELOI GROUP.	3.9 p.m.	A/187	O.3.b.7.1(F.L.T)	7	"HASTY"
	3.23 p.m.	B/187	Machine gun	10	Hostile machine gun firing at our 'plane.
	1.15 p.m.	C/187	O.9.c.3.3	20	Group Order
	2.30 p.m.	"	O.2.c.9.6	22	Registration
	3.13 p.m.	"	O.2.c.7.6	17	Snipers post. Infantry asked for this to be fired on.
	2.45 p.m.	D/187	SUNKEN ROAD - O.2.a.7.5	35	Unsatisfactory
	2.45 p.m.	"	"ARQUE"	5	

OUR TRENCH MORTARS. 41st. D.A. T.M. Batteries did not fire.

HOSTILE ARTILLERY FIRE.

Time	Locality Shelled	Rds.	Nature	Sound or Flash Bearing
8.35 a.m.	Near the BRASSERIE O.6.a.1.1	3 or 4	10.5cm shrapnel	130° from K3
7.45 a.m.	H.35.c.9½.7	12	4.2"	Not located
10.15 a.m.	O.1.d		77mm	140° T.S. from I.31.c.3½.1½
10.35 a.m.) to 11 a.m.)	F.L.T. O.1.2			117° from K9
-do-	F.L.T O.1.2			142° from K9
10.40 a.m.	F.L.T O.2.1			130° from G8
11 a.m. to 12.30 p.m.	"SHOJUD"	20	4.2"	113½° from K9 - H.36.d.8.2
12.30 p.m.	"			114° from K9
12.40 to 2.50 p.m.	"VOORMEZEELE"	35	77mm	139½° from K9 - H.36.d.8.2
12.40 to 3 p.m.	"VOORMEZEELE"	--	77mm	140° H. from K9 - H.36.d.8.2
2.40 to 2.50 p.m.	-do-		77mm	-do-

SECRET

41st. DIVISIONAL ARTILLERY

WEEKLY SUMMARY of OPERATIONS from 13th.
December 1916 to 21st. December 1916.

13th. December

Between 11.30 a.m., and 4.30 p.m., fired about 274 rounds in retaliation on the following Hostile Trench Mortars:-

DESMOND,
DAVID,
DOUGLAS,
DAPHNE,
COOT,
BERTIE
FOOL

Between 1 - 1.30 p.m., fired 130 rounds on SUNKEN ROAD, at 0.13.a.4.2.

At 2.45 p.m., retaliated on CROSS ROADS at 0.15.a.3.1.

Between 12.50 and 1.30 p.m., expended 20 rounds on suspected working party at $0.8.a.9\frac{1}{2}.9\frac{1}{2}$., and vicinity.

At 9.45 p.m., (14.12.16) fired 20 rounds on working party at $0.8.d.8\frac{1}{2}.5$.

At 11.0 a.m., shelled MARTENS FARM, $0.8.a.5\frac{1}{2}.0$.

At 2.30 p.m., fired 10 rounds at HEILE FARM, $0.8.d.9.9\frac{1}{2}$.

At 1 p.m., retaliated on Trenches from $0.13.a.5.2\frac{1}{2}$. to $0.15.c.7.9\frac{1}{2}$.

During the day several S.O.S. tests and registrations were carried out.

At 4.15 p.m., the "duty" gun of "X" T.M. Battery fired 10 rounds on top of enemy's Communication trench at $0.4.a.0.0\frac{1}{2}$., in retaliation.

14th. December

From 9.10 p.m., to 12 midnight our batteries were engaged firing on their S.O.S. lines in consequence of enemy raid on our front line trenches.

At 9.10 a.m., fired a few rounds at Hostile Trench Mortar at 0.12.d.9.1., in retaliation.

At 9.55 a.m., retaliated on Hostile Trench Mortar, "EAGLE".

At 8.45 a.m., fired 86 rounds at Hostile Trench Mortar ANDREW.

At 8.30 a.m., fired a few rounds at N.18.b.7.8., as new work was observed there.

At 5 p.m., retaliated on PLATEAU FARM, $N.18.b.3\frac{1}{2}.6$.

At 11 a.m., shelled the following:-
ESTAMINET, $0.9.c.3\frac{1}{2}.3$.,
DOME HOUSE, $0.8.d.9\frac{1}{2}.7$.,
PICCADILLY FARM, $0.8.a.2\frac{1}{2}.8$.,
and suspected Battalion Headquarters at $0.9.a.0.5\frac{1}{2}$.

15th. December

At 10.30 a.m., registration by aeroplane was carried out.

At 9.15 a.m., a working party was observed at $0.8.d.7\frac{1}{2}.7$, was fired on and dispersed.

At 11.0 a.m., fired 12 rounds at new work at $N.18.b.3.9\frac{1}{2}$, three direct hits being obtained.

At 11.15 a.m., shelled and silenced hostile Machine Guns which were active against our aeroplanes.

At 1 p.m., the operations detailed in our Operation Order No.44, were carried out.

At 1.35 p.m., expended a few rounds on Hostile Trench Mortar FERRIER, silencing same.

At 1.40 p.m., retaliated on hostile Trench Mortar FROSTY.

At 2.30 p.m., fired a few rounds on new work at N.18.b.7½.8½.

18th. December

Between 3.33 p.m., and 3.40 p.m., fired 100 rounds in retaliation for Heavy Trench Mortaring.

Between 1 p.m., and 4 p.m., expended 64 rounds in retaliation on the following Hostile Trench Mortars:-
EMU,
DANIEL,
DOUGLAS,
EVIL,
0.13.a.4.8.
0.7.d.3.1.

At 3 p.m., fired 20 rounds at Trench, N.12.d.8.0. to 0.7.c.2.1.

Between 3.0 p.m., and 4 p.m., fired 50 rounds on trenches 0.7.c.4.4 - N.18.b.9.7., in accordance with Scheme "J" of the 41st.D.A.Defence Scheme.

During the day carried out a few S.O.S.tests.

19th. December

At 3.25 a.m., retaliated on CROONAERT CHAPEL, 0.7.c.4½.4½.

At 3.40 a.m., fired a few rounds on Front Line Trench from 0.7.c.4½.8½ - 0.7.b.8½.5½., in retaliation.

At 10.35 a.m., shelled Front Line Trench, 0.3.d. 0.3. - 0.3.d.6.6., in retaliation for Hostile Trench Mortars firing on our Front Line.

At 11.16 a.m., expended a few rounds on Trench at 0.4.c.7½.7½., in retaliation.

Between 11.30 a.m., and 12.1 p.m., fired a few rounds at Trench Junctions, 0.7.d.5.4. and 0.7.b.8.3., respectively.

At 12.15 p.m., fired 25 rounds on Trenches -
0.2.c.9.6 - 0.2.d.1.7.- 0.2.d.3½.6 - 0.2.d.5.8½.

At 3 p.m., expended three rounds on registration of T.M.ELI.

At 4.30 a.m., fired 60 rounds at Front Line Trench 0.7.c.4½.8½ - 0.7.b.1.1.

Smoke was observed coming from the direction of 0.9.c.4.9., and was fired on.

20th. December

At 9.15 a.m., shelled Hostile Trench Mortar CHARLIE.

At 11.30 a.m., fired 19 rounds at Motor truck at 0.13.a.1.8., with good effect.

At 12.15 p.m., working parties were suspected as being at 0.8.a.3.8. - 0.8.d.6.0., and were fired on.

Several S.O.S.tests and registrations were also carried out.

21st. December

At 1115 a.m., fired a few rounds at working party at about 0.2.c.9.6.

At 9.15 a.m., shelled Hostile T.M.CECIL.

At 10.16 a.m., fired 10 rounds at active Machine Gun at N.12.b.2.9½.

At 12.45 p.m., fired a few rounds at Suspected Dug-Outs at 0.9.c.3½.9½. There dug-outs were registered at 2.30 p.m.

At 12.55 p.m., carried out registration by Aeroplane.
During the day several S.O.S. tests, registrations,
and verification of S.O.S. lines, were carried out.

                                          Brigade Major,
21.12.16.   41st. Divisional Artillery.
HHP

GENERAL SUMMARY.

1. **Enemy's New Works.**

    Work appears to be going on in neighbourhood of HOLLANDSCHES-CHURR FARM.

3. **Observation.**

    St. Eloi Group report very difficult owing to mist.
    Diependaal Group report good.

6. **Guns out of Action.**

            3 18½pdrs.   1 4.5" How.

24/12/16.

Brigade Major,
41st. Divisional Artillery...

SECRET. No.3

41st. Divisional Artillery.

DAILY OPERATION REPORT.

From 6 p.m. 22nd. to 6 p.m. 23rd. Dec. 1916.

OUR FIRE.

	Time	Battery	Target	Rds.	Remarks.
ST. ELOI GROUP.	7 p.m.	A/187	O.9.d.9.8 (POND HOUSE)	20	
	11.20 a.m.	B/187	O.4.d.1¾.4	21	Retaliation
	3.10 p.m.	"	O.4.d.1½.3	18	-do-
	12.1 a.m.	C/187	S.O.S. lines	1	Test S.O.S. (7 Secs)
	1.30 p.m.	"	O.2.c.9½.6	13	Registering 2 guns in new pit.
	11.20 a.m.	"	Working party O.9.a.9.2	10	Working party dispersed
	11.30 a.m.	"	O.2.c.5½.2	15	Working party dispersed
DIEPENDAAL Group.	10.30 a.m.	A/190	O.7.c.4.4½	9	Checking registration
	3.40 p.m.	"	O.7.b.3.3 – O.7.b.7.6½	12	Retaliation for Hostile T.M.
	10.30 a.m.	B/190	N.18.b.5.5	9	Checking registration.
	3.20 p.m.	D/190	DESMOND O.7.b.62.47.	20	Retaliation.

OUR TRENCH MORTARS. 41st. D.A. T.M. Batteries did not fire.

ENEMY'S ARTILLERY FIRE.

Time	Locality Shelled	Rounds.	Nature	Sound or Flash Bearing.
11 A.M. to 12 noon.	DICKEBUSCH & VIERSTRAAT	10	4.2"	119½° & 133½° from K9 H.36.d.8.2
11.20 a.m. to 11.50 am.	F.L.T. in N.12.d		7.7cm	113° from Q6
11.32 to 11.50 a.m.	–		4.2" How.	139° from K9
11.54 a.m.	VIERSTRAAT		4.2" How.	132° from K9
3.15 p.m.	–		7.7cm	111° from K9
3 to 3.15 p.m.	VERMOZELLE	8	7.7cm	111½° from K9 – H.36½.d.8.2
	A few rounds of 7.7cm. at intervals on F.L.T. about N.12.d	12 to 15	7.7cm	Reported by Diependaal Group.

SECRET   app 61   No. 4.

41st. DIVISIONAL ARTILLERY

DAILY OPERATION REPORT.
from 6 p.m. 23rd. to 6 p.m. 24th. Dec.

OUR FIRE.

	Time	Battery	Targets	Rds.	Remarks.
ST. ELOI GROUP.	10 a.m.	A/187	Front Line Trench (O.3.6)	20	"NASTY"
	11.30 a.m.	"	O.9.d.9.8 (POND HOUSE)	30	
	12.30 p.m.	"	DOME HOUSE - O.8.d.9.7.	15	Registration of No. 2 and 3 guns.
	2.20 p.m.	B/187	Hostile Machine gun	16	
	3.25 p.m.	"	Registration	10	
	2.20 a.m.	C/187	S.O.S. Lines	1	SOS Test (50 secs)
	10.45 a.m.	"		4	Hostile M.Guns firing on our 'planes
	10.15 a.m.	"	O.8.d.9.3½	4	German Staff Officers
	11.45 a.m.	"	O.8.d.8.5	15	Working party
				31	Retaliation and testing S.O.S.
	12.15 p.m.	D/187	WHITE CHATEAU and prominent points	42	(1) Registration of gun just placed in position. (2) Registration.
	12 noon	D/190	O.8.d.7½.2	12	
	2.45 p.m.	"	O.9.a.5½.1½	5	Several direct hits.
BELGIAN ARTILLERY	2.7 a.m.	2	O.2.3	1	Test
	10.29 a.m.	2	O.2.3 - O.2.4	18	Registration
	10.35 a.m.	2	O.3.8	10	Retaliation
	11.15 a.m.	2	O.3.8	2	
DIEPENDAAL GROUP	9 to 9.45 a.m.	A/190	Suspected M.G. at O.7.c.4.4 and N.12.d.4.1	12	Slight retaliation
	10.40 a.m.	"	Scheme T3 O.20a.3.9.	30	Retaliation
	10 a.m.	B/190	Suspected M.G. at O.7.c.3.6	10	
	12 noon	"	F.L.T. from N.12.d 4.1 - O.7.c.5½.17	20	Registration
	9.30 a.m.	D/190	MARTENS FARM O.8.d.7.0	12	Retaliation.
	11.40 a.m.	"	Battery at O.15.c.½.6	20	
	1.30 p.m.	"	-do-	20	
	2.30 p.m.	"	Battery at O.15.d.8½.9½	20	
	10.40 a.m.	A/189	Scheme T3 O.20.a 3.9.	30	Retaliation.

ENEMY'S ARTILLERY FIRE.

Time	Locality shelled	Rounds	Nature	Sound or Flash bearing.
8.45 to 10.45 a.m.	SCOTTISH WOOD. Road in rear of ELZENWALLE	180	5.9 & 4.2"	127°30'E from K9 - H.36.d.8.2
12.30 p.m.	DICKEBUSCH	20	4.2"	123°30' E from K9
7.30 to 11 a.m.	H.36.a	150	5.9	105° from I.31.c.3½.½

11 a.m. to 1 p.m.	I.31.c.6.3	16	4.2"	135° from I.31.c.3½.½
1 p.m.	DICKEBUSCH LAKE	8	4.2" How. very high air burst.	Battery at O.15.c.½.6

GENERAL SUMMARY.

1. <u>Enemy's New Work.</u>
    The enemy have rebuilt trench at about O.2.c.7.5. New dugouts at O.9.a.8.3. Parapet from N.12.d.3.0 - N.12.d.3.1 has been considerably strengthened.

2. <u>Enemy's Movements.</u>
    Staff Officers at O.8.d.9.3½. Working party at O.8.d.8.5. Smoke observed to be issuing from O.9.b.½.4½ and O.9.a.5.1. Suspected dugouts at O.9.a.5½.1½. Smoke seen issuing from O.7.c.5.5½ - N.18.b 7½.8½ and O.8.d.9.9. at 8.30 a.m.

3. <u>Observation.</u>
    Very good.

4. <u>Enemy Aircraft activity.</u>
    Very active between 9 a.m. and 11.30 a.m. Three or four enemy planes very active during the morning.

6. <u>Guns out of action.</u>
    18-prs.....3
    4.5"How.....1

25-12-16.

Guy Bullock
for
Brigade Major,
41st. Divisional Artillery.

App 62

S694

SECRET   COPY NO.

ADDENDA TO 41st DIVISIONAL
ARTILLERY OPERATION ORDER
No. 45.

41st Divl. Arty. Operation order No. 45 will be carried out on December 25th.

Zero hour will be 10.45 a.m.

                         ——— Brigade Major
23-12-16.   41st Divisional Artillery.

To all recipients of O.O. No. 45.

War Diary

SECRET

Ref. Map VYTSCHAETE 1/10000
28 S.W.2.

41st Divisional Artillery
OPERATION ORDER NO. 45

INTENTION. The 41st D.A. will carry out a shoot at a date to be notified later in order to damage new work of the enemy at the following points.

O.4.d.1.7   N.18.b.2.9.   O.7.b.4.4.   O.8.d.7½.2

BOMBARDMENTS.

Bombardments will be arranged and carried out as follows:-

By O.C. ST ELOI GROUP

O.4.d.1.7 (White Chateau)

(a) 3 4.5" Hows from zero to 30 minutes after zero
(b) 4 18-prs   "   "   "   "   "   "   "

O.8.d.7½.2   work on new trench.

(c) 3 4.5" Hows. from zero to 30 minutes after zero
(d) 4 18-prs   "   "   "   "   "   "   "

By O.C. DIEPENDAAL GROUP

30 yards each side of O.7.b.4.4 inclusive enemys F.L.T. and gaps filled with brushwood.

(e) 2 4.5" Hows from zero to 30 minutes after zero
(f) 1 Bty 2" M.T.Ms   "   "   "   "   "   "
(g) 4 Belgian guns   "   "   "   "   "   "
(h) 4 18-prs   "   "   "   "   "   "

20 yds each side of N.18.b.2.9 inclusive enemy's F.L.T. and gaps filled with brushwood.

(i) 2 4.5" Hows from zero to 30 minutes after zero
(j) 4 18-prs   "   "   "   "   "   "   "

RATES OF FIRE.

The rates of fire will be as follows.

(a) 1 round per Howitzer per $\frac{3}{4}$ mins
(b) 1   "   "   18-pr   " $1\frac{1}{5}$ "
(c) 1   "   "   Howitzer " $\frac{3}{4}$ "
(d) 1   "   "   18-pr   " $1\frac{1}{5}$ "
(e) 1   "   "   Howitzer " $1\frac{1}{5}$ "
(f) as convenient but the full allotment of ammunition to be fired.
(g) 1 round per gun per 2 minutes
(h) 1   "   "   18-pr per $1\frac{1}{5}$ minutes
(i) 1   "   "   Howitzer $1\frac{1}{5}$ "
(j) 1   "   "   18-pr per $\frac{3}{4}$ "

ALLOTMENT
OF AMMUNITION.

Ammunition is allotted as under.

	AX	BX	BELG	TMs.
(a)		120		
(b)	100			
(c)		120		
(d)	100			
(e)		50		
(f)				40
(g)			60	
(h)	100			
(i)		50		
(j)	160			
TOTAL	460	340	60	40

PREPARATION. O.C. Groups will make all preparations at once to carry out this operation.

Zero hour will be notified later and watches synchronised under 41st D.A. arrangements.

ACKNOWLEDGE.

H. Hutton
Brigade Major
41st Divisional Artillery.

Copy No. 1 FILE.
"   "   2 War Diary
"   "   3 41st Divsn. G
"   "   4 "   "   Q
"   "   5 ST ELOI GROUP
"   "   6 DIEPENDAAL GROUP
"   "   7 189 Bde. (for information)
"   "   8 13th Belg. Rgt.
"   "   9 D.T.M.O.
"   "   10 47th D.A.
"   "   11 16th D.A.
"   "   12 122 Inf. Bde.
"   "   13 123   "   "
"   "   14 124   "   "
"   "   15 10th Corps R.A.
"   "   16 10th Corps H.A.

SECRET.   No. 5

41st. DIVISIONAL ARTILLERY
DAILY OPERATION REPORT.

From 6 a.m. 25th. to 6 a.m. 26th. Dec.

	Time	Battery	Target	Rds.	Remarks.
ST. ELOI GROUP	10.45 to 11.15 a.m.	A/187	O.8.d.7½.2 (New work)	100	Operation Order No. 45.
	10.45 to 11.15 a.m.	B/187	O.8.d.1.7 (New work)	100	-do-
	9.30 a.m.	"	Registration	6	
	2.30 a.m.	C/187	O.2.c.5.7½	10	Retaliation called for over O.2.7 by Group.
	2.15 a.m.	"	S.O.S. Lines	1	Sent S.O.S.
	2.7 p.m. to 2.30 p.m.	"	O.2.c.8.5	16	Registration of R.G. Emplacement.
	8.30 a.m.	D/187	O.2.a.12.60	2	Group Order
	10.45 a.m.		O.2.c.95.50	2	-do-
	10.45 a.m. to 11.15 a.m.	"	O.8.d.1.7) New O.8.d.7½.2) work.	120 40	Operation Order No. 45
	4.45 p.m.	"	O.2.d.18.80	10	Group Order
			O.2.c.95.50	5	-do-
			O.8.a.45.57	5	-do-
	10.45 a.m. to 11.15 a.m.	B/190	O.8.d.7½.2 New work	80	Direct hits observed.
DIKKEBUSCH GROUP	10.30 p.m.	A/190	S.O.S Test	1	
	10.45 a.m. to 11.15 a.m.	"	O.7.b.4.4 New work	100	Operation Order No. 45.
	10.45 a.m. to 11.15 a.m.	C/190	N.18.b.2.9 New work	160	-do- Observed to be very effective.
	10.45 a.m. to 11.15 a.m.	A/190	O.7.D.4.4 N.18.b.2.9 New work	100	Operation Order No. 45. Observed to be very effective.
BELGIAN ARTY.	10.4 a.m.	2	O.2.3	1	Test
	10.8 a.m.	2	O.2.7 - O.2.4	10	Registration
	10.45 a.m.	2	O.7.b.3½.5 - O.7.b.8½.6	30	Operation Order No. 45
	10.45 a.m.	2	O.7.b.8½.5 - O.8.c.3½.1	30	-do-

OUR TRENCH MORTARS. Y Battery took part in the shoot yesterday in accordance with Operation Order No. 45. Two Trench Mortars fired on to enemy's front line at O.7.b.4.4. 40 rounds were fired with good result. Retaliation normal, consisting of 'Fishtails' 'Minnie' 'Minenwerfers and 7.7cm shells on the F.O.T. and GREGORY LANE.

ENEMY ARTILLERY FIRE.

Time	Locality Shelled	Rds.	Nature	Sound or Flash bearing.
9.40 a.m.	N.36.c.5.3	10	7.7cm	96½° from EP
10.30 to 11 a.m.	N.36.d.8.7	22	7.7cm	130° from I.31.c.8½.5
9.49 a.m. to 10.15 a.m.	I.31.c.1.6	11	4.2"	105° from I.31.c.3½.5

GENERAL SUMMARY.

1. <u>Enemy's New Works.</u>

    A piece of corrugated iron was observed lying over F.L.T. at about O.3.d.1.6.

2. <u>Enemy's Movements.</u>

    A man was observed carrying a duckboard out of a trench at O.8.d.5.3 at 9.45 a.m. yesterday.

3. <u>Observations.</u>

    Observation good between 2 and 3 o.m. Enemy's reply to our bombardment was feeble.

6. <u>Guns out of action.</u>

    18-prs.....3   4.5" How....1

26-12-16.

Brigade Major,
41st. Divisional Artillery.

SECRET.

ADDENDA to 41st DIVISIONAL
ARTILLERY OPERATION ORDER no. 46.

Operation Order No. 46 will be carried out on
December 30th.
Zero Hour will be 1.45 p.m.
ACKNOWLEDGE.

[signature]

Brigade Major
25-12-16.   41st Divisional Artillery.

SECRET.   Ref. Map WYTSCHAETE
1/10.000 28 SW 2.

41st DIVISIONAL ARTILLERY OPERATION ORDER
No. 46.

INTENTION.   The 41st D.A. will bombard hostile trench Mortars
about O.7.d.25.55, N.18.b.95.30., O.7.c.40.40 and
O.7.c.97.87 on a date to be notified later.

BOMBARDMENTS.   The O.C. Diependaal Group will arrange bombardments
in accordance with Appendix A.
The O.C. St. Eloi Group will arrange bombardments
in accordance with appendix B.
The Xth Corps H.A. will be asked to co-operate in
accordance with appendix C.

AMMUNITION   Expenditure of ammunition and rates of fire will
RATES OF FIRE.   be as shewn in appendices A, B, & C.

PREPARATION.   Officer Commanding Groups will make all arrangements
at once for carrying out this operation.

Zero hour will be notified later and watches will
be synchronised under 41st D.A. arrangements.

ACKNOWLEDGE.

                                        Brigade Major

24-12-16.   41st Divisional Artillery.

Copy No. 1 FILE
Copy No. 2 War Diary
  "   " 3 St Eloi Group
  "   " 4 Diependaal Group
  "   " 5 41st Divsn. G
  "   " 6 41st Divsn. Q
  "   " 7 10th Corps H.A.
  "   " 8   "   " R.A.
  "   " 9 10th Corps
  "   " 10 47th D.A.
  "   " 11 16th D.A.
  "   " 12 122nd Inf. Bde.
  "   " 13 123rd "   "
  "   " 14 124th "   "
  "   " 15 D.T.M.O.
  "   " 16 189th Bde.

APPENDIX A.

GUNS	TIME	TASK	Co-ordinates	rds per gun per min	A	AX	BX	TM	TOTAL
2 4.5 Hows	Z to 15' after Z	Bombard	0.7.c.4.4.	$1\frac{1}{3}$		40			40
1 M.T.M.	"	"	"	$\frac{1}{3}$				15	15
2 18-prs	"	Barrage	0.7.c.3½.3 − 0.7.c.3½.5	1	10	20			30
2 18-prs	"	"	0.7.c.5.5. − 0.7.c.5.3	1	10	20			30
			0.7.c.5.3.						
1 M.T.M.	"	Bombard	0.7.d.2½.5½	1				15	15
2 18-prs	"	Barrage	0.7.d.2½.6½ − 0.7.d.1½.5	1	10	20			30
			0.7.d.2.4.						
2 18-prs	"	"	0.7.d.2.4 − 0.7.d.3½.4½	1	10	20			30
			0.7.d.2½.6½						
2 4.5 Hows	"	Bombard	0.7.c.97.87	$1\frac{1}{3}$		40			40
1 M.T.M.	"	"	"	$\frac{1}{3}$				15	15
2 18-prs	"	Barrage	0.7.c.88.90 − 0.7.c.90.82	1	10	20			30
			0.7.c.98.82						
2 18-prs	"	"	0.7.c.98.82 − 0.7.c.98.90	1	10	20			30
			0.7.c.88.90						
2 4.5 Hows	"	Bombard	N.18.b.95.30	$1\frac{1}{3}$		40			40
2 18-prs	"	Barrage	N.18.b.9.4 − N.18.b.8½.3	1	10	20			30
2 18-prs	"	"	N.18.b.8½.3 − 0.13.c.0.2	1	10	20			30
2 18-prs	"	Give covering fire	N.12.d.3½.1½ − N.18.b.6.9	1	15	15			30
			TOTAL		95	175	120	45	435

Appendix B.

GUNS	TIME	TASK	Co-ordinates	rds per gun per min	H.A.	A	AX	BX	TM	Blg.	Total
2 4.5 Hows	Z to 15' after Z	Bombard	0.7.d.25.55	$1\frac{1}{3}$				40			45
3 18-prs	"	Give covering fire	0.7.a.9½.1½ – 0.7.c.3½.5	1	22	23					85
					22	23	40				435
					95	175	120	45			45
			TOTAL								
			From Appendix A								
			From Appendix C	45							
			GRAND TOTAL	45	117	198	160	45			565

APPENDIX C

1 6" How.	Z to 15' after Z	Bombard	0.7.c.40.40	2/3							10
1 6" How.	"	"	0.7.d.25.55	2/3							10
1 6" How.	"	"	0.7.c.97.87	2/3							10
1 6" How.	"	"	N.18.b.95.30	2/3							10
1m6" How	"	"	"	1/3							5
1 6" How.											45

SECRET   COPY NO. 5

41st DIVISIONAL ARTILLERY
OPERATION ORDER NO. 47.

Intention.

The Medium Trench Mortars of the 41st Divisional Artillery will carry out bombardments with silencers on December 27th from 12 noon to 12.25 p.m. and from 8 p.m. to 8.25 p.m.

TARGETS. X/41 will bombard 0.4.a.2½.3   and 0.4.a.4½.4½
           Y/41   "   "   0.7.c.5.6.   "   0.7.b.4.3.
           Z/41   "   "   0.8.a.3.9½

RATE OF FIRE.

Each Mortar will fire 15 rounds on each occasion.

COVERING FIRE.

O.C. ST ELOI GROUP will arrange covering fire for X/41 and Z/41 on the enemy's support line from 12 noon to 12.25 p.m.

O.C DIEPENDAAL GROUP will arrange covering fire for Y/41 on the enemy's support line and pay especial attention to the HOLLANDSCHESCHUUR SALIENT and the BOIS QUARANTE from 12 noon to 12.25 p.m.

100 rounds per group are allotted for this purpose.

TIME.   Watches will be synchronised under 41st D.... arrangements.

ACKNOWLEDGE.

                                            Brigade Major

23-12-16.   41st Divisional Artillery.

Copy No. 1   War Diary
  "   " 2   File
  "   " 3   St Eloi Group
  "   " 4   Diependaal Group
  "   " 5   122nd Inf. Bde.
  "   " 6   123rd   "   "
  "   " 7   124th   "   "
  "   " 8   41st Divsn G
  "   " 9   "   "   " Q
  "   " 10   16th D.A.
  "   " 11   47th D.A.
  "   " 12   D.T.M.O.
  "   " 13   13th Belg. Rgt.
  "   " 14   Xth Corps
  "   " 15   "   "   R.A.
  "   " 16   "   "   H.A.
  "   " 17 - 20 Spare.

War Diary

SECRET   COPY NO. 2

41st DIVISIONAL ARTILLERY
OPERATION ORDER NO. 48.

INTENTION. The Trench Mortars will cut wire on 31st December/16 and 1st January/17.
This operation will be carried out as follows :-

ARRANGEMENTS.

(a) On December 31st one Medium Trench Mortar will cut wire from $0.4.a.1\frac{1}{2}.2\frac{1}{2}$ to $0.4.a.3.4.$ from 3 p.m. to 3.30 p.m.

(b) On January 1st 1917 one Medium Trench Mortar will cut wire at $0.4.a.5\frac{1}{2}.6$ from 3 p.m. to 3.30 p.m.

O.C. St Eloi Group will arrange covering fire for these Medium Trench Mortars on enemy's support line. For this purpose 50 rounds are allotted each day.

The D.T.M.O. will arrange details for the firing of the Medium Trench Mortars.

ALLOTMENT OF AMMUNITION. For Shoot (a) 20 rounds M.T.M. will be fired.

For Shoot (b) 30 rounds M.T.M. will be fired.

TIME. Watches will be synchronised under 41st D.A. arrangements.

ACKNOWLEDGE.

                                                       Brigade Major

27-12-16.   41st Divisional Artillery.

Copy No. 1 FILE
" " 2 War Diary
" " 3 D.T.M.O.
" " 4 St Eloi Group
" " 5 41st Divsn G.
" " 6 " " Q
" " 7 10th Corps Q.
" " 8 " " H.A.
" " 9 " " R.A.
" " 10 Dieperdaal Group
" " 11 16th D.A.
" " 12 47th D.A.
" " 13 13th Belgian Rgt.

SECRET

41st. DIVISIONAL ARTILLERY

DAILY OPERATION REPORT
from 6 p.m., 30.11.16 to 6 p.m., 1.12.16.

OUR FIRE:-

Time	Battery	Target	Rds	REMARKS
DIEPENDAAL GROUP:-				
11.0 a.m.	A/190	BOIS QUARANTS	50	Group Shoot
" "	B/190	Enemy Trench) O.7.a.9.1.to) O.7.c.5.9.)	60	" "
" "	D/190	BOIS QUARANTES	40	" "
ST. ELOI GROUP:-				
12.10 a.m.	C/187	S.O.S. Lines	1	Test S.O.S.

OUR TRENCH MORTARS:-

At 12.15 p.m., X/41 T.M. Battery fired 32 rounds with good results. The rounds were observed to fall in the wire and Front enemy Trench. Two of these rounds were "duds".

ENEMY'S ARTILLERY FIRE:-

NIL.

GENERAL SUMMARY:-

OBSERVATION:-

Impossible in consequence of thick mist.

CASUALTIES:-

PERSONNEL:-

NIL.

GUNS OUT OF ACTION:-

18 pdr.

1.

BRIGADE MAJOR,
41st. Divisional ARtillery.

2.12.16.
HHP

SECRET

41st. DIVISIONAL ARTILLERY

DAILY OPERATION REPORT
from 6 p.m., 1.12.16 to 6 p.m., 2.12.16

OUR FIRE:-

Time	Battery	Target	Rds.	Remarks
DIEPENDAAL GROUP				
2.0 p.m.	C/190	Hostile front line in N.12.d)	3	Checking registrations for O.O. No.39
2.30 p.m.) to 3.30 p.m.)	A/190	Hostile front) line)	20	Registration
3.0 p.m.	D/189	SUNKEN ROAD in) N.18.b.)	6	
ST. ELOI GROUP				
3.45 a.m.	B/187	Test Round	1	
12.25 a.m.	C/187	O.2.c.8½.6.	1	Test S.O.S.
3.40 a.m.	"	O.2.d.3½.1½.	1	"
3.46½ a.m.	"	FRONT LINE TR.	30	Registration of 8 guns.
3. 0 p.m.	D/187	ROAD N.18.b.8. 2½.to O.13.a.4. 8½.		

OUR TRENCH MORTARS:-

Two Medium Trench Mortar Batteries took part in operations in accordance with this Office Operation Order No.39.
    X/41 Battery fired 65 rounds, including 15 for registration purposes.
    Y/41 Battery fired 56 rounds, including 6 for registration purposes.
    Targets of X/41 Battery - Enemy's front line between O.4.a.3.4. and O.4.a.4.4½.
    Targets of Y/41 Battery - Enemy's wire from N.18., A.,2., 9½., to N.18.B.b.1.1½.
    Casualties - Nil. Observation impossible - Night firing.
The behaviour of the men was excellent.

ENEMY'S ARTILLERY FIRE:-

Time	Locality shelled	Rds.	Nature	Sound or Flash bearing
1.30 to) 3.0 p.m.)	Trenches in front) of VIENTRATT.)	100	T.M's & 15.0 cm.	OOSTERVERNE

GENERAL SUMMARY

OBSERVATION

Very Bad, in consequence of mist.

CASUALTIES

Personnel:-

NIL

GUNS OUT OF ACTION

NIL

LATER:-

REPORT on OPERATIONS of night 2.12.16/ 3.12.16.

The raiding party arrived at Battalion Headquarters at 10 p.m., and were in position in the front line trench at 11.10 p.m. They commenced to move into NO MAN'S LAND at 11.58 p.m., and got into position without casualties. The opening Battery commenced at 12.4½ a.m., and the bursting of the shells was good both as regards range and fuze. The enemy retaliated with Trench Mortars on our front line, but not heavily. Hostile Machine gun fire was almost entirely kept down by our Artillery.

At 12.35 a.m., the raiders moved forward and entered the trench. On the right some concertina wire was encountered but did not prove a serious obstacle - on the left got in without any difficulty. Both parties took prisoners bearing the number,133, on their shoulder straps. Three prisoners were brought back. Two dug-outs were bombed and casualties inflicted, estimated at 12. Our own were about 10 slightly wounded.

The Infantry Raiding Officers spoke well of the "Box" barrage, and Officer Commanding Operation seemed satisfied with our support. The enemy displayed a very varying selection of lights.

Reports on the condition of the hostile trenches were conflicting. The raiders returned at 12.58 a.m.

There was no hostile shelling in rear. No casualties to guns or personnel at the Batteries.

BRIGADE Major,
41st.Divisional Artillery.

3.12.16.
MRF

SECRET   Ref map WHYTSCHAETE
                                          28 S.W.I" 1/10000

                    41st Divisional Artillery Operation
                            Order No. 39½

INTENTION: The 41st Division will carry out a raid on December 2nd, 1916.
                Point of entry N.18.b.28 — N.12.d.60

BOMBARDMENTS   On the day of the raid BOMBARDMENTS and barrages will be arr-
& BARRAGES.   anged and carried out as follows:-

                Those in SCHEDULE A by O.C. DIEPENDAAL GROUP
                  "   "   "   B "   ST ELOI GROUP
                  "   "   "   C "   16th D.A.
                  "   "   "   D " G.O.C. Xth Corps H.A.

RATES OF   The time and rates of fires will be as laid down in
  FIRE.   Schedules A,B,C,& D.

LIAISON   MAJOR N.H. HUTTENBACH is detailed as Liaison Officer with
OFFICER.   Officer Commanding the operations.
                During the operations he will be in direct communications
                with the G.O.C. R.A.

AMMUNITION   The allotment of ammunition is shewn in Schedules A,B,C & D.
                The total ammunition expenditure is shewn in Schedule E

PREPARATION.   Officers commanding Groups will make all arrangements necessary
                for carrying out this operation.

ZERO HOUR   Zero hour will be notified later and watches will be
                synchronised under 41st Divisional Artillery arrangements.

7.   C/189 & D/189 are placed at disposal of O.C. DIEPENDAAL
                Group for this operation.
                The Howitzers in position at H.35.a.8.8. and N.4.c.9.8 will
                be under orders of O.C. ST ELOI GROUP for this operation.
                The Howitzers in position at H.30.a.7.8. will be under
                orders of O.C. DIEPENDAAL GROUP for this operation.

8.   All previous orders and amendments regarding 41st D.A. O.O.
                No. 39 are cancelled.

10.   ACKNOWLEDGE.

                                                    Brigade Major
28-11-16.   41st Divisional Artillery

    Copy No. 1 War Diary
      "   " 2 FILE
      "   " 3 41st Divs   G
      "   " 4   "   "   Q
      "   " 5 16 D.A.
      "   " 6 47th D.A.
      "   " 7 Xth Corps R.A.
      "   " 8   "   "   H.A.   13 - 21 DIEPENDAAL GROUP
      "   " 9 124th I f Bde   22 - 34 ST ELOI   "
      "   " 10 Staff Capt   35 - 39 Spare.
      "   " 11 7t Belgian Regt.
      "   " 12 D.T.M.O.

SCHEDULE A.
REGIMENTAL GROUP.

	Guns	Period	Task	C-ordinates	Rds. per gun per min	A	AX.	EX.	EFlO.	Total
(a)	8 18-prs	30' bef re Z t. 5' before Z	Bombard	N.18.b.2.8, N.12.d.3½.1 N.12.c.6.0	2	200	200			400
(b)	8 18-prs	5 bef re Z t. Z.	"	- do -	2	80				80
(c)	2 18-pr	30' before Z t 5' before Z	"	N.18.b.1½.6 - N.18.b.2.6	2	50	50			100
(d)	2 18-pr	- do -	"	N.18.b.5.7½ - N.18.b.4½.6½	2	50	50			100
(e)	2 18-prs	5' bef re Z t. Z	"	N.18.b.1½.6 - N.18.b.2.8	2	20				20
(f)	2 18-prs	- do -	"	N.18.b.3.7½ - N.18.b.4½.6½	2	20				20
(g)	4 4.5" Hows	15' bef re Z t. 10' af er Z	"	N.12.d.9.1 - 0.7.c.2.2½	2	40				40
(h)	4 4.5" Hows	- do -	"	N.18.b.4.4½, N.18.b.9.1½	2			200	200	200
(i)	2 Medium T.M.	15' before Z t. stop	"	N.18.b 8.8½ 0.1.a.0.8.	2				200	200
(j)	8 18-prs	Z to 10' after Z	Barrage	N.18.c.2.9½ N.18.b.1.1½	-	50				50
(k)	2 18-prs	- do -	"	N.18.b.6.9½ H.12 c 8½.1	4	320				320
(l)	2 18-prs	8 do -	Bombard	N.18.b.1½.6 N.18.b.2.9.	4	80				80
(m)	2 18-prs	- do -	"	N.18.b.5.7½ N.8.b.4½.6½.	4	80				80
(n)	4 18-prs	- do -	"	N.18.c.9.1 0.7.c.2.2½	4	80				80
(o)	8 18-prs	10' after Z to stop	Barrage	N.18.b.4½.6½ - N.18.b.7.8.	1	160				160
(p)	2 18-prs	- do -	"	N.18.b.8.9½ N.12..8½.½	1	480				480
(q)	2 19-pr	- d -	Bombard	N.18.b.6.9½ N.18.b.2.8	1	120				120
(r)	2 18-prs	- do -	"	N.18.b.1½.6 N.18.b.2.8	1	120				120

Guns	Period	Task	Co-ordinates	rds. per gun per min	A	AX	EX	RFLG	TM	Tot. l
2 18-prs	10' after Z to stop	Bomb. n.	N.18.b.3.7½ - N.18.b.4½.6½	1	120					120
2 18-prs	- do -	"	N.1.d.9.1 - 0.7 c 2.2½	½		120				120
2 18-prs	- do -	"	E.18.b.4.4½ R 18.b.9.1½	½			120			120
4 4.5" Hows	- do -	"		½				120		120
4 4.5" Hows	- do -	"	N.18.b.2.8½ 0.13.a.4.8.	½					480	480
			TOTAL AMMUNITION		120	120	240	120	120	
			TOTAL AMN for Sheet 1.		1820	620	640		50	3130
			GRAND TOTAL							

SCHEDULE P
ST ELOI GROUP

Guns	Period	Tack	Co-ord tes	rds per gun per min	A	IX	FX	BELG	TM	Total
(a) 12 Bdlr.	30' before Z to Z	Bombardm't	0.7.c.4.4. 0.7.c.5.9½	2			720			720
(b) 4 4.5"	15" no before Z to 10' after	"	0.9.b.2.6½ 0.3.c.8.0	2		200				200
(c) 4 4.5"	-- do --	"	-- do --	2		200				200
(d) 8 18-prs	5' before Z to Z	"	PICCADILY FM 0.8.d.3.7.	2				80		80
(e) 16 18-prs	-- do --	"	0.3.d.1.8½ 0.3.d.5.9½	2				160		160
(f) 4 T.M.	5' before Z to stop	"	0.2.c.9.6. 0.2.d.7.5½	2					50	50
(g) 12 Belg	Z to 108 after Z	"	0.4.c.3.4. 0.4.d.4.4½	5		600				600
(h) 8 13-prs	Z to 10' after Z B/184	"	0.7.c.4.4. 0.7.c.5.9½	4				320		320
(i) 4 18-prs	-- do --	"	0.3.d.1.8½ 0.3.d.5.9½	4				160		160
(j) 12/18-prs	-- do --	"	0.2.c.6.3. 0.2.c.9.5.	4				480		480
(k) 12 Belg	10' after Z to stop (estimate two hour)	"	0.2.c.9.6. 0.2.d.7.5½	2		1440				1440
(l) 4 4.5"	-- do --	"	0.7.c.4.4. 0.7.c.5.9½	¼		120				120
(m) 4 4.5"	-- do --	"	0.9.b.2.6½ 0.3.c.8.0	¼		120				120
(n) 8 18-prs	-- do -- B/184	"	PICCADILY FM 0.8.d.3.7.	¼				240		240
(o) 4 18-prs	-- do --	"	0.3.d.1.8½ 0.3.d.5.9½	¼				120		120
(p)12 18-prs	-- do --	"	0.2.c.6.3. 0.2.c.9.5.	¼				360		360
		TOTAL AMUNITION			1920	640	2760	50	6370

SCHEDULE C
15th Divisional Artillery.

GUNS	Period	Task	Co-ordinates	Rds. per gun per min	A X	TOTAL
(a) 4 18-prs	30' before Z to Z	Bombard	N.24.a.7.2½ - N.18.d.1.1¾	2	240	240
(b) 2 13-prs	Z to 10' after Z	"	N.24.Z.7.8¼ N.18.d.1.1½	4	160	160
(c) 4 18-pr	10' after Z to stop estimated 1 Hour	"	N.24.a.7.8¾ N.18.d.1.1¼	¼	120	120
					520	520

TOTAL AMMUNITION

SCHEDULE D
Xth Corps H.A.

GUNS.	Period	Task	Co-ordinates	Rds. per gun per min	H.A.	TOTAL
4 6" Hows	30' before Z to 15' before Z	Bombard Support line	N.18.b.3.7¼ - 5½.6¾ - 5.7 6.3¾	1	60	60
2 6" Hows	15' before Z to Stop	Bombard	0.13.d.0.8 - 0.13.c.9.7½ 0.13.c.6.1	⅓	37	37
"	- do -	"	0.13.c.4.8. - N.18.b.9.2.	⅓	37	37
2 6" Hows	- do -	"			10	100
60-prs & 4.7"	Throughout operation	Counter Bty on active hostile Batteries in area.			100	100
					334	334

TOTAL AMMUNITION

SCHEDULE AE

AMMUNITION EXPENDITURE.

	A	AX	BX	BELG	TM	HA	TOTAL
SCHEDULE A	1820	620	640		50		3130
SCHEDULE B		1920	640	2760	50		5370
SCHEDULE C		520					520
SCHEDULE D						334	334
GRAND TOTAL	1820	3060	1280	2760	100	334	9354

Secret.
Scale 1:10,000

HQ RA 41 Div
Vol 8